SALT HORSE

MEMOIR OF A MAVERICK ADMIRAL
CLAUDE LIONEL CUMBERLEDGE

INTRODUCED AND EDITED BY ROBIN KNIGHT

Whittles Publishing

Published by
Whittles Publishing Ltd,
Dunbeath,
Caithness, KW6 6EG,
Scotland, UK

www.whittlespublishing.com

ISBN 978-184995-572-0

Printed and bound in Great Britain by
TJ Books Limited, Padstow, Cornwall

MIX
Paper from
responsible sources
FSC® C013056

CONTENTS

ACKNOWLEDGEMENTS

This memoir has a curious history. The 500-page manuscript was written in 1936–38 by Claude Cumberlege following publication of *Master Mariner*, his volume of short stories about the sea, in June 1936. *Master Mariner* is a clever mixture of fact and fiction, and includes many tall tales derived from a lifetime at sea. The Admiral titled his second effort *Salt Horse*, and began it in 1936 while living at El Canuto, Andalucía, ostensibly so that his young son Mistral, then two years old, would 'know how your father passed his life'. Cumberlege was then about 60. He finished the manuscript at the end of 1938. Once war had broken out in Europe in 1939, and Cumberlege had left the French Riviera for Sussex in 1940, the time was never right to publish, although he arranged for the original to be clean-typed.

Several copies of the memoir existed. Two belonged to Mistral and Tarik Cumberlege, by then both living in California. In 2016, when I was researching the biography of the Admiral's oldest son, Michael, Tarik sent me his copy. *The Extraordinary Life of Mike Cumberlege SOE* was published in September 2018, and took some material from *Salt Horse*. After that, I moved on to a new project; this book, *Leaders*, was published in late 2021. Looking around for another venture, I remembered that I had a copy of *Salt Horse*.

By then, all of the Admiral's six children except Claudine had died. She lives in Majorca, and has graciously granted me copyright and agreed that I could edit the manuscript. Shortly after, Whittles Publishing, in the far north-east of Scotland, offered me a contract to publish the book.

The Admiral had written at least 150,000 words, and this had to be edited down to about 100,000. It also had to be updated and, in places, explained – hence the footnotes and occasional explanations in square brackets. His use of language reflected the values and culture of the times. I have modified it in places, but not all, in order to leave you with a feel for his outlook. While I was doing this, it became apparent to me that an Introduction and an Afterword were needed to sketch in the family background and to take the Admiral's story up to his death in 1963.

My thanks are due first and foremost to Claudine Cumberlege, who agreed to this project and also provided some family images. Secondly, to publisher Dr Keith Whittles and Sue Steven, to wordsmith Caroline Petherick and to designer Emma Aldous for supporting and overseeing the memoir to publication so admirably. Thirdly, to an old school friend, Rear Admiral Mike Harris, who I prevailed upon to write the Foreword; his long-standing interest in naval history shines through in what he has written. Fourth, to the invaluable Juan Dibos of Cochabamba, Bolivia, who contributed precious images and recollections about his mother Diana, the Admiral's second child. Other photos were collected from far and wide; my thanks are due to a number of collections and archivists, especially in Australia.

Photos add immeasurably to a book of this sort in which so many relatively recent events and individuals have slipped from public awareness. Images were collected from far and wide, in particular from the Imperial War Museum (IWM), the Australian War Memorial (AWM), the Gibraltar National Museum, Mauritius Images, BRNC Dartmouth, the Macleay River Historical Museum, the University of Newcastle in Australia, the Mary Evans Agency, the National Portrait Gallery (NPG) and the National Maritime Museum, and there are several from the public domain (PD). Every attempt has been made to track down copyright holders.

I have enjoyed resurrecting this life and memoir, and I hope that you will feel the effort has been worthwhile. The world in 2023 is so utterly different to that which the Admiral knew that such larger-than-life maverick characters, who lived their lives in the last century and before largely on their own terms, become harder and harder to imagine, let alone replicate, today. Long may the memory of Claude Lionel Cumberlege endure.

FAMILY TREE

There are over 20 great-grandchildren and great-great-grandchildren; too many to fit here, but it is hoped that a full family tree will become available online.

Bulstrode Whitelock Cumberlege (1804–1874)
m Isabella Susanna Mundell (1803–1838)

Alexander Bulstrode Cumberlege (1831–1911)
m Emily Florence Broadwood (1852–1937)

Claude Lionel Cumberlege (1877–1963)

m1 Laetitia Couldwell (1884–1930)

- 1. Michael Bulstrode Cumberlege (1905–1945)
  m Nancy Wooler
  - 1. Marcus (1938–2018)
    - 1. Eunice (1967–)
      - 1. Julia (2010–)
- 2. Diana Cumberlege (1910–1989)
  m1 in 1931 José Avial
  - 1. José Maria "Joe" Avial (1930/1–)
    m Laura Bell
  - 2. Paloma Avial (1932/3–)

  m2 in 1937 Jorge Dibos Valdeavellana
  - 3. Jaime Valdeavellana (1938–)
    m2 Martha Luz
  - 4. Maria Christina "Nena" Valdeavellana (1940–)
  - 5. Jorge "Coque" Valdeavellana (1938–)
    m Isabella "Bey"
  - 6. Juan Miguel "Piti" Valdeavellana (1946–)
    m Grace

m2 Nora Kirby (1907–1992)

- 3. Mistral Cumberlege (1933–2019)
  - 1. Henry Cumberlege (1974–)
    m Suchada
- 4. Tarik Cumberlege (1936–2011)
  m Janet Lee Hartman (1939–)
  - 1. Christopher Cumberlege (1960–2001)
    m Carey Lynn Brannon (1964–)
  - 2. Tarika Cumberlege (1966–)
    m Edward Benno Brink(1949–)
- 5. Claudine Cumberlege (1938–)
  m1 Prince Sapeha
  - 1. Mikush Sapeha (1966–)

  m2 Peter Matson
  - 2. Adam Matson (1977–)
  - 3. Ivanna Matson (1979–)
- 6. Luis/Louis (Loulou) Cumberlege (1941–2019)
  m1 Vera
  - 1. Nicholas Cumberlege (1986–)
  - 2. Daniel Cumberlege (1989–)
    m Vanessa Estelles

  m2 Jenny
  - 3. Luke Cumberlege (1992–)

TIMELINE

Claude Lionel Cumberlege, 1877–1963

1877	born 9 June in St John's Wood, London
1885	attends Field House Preparatory School, Rottingdean, Sussex
1889	aged 12, enters HMS *Britannia*, Royal Naval College Dartmouth in Devon
1892	joins HMS *Tourmaline* as a midshipman
1896	returns to England end April. Joins the battleship HMS *Royal Sovereign* in August
1897	by now a sub-lieutenant, appointed second-in-command of the destroyer HMS *Decoy*
1898	becomes executive officer in the destroyer/torpedo boat HMS *Halcyon*
1899	aged 22, promoted to lieutenant end June
1901	appointed watchkeeping lieutenant in the cruiser HMS *Furious*
1902	aged 23, assumes command of the Gibraltar Torpedo Boat Squadron
1904	marries 21-year-old Sarah Laetitia Crossley Couldwell in Gibraltar
1905	eldest child, Claude Michael Bulstrode, is born in October in London
1905–07	commands the Malta-based destroyers HMS *Banshee*, *Locust* and *Albatross*
1908	takes command of HMS *Hussar*, the C-in-C Mediterranean's 'yacht'
1910	a daughter, Diana, is born in July in London
1910	transferred to a cruiser, HMS *Hogue*, in August
1910	cited in a divorce case involving a fellow RN officer
1911	commands the torpedo gunboat HMS *Speedy*
1911	promoted to commander in June
1911–13	commands the destroyers HMS *Kale*, *Fury* and *Lurcher*
1913	seconded for three years to the Royal Australian Navy (RAN) in November
1913	commands a flotilla of three destroyers in RAN, including his ship HMAS *Warrego*
1914	takes part in the Australian capture of Rabaul in the German colony of New Britain
1914–15	ventures 400 miles up the Sepik River in New Guinea, seeking a German warship
1915	promoted captain RN/RAN in June
1916	commands the cruiser HMAS *Encounter*
1916	in October takes command of the newbuild cruiser HMAS *Brisbane*
1919	becomes flag captain and chief of staff in the battlecruiser HMAS *Australia*
1919–20	wife Laetitia, and daughter Diana, visit Australia
1920	transfers to HMAS *Melbourne*, flagship of the Australian Navy, as flag captain
1921	resigns from RAN end year. Returns to UK
1922	promoted rear admiral, retires from RN aged 45. Lives alone in Henley on Thames.
1922	in November purchases a retired Belgian pilot mail ketch, the 170-ton *L'Insoumise*
1923	fits out and adapts *L'Insoumise* for cruising
1924	first voyages in *L'Insoumise*

1925–28 bases in St Jean-de-Luz (summer) and Bayonne (winter)

1929 docked in Gibraltar. Daughter Diana marries a Spanish landowner, José Avial

1930 Laetitia dies of cancer in Paris. Unclear if the couple have divorced

1930–33 centres life year-round in St Tropez. Swaps *L'Insoumise* for smaller *Fleur de Lys*

1933 marries Nora Kirby; a son, Mistral, is born on *Fleur de Lys* in St Tropez in September

1935 moves on shore. Rents El Canuto, a farmhouse in Andalucía, Spain

1936 leaves Spain as Civil War starts. Son-in-law José Avial murdered. Diana flees to UK.

1936 moves back onto *Fleur de Lys*. Another son, Tarik, is born in Gibraltar

1937–38 settles in Cap d'Antibes, France. Diana marries a Peruvian, Jorge Dibos Valdeavellano

1939 builds a house in Cap d'Antibes. Daughter Claudine is born

1940 flees France via Spain following Axis invasions. Settles in Sussex, in Diana's house

1941–45 joins Home Guard. Has second operation, probably for cancer

1941 a son, Luis – the Admiral's sixth child – is born in England

1945 supports daughter-in-law Nancy's search for his missing SOE war hero son Michael

1945 returns to Cap d'Antibes end year

1946 in November Michael is declared dead, shot by SS in Sachsenhausen Camp February 1945

1958–59 leaves Cap d'Antibes after belt-tightening French currency upheavals

1960 settles in Majorca

1962 with Nora, opens the Sea Club

1963 dies in Majorca on 22 November, aged 86

FOREWORD

Robin Knight has done us the favour of editing the memoirs of a splendid early-twentieth century Yellow Admiral,[1] a breed no longer to be found amongst us.

Born in 1877, Claude Cumberlege spent his early years in the Royal Navy of the Edwardian era, leading up to the First World War. Born the same year as the ill-starred Sir Dudley Pound, First Sea Lord for much of the Second World War, they joined *Britannia* together, but were entirely unalike; Pound was an example of the mainstream orthodox officer while Cumberlege was not, being cast more in the mould of a Beatty, his private life included.

His first ship was the rather beautiful sail-and-steam corvette *Tourmaline* in which he spent three years in North America and the West Indies. On reaching the rank of lieutenant in 1897, having done a few months in a battleship, he decided that he would prefer life in destroyers, and asked the Secretary of the Admiralty to send him to one, which that official duly did. It was the first of his several personal requests, a practice generally frowned upon but in his case wholly successful.

Cumberlege then went as First Lieutenant of the torpedo gunboat *Halcyon,* under a middle-aged commander as her captain. For the best part of three years she was based in the Mediterranean, where Claude had a whale of a time. He became, for example, adept at relieving Malta dockyard of the necessities of a first lieutenant's life, such as enamel paint and gold leaf, and the nearest he came to danger was when his commander-in-chief – the formidable Jacky Fisher, a ballroom dancing enthusiast – tried to cut him out on the dance floor, only to be prevented by the fearlessness of his partner, who turned Fisher down flat.

This happy life came to an abrupt halt when he was appointed, as recommended by his unimaginative captain, to a cruiser as a watchkeeper, a tedious existence. His chance to escape arose in Gibraltar, when he heard that the job of running the torpedo boats there was about to become vacant. Claude solved his own problem and changed his career path by sending a telegram to the Secretary of the Admiralty volunteering for the job. Astonishingly, he was successful: 'From the day I joined that perfect little vessel (Torpedo Boat No. 93) until the day (in 1922) that I was invited to quit His Majesty's Active Service, except for a few weeks on gunnery and torpedo courses, I was continuously in command of Her/His Majesty's ships of war.'

As one reads this book it becomes clear that Cumberlege's character was individualistic and, almost more importantly, deeply empathetic. Working personally for the admiral superintendent, he found no difficulty in assuming the role of captain of an HM ship – which is rankless – and getting on well with his admiral as well as with visiting flag officers and captains. 'Probably I expected to rise to exalted rank, but I never dreamt of it,' and 'it was here that I met, and loved for ever, Lord Charles Beresford and Prince Louis [of Battenberg]': the latter went out of his way to ensure Cumberlege's promotion to commander in 1911.

By 1913 Cumberlege felt that he had done it all in the peacetime Royal Navy, and responded by telegram to an Admiralty Weekly Order advertising a loan appointment to the Australian government to organise its destroyer flotilla: 'Others applied by letter and wasted 48 hours.' So it was that he spent the First World War

1 In the normal course of events a post captain was promoted to admiral before his retirement, but the wartime plethora of captains and the comparatively few admiral-level jobs available resulted in most of those captains being created Yellow Admirals on retirement instead.

in Australian waters, doing well. But in 1922 he was one of thousands who found themselves on the streets as a result of the Geddes Axe.[2]

At this point Cumberlege, supported by some private capital, decided that he would spend the rest of his life afloat, which he did in the Mediterranean in large sailing craft, first an ex-Belgian pilot ketch, and then a 62-foot American schooner, enjoying the title of Admiral, which he had achieved on retirement.

A combination of age, the Spanish Civil War and the Second World War drove him ashore to the South of France and finally to Majorca. In 1933 he married for a second time, someone 30 years younger than himself, yet both of them enjoyed life as energetic Riviera drones.[3] His wife, Nora, could and did remain active long after he did, leaving him at the end to wonder if his youngest son was his at all.

As Charles de Gaulle once said, 'Old age is a shipwreck'.

Rear Admiral Michael Harris

Naval historian, and captain of HMS *Cardiff* in the Falklands War

2 Sir Eric Geddes, Director-General of Munitions and Railways in the First World War, and Minister of Transport shortly afterwards, introduced sweeping government spending cuts in education, housing, transport, and civil and military infrastructure.

3 P.G. Wodehouse's idle young men

Part One
In the Navy 1889–1922

Introduction

When Claude Cumberlege was pondering what to call the schooner he had acquired in 1931 by swapping his Belgian pilot ketch, *L'Insoumise*, he came up with the name *Fleur de Lys*. It was a deliberate bow to his origins; the Cumberlege family claims to be of Huguenot stock, and its coat of arms, replete with lilies, reflects this early French background.

The Cumberlege coat of arms (Cumberbatch family history)

By the 19th century, however, the family's fortunes had become rooted firmly in India. Claude's grandfather, Bulstrode Whitelock Cumberlege, had been born in Banbury, Oxfordshire, in 1804. In his twenties he joined the East India Company (EIC) in London. By 1833 he is listed as a lieutenant in the 7th Native Infantry regiment run by the EIC. Mostly he lived in Arcot, a town in southern India on the route between Bangalore and Chennai, and was married there in about 1830 to Isabel Mundell. Five years later he became a major general in the EIC. In 1838 his wife died. He never remarried, and retired as a major general in 1865, returning to England and dying there in 1874.

Bulstrode's son Alexander was born in Arcot in 1831. Claude described him once, to introduce two of his sons, Mistral and Tarik, to a grandfather they had never known. In his words:

> Daddy was born in 1831 and went to school in Normandy at Monsieur Carpenter's establishment – until he and his brother Cleland were expelled because the old Frenchman could not cope with two quite ordinary English boys who invented strange games. My father then 'went for a soldier' and applied for, and received, a commission in the Army of the East India Company. I imagine that his father Bulstrode arranged this matter because the latter was at the time the General commanding the cavalry of the E.I.C.

The East India Company ship *Windsor* leaves St Helena in 1847 with Claude Cumberlege's father on board bound for India (Wikipedia/PD*)

> Alexander had to go to London to be interviewed by the E,I.C. Board. On arrival he was told by the porter to 'go in and make your bow to the gentlemen'. According to Father, the gentlemen were a group of old fossils. He presented his papers to them and was directed to join the *Windsor* Indiaman at Portsmouth which was sailing shortly for Hindustan. On his way out of the offices, the porter gave him a copy of the 'Company Regulations' for which he had to pay 18/6d. He told me that he never opened the book.

In Portsmouth Alexander overslept and missed the sailing of the *Windsor* by an hour. 'She be lying 'ove to at Spithead by now,' a waterman told him. Giving the man a guinea, he asked him to row after the *Windsor*. When the sporting fellow reached her, 'he clambered up the starboard ladder, as mail for the Peninsula was being hoisted on the port side, and voyaged for 104 days to Madras'.

The year was 1847 and Alexander was 17 years old. A decade later, when the mutiny/First War of Independence broke out, he was teaching the Nizam of Hyderabad's army to shoulder arms; together with two other Englishmen and two troops of the Nizam's cavalry who remained loyal, he was part of a force which kept the 10,000 men of the Tantia Tope's[1] army on the run. Alexander, said Claude, 'personally captured Tantia Tope'. Three years later, he was appointed captain of the 41st Native Infantry based in Madras (Chennai). His last appointment was in 1867 as Deputy Commissioner Central Provinces Sambalpuri, midway between Nagpur and Calcutta.

The Indian Mutiny 1857 – Tantia Tope (Britannica)

In 1875, after the EIC Army had been disbanded, Alexander became a colonel in the Indian Army. He retired the following year and returned to England aged 46. He said once that his favourite sports in India were tiger-hunting on foot and pig-sticking on horseback, and that his hobby was horses – something he certainly indulged during his retirement. A year or two before he retired he married Emily Broadwood, more than 20 years his junior. He never worked again. Emily's family was well to do, having created the firm which had evolved the spinet into the piano,[2] and

Alexander Bulstrode Cumberlege, Claude's father, in 1870 (Family collection)

1 Tantia Tope (1814–1859) was a general in the Indian Rebellion of 1857. Despite lacking formal military training, he is considered to have been the best and most effective rebel general. After the British had reoccupied Cawnpore Tope advanced with a force and obliged General Windham to retreat. Later he came to the relief of Rani Lakshmana of Jhansi and with her seized the city of Gwalior. However, he was defeated by General Napier's British Indian troops at Ranod, and after a further defeat at Sikar abandoned the campaign. A witness at his trial described Tantia Tope as 'a man of middling stature, with a wheat complexion and always wearing a white churidar turban'. Tope was executed by the British government at Shivpuri on 18 April 1859.

2 John Broadwood (1732–1812), a Scottish joiner and cabinetmaker, went to London in 1761 and began to work for a Swiss harpsichord manufacturer, married the owner's daughter and became a partner in the firm in 1770. As the popularity of the harpsichord declined, the firm concentrated on the manufacture of pianos. By 1808 the firm was trading as John Broadwood & Sons Ltd, a name it retains today. Ludwig van Beethoven received a six-octave Broadwood in 1818, a gift from Broadwoods which he kept for the rest of his life. Frédéric Chopin played Broadwood instruments in Britain, including at the last concert of his life, given at Guildhall, London, in 1848.

in the family Emily is reputed as a young girl to have spent a lot of time in 1859–60 yachting in a schooner, *Camilla*.[3] 'She was the kindest mother a boy ever had' reflected Claude on one occasion. She died in 1937. Alexander died in 1911.

Alexander and Emily had three children: Cleland (born 1875), Claude (born 1877) and Mary Nathalie (born 1879). Cleland was educated at Eastbourne College, and after Sandhurst joined the Imperial Yeomanry and took part in mounted operations in the Transvaal during the Boer War in South Africa 1900–02, for which he was decorated. Given a Commission in the Bedfordshire Regiment, he became a lieutenant in 1904. During the First World War he served on the Western Front for three years and, by then a major, was awarded the DSO 'for distinguished service in the field' following the battle of Neuve Chapelle in March 1915. Promoted to lieutenant colonel in 1919, he was awarded an OBE as Officer Commanding the Depot of the newly-amalgamated Bedfordshire and Hertfordshire Regiment in 1921. He died in 1946. His son, also named Cleland[4] and also an Army officer, died under a German air attack while escaping with his cousin Michael, Claude's oldest child, in a Greek caique from Crete following the German invasion in 1941.

Emily Cumberlege, Claude's much-loved mother (Family collection)

Cleland Bulstrode Cumberlege (Family collection)

Claude's nephew, Major Cleland Cumberlege RA, killed escaping from Crete with Mike Cumberlege in 1941 (Family collection)

3 The 19th-century racing yacht *Camilla* had originally been named *America* and under that name had on 22 August 1851 won the Royal Yacht Squadron's 53-mile (85 km) regatta around the Isle of Wight by 18 minutes, to be awarded the squadron's One Hundred Sovereign Cup; it was later renamed the America's Cup after her. The yacht, bought as *Camilla* by an English boatbuilder in 1858 and rebuilt, was sold to an American in 1860 and, renamed *America*, returned to the USA, to be owned by the US Naval Academy.

4 Cleland Alexander Martin Cumberlege (1906–41) was a major in the Royal Artillery attached to the SOE Para-Naval Section. Previously he had been on General Wavell's staff in the Libyan campaign. He was killed on 31 May 1941 when a Me109 strafed the caique *Athanassios Miaoulis*, in which he was escaping from Crete to North Africa.

CHAPTER 1

Early years 1877–1889

The early pre-Dartmouth and pre-Royal Navy days of Claude Cumberlege in the late 19th century. His family moved around southern England before settling near the sea at Lewes, Sussex.

I was born in 'The Wood' – St John's Wood in London – in June 1877. My brother Cleland was two years older than me, and Mary Nathalie (or Noonie, as we called her) was two years younger. She was the loveliest girl I ever knew, and died too young. We migrated to Hampstead, then Hove, and eventually to an old house called The Gables at Southover, Lewes, with a horse chestnut tree at the bottom of a biggish garden. I was sent to school first at Burncoose House at Hove, run by Aunt Emma and Aunt Lizzie.

Suddenly, I found myself at a proper boys' school – Field House, Rottingdean, kept by the brothers Jimmy and Billy Hewitt and their sister Sophie. My brother was ten and I was eight. We walked hand in hand through a hall. A dozen or so boys surrounded us new boys. 'Are you Liberal or Conservative?' they shouted at us. I had never heard these terms. Nor did I know that a General Election was looming [it was 1885[5]], and that the choice was between Mr Gladstone and Lord Salisbury. The word 'Liberal' seemed to me to have a more comfortable ring to it than 'Conservative' so I brightly answered 'Liberal'. Crash, a fist landed on my nose and down I went, while my brother, with a glance at the result of my political leanings, shouted 'Conservative' and became a popular character. After a certain amount of pummelling I turned my coat – but from that moment developed a distaste for the very word 'politician' which has never left me.

Field House School, Rottingdean was damnable. The food was filthy, the French teacher smelled. One day after the holidays, we came back to find a complete revolution. Two young upstarts had taken over from Jimmy and Billy and Sophie. There was fresh paint everywhere, and a bathroom and icy-cold water in the bath which every boy had to plunge into and out of under the watchful eye of one of the new owners. A drill sergeant drilled us. Games became compulsory, and distasteful. Our hampers from home were commandeered and handed out to all and sundry. Worst of all, top hats and Eton jackets were ordered as rig-of-the-day for Sundays. My old man vetoed the top hat and sent us back to school with brown billycock [bowler] hats which had just come into fashion; we were regarded as moral lepers by the owners and with envy by the other boys.

Another fly in the ointment was the periodic arrival of my father and a couple of horses for his sons, always coinciding with nearby hunting fixtures. At home, I was put up on two-year-old thoroughbreds at the age of eight. In winter, we hunted

5 In the 1885 general election Gladstone's Liberals won most seats and the popular vote, but not an outright majority; the balance was held by the Irish Nationalists. This led to a split in the Liberal Party and another election in 1886.

Field House School, Rottingdean, in 1885 (PD)

three or four times a week. In summer, we had the Downs and beautiful places where adders lived. There was Seaford where we bathed, and Newhaven where Scandinavian timber brigs smelling of sweet pine logs and tarred rope docked. And then, the hell of going back to school! In all my life since, I have never known such agony of mind. I never cried at the time, but that first night in bed at school – the utter misery of it! I used to cry myself to sleep. I loathed school, but perhaps it was a matter of comparison. We had such wonderful times in the holidays.

One summer holiday I was fairly bowled out.[6] I had been going to Brighton and using my pocket money to take sea trips in Captain Collins' *Skylark* (a yawl). I hadn't mentioned this to a soul at home because I thought objections might arise. One day as I was landing, I met a friend of the family on the beach. It never entered my head to warn him to say nothing. Next day, he turned up for lunch and, quite innocently, gave the show away. There was no trouble, but arising from this it was decided that I should go into the Royal Navy. My brother was preparing for the Army and Sandhurst. There was talk of sending me to a crammer, but the headmaster of Rottingdean guaranteed I would pass the entrance exam if I stayed at the school. Thanks to Mr. Nye, the village schoolmaster at Southover, I did pass; every evening, he arrived at home to cram me with mathematics.

Prior to the exam, I had to go to London for my medical. My turn to be examined came. I was shown into a dressing-room and told to strip. Moments later I walked, completely naked, into a room with four or five elderly gentlemen sitting round a table. The examination began. My hearing was tested. I was told to hop across the room on one leg. Then I was told to hop across the room on the other leg. Halfway back, I stopped, realising that I was hopping on the same leg. Everyone burst out laughing – no one had noticed my mistake. At length, it was over. I passed. Next was the crucial 'Passing In' exam. It must have lasted days, as Mother and I stayed at Morley's Hotel on Trafalgar Square and I recall trudging back to the hotel along the embankment with snow on the ground, accompanied by a boy called Wrottley.[7] I passed into the *Britannia* – by the skin of my teeth! I was 54th out of 55 boys selected. Thanks to Mr. Nye, in Arithmetic I got 149 marks out of 150, which must have saved me.

By the time I left Rottingdean I was 12 years old, head monitor and captain of the football team. I am sure my dislike of the school stemmed from my complete freedom of action at home in the holidays. I have never been back. While at the school I met two celebrities; one was Lord Jellicoe, whose younger brother[8]

---

6 In *Master Mariner* Cumberlege gives a fuller version. He wrote that he often watched the sea and the ships that sailed on it from the cliff above Rottingdean: 'One lovely day in the 1880s I counted 150 vessels in sight at once, almost all sailing ships.' Another day he was standing in a 'motley crowd' by *Skylark* as Captain Collins, shouting appeals for passengers for a trip on the ship, spotted young Cumberlege, called him 'young shaver' and beckoned him up the gangway. 'This was all I needed.' It was a memorable voyage back to Brighton's shingly beach. Cumberlege was hooked and spent all his pocket money on more sea trips. One day Collins gave him the tiller. All went well and he was complimented. It was then, walking up the beach, that he ran into a 'seafaring uncle' returned from foreign parts; he had come to see Cumberlege's mother after a voyage to the West Indies. When he arrived for lunch the following day, the *Skylark* story emerged.

7 Captain Francis Robert Wrottesley, DSO (1877–1954), the son of a vicar, had been born in Chichester. He commanded the 14th Kite Balloon Section RNAS in the Persian Gulf in 1916–17, lending valuable spotting services to the Army and riverine gunboat operations, and was awarded a DSO. He retired from the RN in 1919.

8 Edmund Henry Jellicoe (1875–1904) was promoted to the rank of lieutenant on 30 September 1898. Shortly after being appointed in command of a destroyer on the China Station, he was found dead in his cabin with a gunshot wound to the head. A Court of Inquiry determined that he had killed himself while suffering from a mental debility.

was a crony of mine and joined *Britannia* a year before I did; the other was a famous watchmaker called Benson.[9] The whole school was walking on the cliffs one Sunday morning when we were confronted by a very picturesque-looking old gentleman with white hair who gave us a harangue on the stupidity of wearing top hats, which we all enjoyed. He then produced the most wonderful-looking watch. It had been made for him by his firm as a present on his 70th or 80th birthday at a cost of £7,000.[10]

Eventually I caught the train at Brighton gladly and left Rottingdean in 1889. A curious man with white patches of hair at the back of his head and a tape measure called and said he knew how to make naval uniforms. His name was Mr. Gieve. He went back to his shop in High Street, Portsmouth, and shortly after a parcel containing my round jacket and my monkey jacket, both in blue cloth, and brass buttons arrived. I put them on and lorded it over other poor devils in plain clothes out skating in the marshes. And then the day came when I had to join the *Britannia* at Dartmouth.

9 In Victorian London J.W. Benson was the watch-maker of choice.

10 Worth almost £1 million today.

CHAPTER 2

At Dartmouth

Claude Cumberlege joined HMS Britannia *at Dartmouth as a cadet in the Royal Navy in 1889, aged 12. He would remain at the training establishment on the River Dart for the next three years.*

Father took me from London; I would have been a bit lonely going on my own. All the other cadets were joining with friends and cronies from crammers. We called at his club, the Junior in Charles Street, and then caught the train to Dartmouth from Paddington. At the station, we got into a carriage with other boys in uniform, one of whom looked very old and superior. He was one of the two Chief Captains of Cadets and had been on *Britannia* for over 18 months. I suppose he was a little over 14 years of age! His name was Parker[1] and his duty was to keep an eye on newly-joining cadets. Parker was splendid – a little aloof, but kindness itself. Immediately, I sensed in him the beginnings of discipline as I was to know it in all my years at sea. Human he was, too, boyishly enjoying the buns my old man bought at the first stop.

We were joining one day ahead of the others to allow us 24 hours to shake down in our new surroundings. Father left me at Kingswear, where it was raining cats and dogs. Here we tumbled into a little steam pinnace called the *Osprey* and went up the Dart calling *en route* at the hospital to be vetted for any lurking measles. Finally, we arrived alongside a vast, old three-decker called *Britannia.*[2] I ran up the gangway with the others and, going through a rather low entry port, found myself afloat. It was all rather staggering. Terribly clean. Great beams near one's head so that tallish men had to bend. Polished wooden decks, white paintwork, a bugle call, cadet corporals calling out 'At the double!' Tea and jam with Devonshire cream followed. Bed at the bugle – but not on four legs. Instead, we slept in rows and rows of white canvas hammocks, taut up under the beams, almost touching each other. Below the hammocks lay serried ranks of sea chests, each with a brass name plate, a black lid and a white body. I fell out of my hammock once, but never again. For the next five years of my life my bed was to be a hammock like the one in *Britannia*.

Very, very early next morning I woke to hear distantly a long, drawn-out wail of a whistle. It seemed to last minutes, then a pause, then still very far away a deep, raucous voice – 'All Haaaands!' Again a pause, and again the long, long pipe of a whistle, suddenly cut short on a rising note followed by the crash of the great voice, taken up and repeated by others. 'Lash up and stow hammocks!' 'Turn out, turn out, turn out!' 'Rise and shine, rise and shine, rise and shine!' 'Lash up and stow,

---

1 Henry Wise Parker, CB, CMG 1875–1940. Took part in the Battle of Jutland 1916. Promoted admiral 1925.

2 HMS *Britannia*, previously the battleship HMS *Prince of Wales*, served as the base to train RN officer recruits from 1869 to 1905 when it was replaced by a purpose-built shore establishment in Dartmouth.

HMS *Britannia-Hindustan* in 1890 (BRNC Dartmouth)

lash up and stow!' It was the voice of the Boatswain's Mate calling the ship's hands, somewhere far away in *Britannia*. For our [cadets'] accommodation was on the middle deck of the *Hindustan*,[3] an old wooden two-decker which was connected to the *Britannia* by a covered bridge. The whistle was not intended for us. Perhaps I fell asleep again; it was snug and warm in my hammock. I certainly didn't feel a bit like rising, let alone shining.

Suddenly, there was the blare of a bugle on our deck as a young drummer blew Reveille. With this cursed row also arrived two corporals. 'First term through the bath, first term through the bath!' came the order, together with shakings of hammocks. Now we knew our time had come to show a leg. Scrambling out, we shed our pyjamas, grabbed a towel, rushed forward and plunged into a large tank of cold salt water in the fore part of the ship. Curiously, after the first annoyance of having to turn out at all, this quick dip with 50 other boys was really enjoyable

The first day followed. We were literally shown the ropes, ate our meals (not at all bad) and generally found our feet. That evening, all the other 'terms' arrived. We were the 'News'. Above us were the 'Threes', the 'Sixes' and the 'Niners'. At one time I must have known why the terms were labelled like this – probably something to do with the amount of time spent on board. The 'Threes' had just emerged from the 'New' stage and could be fagged [made use of] by the 'Niners' who were fourth term, but not by the 'Sixers' or by third-term boys. The 'Sixers' could fag the 'News', but not the term (the 'Threes') immediately below them,

3 HMS *Hindustan* was launched in 1841. In 1865 it became an auxiliary to *Britannia* at Dartmouth and continued in this capacity to 1905.

and were immune from being fagged themselves. The 'Niners' were the top dogs and behaved accordingly. The second term, the 'Threes,' patronised us 'News' but were not allowed to fag us. The third term, having just arrived at the stage where it was unfaggable, had the right to fag the 'News'; it went the whole hog with its new-found power. The fourth term had more or less grown out of the delights of the slave driver and regarded 'News' as beneath its notice.

I doubt if any scholastic establishment in the United Kingdom had such a collection of stupid traditions. To wear one's jacket unbuttoned or to wear a stand-up collar or a cap at the back of one's head without permission was worth half a dozen (lashes) with a 'togie' [twisted or braided rope] as a 'bumming' was called. It was absolutely impossible to make friends with any boy outside one's own term. For a more senior boy to show kindness to a new boy was regarded as bad form. One of those who did was sneeringly called 'Ma News' by his peers. Once the other terms had arrived, immediately and instinctively us first termers withdrew into the thin shell of our term. We loathed our immediate superiors with a deadly hatred, and funked the rest. At Rottingdean I'd had a great crony called Jellybags. Now he was a third or fourth termer. I longed to see him and talk of old times. Once, I came face to face with him, passing along the main deck. 'Hello, Jellybags,' I said. 'Oh, er, it's Cumberlege … er … have you got leave to cheek [talk to an older cadet]? Just say I gave you leave if anybody asks.' And he hurried away and never spoke to me again in *Britannia*. How these ridiculous customs were allowed to go on for so long, with no discouragement from the authorities, baffles me now. Possibly, a regularised form of fagging was seen as good disciplinary tuition provided it did not lead to abuses. But even naval cadets are not all cock angels, and there were abuses.

This led to a riot when a boy in my term was damned if he would stand it any longer and calmly went home on a weekend visit to his people, and absolutely refused to return to the ship. The newspapers took up his case and there was a red-hot scandal. We juniors were all questioned separately. 'Have you ever been fagged for money?' I was asked. 'No, Sir,' I replied. I didn't say that I had often been fagged to buy sweets and buns ashore out of my own pocket money (one shilling), smuggle the 'stoodge' on board in my socks and seat of my trousers, retail it for double the cost and hand over the surplus to the young gentleman who had fagged me. Fagging, though, did have the effect of sharpening one's wits. To get past the lynx-eyed corporal of the gangway with a couple of blackberry and cream buns lashed to one's crutch, sweets in each sock and a few hap'orths of 'stickjaw' [toffee] in one's armpits, took some doing. I found a bland smile and honest look invariably was successful. The result of the hoo-ha was that two or three boys were made to withdraw. Most of us were rather sorry about it as they were not bullies and infinitely preferable to some of the niggling little swine who exploited one to keep themselves comfortable on board. None of this, incidentally, involved sex; the 'homo' type did not exist in *Britannia*.

A very unpleasant side of the old ships, however, was the punishments. They were damnable. Any charge of misdemeanour laid by the Lieutenant of the Term invariably was followed by a punishment – extra drill tearing around the great expanse of concrete tennis courts on shore carrying a couple of Indian clubs[4] for an hour with one two-minute stand-easy in the middle. And the inhuman Lord of the Admiralty who invented 'standing at ease' for a solid hour facing the paintwork without moving a muscle after everybody else was comfortably in their hammock ought to have been hanged at his own yard arm. At least the running-round punishment made one fitter. I discovered that the coveted position in the string of delinquents running

4 A type of wooden exercise equipment used to develop strength and mobility. They can range in weight from a few pounds to special clubs of up to 100 pounds.

around the courts was the leader. If one really piled on the pace until the wretched tail of the column was lurching and gasping, Dunn, the Marine Sergeant, would suddenly call out: 'Fall out, Mr. Cumberlege, and stand at ease.' How one enjoyed those two minutes watching the pitiful bandits swearing to themselves to lead a better life in future as they toiled!

It may seem that the old ship was a gloomy sort of place, but how I loved it! Our Naval Instructor, old Lane, was a marvel. He knew us all so damnably intimately. We had an awful lot to learn – probably too much for ordinary little boys. But somehow, he got it into us. Don't forget that I had passed into *Britannia* 54th out of 55 boys that term, so I was almost the fool of the family. At the end of my second term, I had gone up a dozen places. The other Instructors were a quaint lot. Badger Bill taught us Naval History, 'Stinks' taught Physics, two Instructors taught Drawing -- mechanical and free hand – and two droll men, Delbo and Brunel, taught French. Delbo was an enormous Basque with a full beard and as strong as a prize fighter – he used to hold us at arm's length by the ears. Brunel pretended he knew no English and pretended to be violent-tempered. He used to warn us: 'Mod you larf, mod you spik – deux mods make one indeef,' which meant that if one got two 'moderate attentions' against one's name, entailing an hour's run for each, the two automatically resulted in an 'indifferent attention', which led to an additional two hours' extra drill and a serious report to headquarters. Fortunately, I rather shone at French, having been well grounded in it at Rottingdean. Then there were the Seamanship Instructors – very earnest old chief petty officers and splendid men. There were wonderful ships' models down below in *Britannia*, and at that time we learnt all about masts and yardarms. Enthralling! It was certainly awfully hard work, but we simply had to learn.

We got ashore by rowing in a big ship's cutter. It was a matter of a few minutes to the land opposite the ships. Here every known game worth playing could be played, with a pack of beagles thrown in. One was never forced to play any particular game, but there were always pretty keen eyes on the outlook for talent, especially rugby and cricket. At Rottingdean I had played football and I didn't take up rugby until I went to sea. At cricket I never made more than six runs and found fielding irksome. Instead, I was most attracted to the water. There were boats by the dozen – four-oared gigs and skiffs, a couple of schooner yachts and about a dozen very good little half-decker sloops or cutters.

Beagling had its advantages, especially if we knew some hospitable folk in the neighbourhood who were good for a first-rate tea. A run with the beagles also carried with it the right to a hot, fresh water bath on returning on board. One of the big baths was used for this, and about a dozen of us piled in together. If you got in with the first batch it was possible to get a second bath. The trick was to get into a corner, right under the corporal's nose where the side of the bath cast a shadow, and lie doggo with one's nose just out of the water. Often enough the corporal would not notice anyone there as he cleared the bath. It was not always necessary to actually go beagling to secure a bath. All one had to do, after carrying out whatever adventure one had decided on for that afternoon such as robbing an orchard or gathering beech nuts, was to smear plenty of red Devon earth on one's flannel trousers and look as if one had been out with the beagles. It was always good for the wits to outmanoeuvre taskmasters!

The River Dart was full of interest in those days, and in summer time it was great fun if one could get on the right side of old Dunn, the keeper of the boats, to go out in a skiff. Dunn hated letting any of 'his' boats out of his sight. He soon got to know those who took little care of them. Even so, it was part of the play to use all one's tact and persuasive powers when applying for a boat. Every sort of ship had a lot of interest, and the river always had a number of unusual vessels in it, mainly Scandinavian. The Dart was quite a big coaling port at that time as well as being used by the Cape mail liners as their port of departure. Now and again some great full-rigged sailing ship would come into the river, so stretched in her spars that she had to anchor below the telegraph wires which stretched from the Dartmouth side to the Kingswear side. Nearly always there were many beautiful little West Country brigs and brigantines and topsail schooners to see. Dartmouth, if narrow at the entrance, was much used too as a port of refuge in bad weather.

The little sailing sloops in Dunn's personal flotilla were grand fun. They were rigged with a boom mainsail and a jib, and were decked forward and round a well at the side – not over-canvassed and very still and believed to be uncapsizeable. This theory I proved to be erroneous, deliberately. One blustery day with a couple of other scoundrels I managed to capsize the *Foam* after a difficult manoeuvre that involved flattening aft the sheets as a handy heavy gust came down. Over she went, to our infinite delight. The schooners were used on half-holidays, but only one of them, the *Siren*, was permitted to poke her nose outside the harbour.

Just like an ordinary school, we had holidays, and while I always hated leaving home again, I never felt the same hell going back to *Britannia* that I had when re-joining Rottingdean. Once I was a 'Sixer', life was almost perfect. By then, one had got used to discipline, one was no longer fagged and one could toy with one's new-found powers over the contemptible 'News'. I had also got sufficiently artful to be able to circumvent the corporals on all normal occasions. By the time I became a 'Niner' or fourth term [last term] boy, I had gained a lot more. By then one had begun to realise that somewhere there were big ships which went to sea with officers. The guardians of the peace more or less left one alone. The only fly in the ointment was the knowledge that at the end of the term loomed that dreadful examination which would determine one's life work or not.

The nearer that time came, the harder I worked. I knew, and Instructor Lane was always rubbing it in, that I was less than ordinary at study. When at length the exam began, a great pal of mine and I used to climb through a sort of hatchway or skylight on the poop [deck] into our study, which was otherwise locked after hours. There, under a shaded lamp, we swotted up the next day's subject into the small hours. We were never bowled [found] out, but now, looking back, I sometimes think that it was perfectly well known to the authorities, and that we were mercifully disregarded. Finally, it was all over. My dear friend Dod Bernard failed, with six others. I passed by the skin of my teeth and found myself designated a 'young gentleman' [midshipman]. I went home, aged 15, and had a glorious long *leave* – no more holidays for me!

CHAPTER 3

midshipman at sea

Midshipman Claude Cumberlege joined HMS Tourmaline *in 1892. He spent the next three years at sea in the ship, journeying to the Caribbean and the east coast of North America.*

HMS *Tourmaline* (Wikipedia)

I wrote a polite letter to the Secretary of the Admiralty suggesting that I be appointed to a ship on the Australian Station. It was the farthest from England, and I felt a passionate urge to see the world as quickly as possible. A courteous reply was received stating that there were no vacancies. Instead, I was appointed to the *Tourmaline*, then refitting in Sheerness, before proceeding to the North American and West Indian Station for a three-year commission.

The day to join arrived. I put on my round jacket and girded on my brand-new dirk. My parents and sister saw me off from Hassocks station. My brother[1] accompanied me to Sheerness; he was two years older than me and preparing for Sandhurst. There were no tears on parting; it was all too exciting. Father had, however, given me some advice: 'If you ever get a dose of clap [gonorrhoea], go straight to the doctor.'

Next day I went on board my first sea-going ship. *Tourmaline* was called a corvette. She was the last of her class to be employed as a fully-commissioned ship on a foreign station and had been built in 1874. Her displacement was 2,120 tons, she was rigged as a barque and had a steam engine which drove a detachable propeller and could make 4½ knots. A very pretty ship in front, her general appearance was spoilt by a heavy-looking stern. She carried eight 5-inch guns, four on each broadside on the upper deck, and four 6-inch guns mounted on a sponson [gun platform]. There was a raised forecastle called the top gallant forecastle, and a raised poop. The big double wheel was placed just under the forward end of the poop.

Amidships, there was a collapsible funnel which could be screwed down more or less out of sight when the ship was under sail. Here, too, were stowed the bigger boats 'on the booms,' a 42-foot sailing launch and a steam cutter. Two sailing cutters, one on each side of the poop, could be hoisted up to davits, and there was a whaler and the captain's galley. Bulwarks, or 'netting', pierced with closing ports for the broadside guns, joined the top gallant forecastle to the poop, thus presenting

1 Lt Colonel Cleland Bulstrode Cumberlege, DSO (1875–1946). He fought in the Boer War 1900–02. Commissioned into the Bedfordshire Regiment in 1901, he was awarded the DSO in 1915 after being wounded severely at the Battle of Neuve Chapelle.

an unbroken line fore and aft. The bulwarks were about 7 feet high and were fitted for the hammocks of the 250-strong ship's company including a dozen Royal Marines.

Some of the officers had not joined, but I found three or four other cadets from my *Britannia* term, and we had the run of the ship for 24 hours. We went down to the gunroom – our home for the next three years – to explore. It smelt of cockroaches and horsehair cushions damaged by 20 years of salt water. Superficially, it was clean and painted white – a small, dark room lit by three square port holes with bullseyes of glass. By night, a swinging oil lamp gave light. A table and chairs almost completely filled the room. A hatch led into a tiny pantry, and a settee ran along the ship's side. When everybody sat down for a meal, five sat on the main settee, five in chairs and one on the chair at the head of the table. When I joined there were a dozen members of this Mess although more joined later – a Sub-Lieutenant, Assistant Paymaster [AP], Assistant Engineer, Assistant Clerk, an RNR Sub-Lieutenant and seven Midshipmen.

Normally, the gunroom was rarely bung full. Even so, I usually had to sit on the edge of the settee to read or write. The Sub-Lieutenant was in complete command. He was a good-natured sort but without much character. He ruled by 'dint of whip and horrible black-hole', and for months a day hardly passed without a dirk scabbard laid on my bottom. It didn't hurt but I think the Sub. liked to demonstrate his authority. Next to the Sub. was Bill Lee, the AP, an engaging personality. I became quite fond of Bill. He was terribly strong, aged about 23. He never attempted to beat us [midshipmen]; if you annoyed him, he banged you on the nose or threw you bodily out of the Mess. We midshipmen were no cock angles but we were a fairly decent lot.

I admired the senior midshipman, Bom Davy,[2] tremendously. He was teetotal and a good example to us younger ones. The Sub. certainly was not, and was often, in his words, 'as drunk as a bloody fart'. Of course, sometimes we all got tight but always on 'proper' occasions such as the Queen's birthday or my birthday or any old birthday. Then we were sick and that was the end of it. We shirked work as much as possible, slept on watch (with one eye open) and stuck to each other like jam in a blanket. Our sea chests were in a row outside the gunroom and we slept in hammocks under the beams, over our chests. There was no privacy, ever, for us. We bathed in two tiny tin dishes open to the world. We dressed at our chests in public. We swapped or lent or took each other's clothes when necessary. We read and sometimes wrote, each other's letters. Our Naval Instructor (also the ship's chaplain) was on his first ship, like us. He was pleasant, but we were unkind to him. Any excuse to get out of 'school' was seized on.

We paid a shilling a head towards our messing, and there were other small subscriptions monthly. Junior members of the Mess were allowed to spend ten shillings a month on 'wines', seniors 15 shillings. We were not allowed spirits, and smoking was forbidden until we were 18. We could spend as much as we liked, or could afford, on 'extras'. The food was, frankly, poor and inadequate. Afternoon tea – jam, soft drinks – was an 'extra', as was every mortal thing one might want.

As far as the work of the ship went, we were divided into watches under the lieutenants, commanded various boats and their crews, and had our different stations when making sail such as 'Midshipman of the Fore and Main Tops and Cross Trees'. I picked up a very good number.; the Navigating Lieutenant unwisely chose me as his assistant, known as 'Tankie,' and with that role went the very amusing one of the Captain's ADC or, more popularly, the his 'doggie' [dogsbody]. As Tankie, I kept no watch and was supposed to assist the Navigator. Of course, I did nothing of the sort. I also had to keep a copy of the Fair Log which was sent periodically to the Admiralty. I did this religiously, but it was sent back as one of My Lords Commissioners

2 Captain Edward Guy Wright Davy, RN (1866–1939).

could not read a thing; I couldn't read it myself! I simply couldn't keep awake over the job. There is nothing duller than an ordinary ship's log – and my ink pen trailed on in unintelligible nightmare hieroglyphics! As for being the Captain's doggie, everything went well. One just stood about and waited until the skipper sang out 'Midshipman! Go and tell the officer of the forecastle that he's a bloody idiot!' 'Aye, aye, Sir.' I always repeated the order suitably embellished.

By April 1893 we were 'Ready for Sea'. Before sailing on the long voyage to Bermuda we were inspected by the Admiral at the Nore, Sir Algernon Heneage,[3] known throughout the Service as 'Pompo'. W.S. Gilbert has not portrayed a droller character. Imagine the scene. The ship was all spick and span. The officers, headed by the Captain, had gathered at the gangway. The yards were manned by bluejackets. The Royal Marines in their scarlet coats were drawn up as Guard of Honour. The trumpets were ready to blow a fanfare, the Boatswain and his mates to pipe [aboard]. The Admiral's barge drew alongside. As he stepped out attended by the Flag Lieutenant, Secretary and other minions and mounted the gangway, the pipes shrilled a respectful welcome. He arrived at the top of the gangway. The trumpets blared a salute, the Guard crashed to the 'Present' [arms]. Then silence. The great man stood in the entry port – a huge red face topped with little curls round his hat, dressed in the newest uniform imaginable so that it looked as though it had been sent from Gieves[4] that morning.

The Admiral looked as if he might explode. He raised his right hand with two fingers stuck out in a white kid glove. His gaze settled on our Navigator, a splendid-looking man with a big red beard. He shook his fingers under the Navigator's nose, his face alive with ill-suppressed emotion. 'Captain Poore!'[5] he gasped. 'Captain Poore. This officer's beard should be short.' Gasp. 'Crisp.' Gasp. 'And trrrrimmmed, Sir! See to it!' Everyone was inspected and everything turned inside out. Just before the Admiral left, he said, 'I wish to see the young gentlemen.' He tore us to ribbons. All was wrong, although we had hardly had our new uniforms a fortnight. 'There is grease and dirt on the seat of this young officer's trousers,' he said, wagging two fingers. 'Stop his leave, Captain Poore, stop his leave. And why is this young gentleman's dirk-knot of a different pattern, Captain Poore? Stop his leave, Captain Poore. Stop his leave.' The ship then received a first-class Inspection Report, and all the midshipmen were given 48 hours' leave to bid farewell to their families for three years.

At this time in the Service the gap between a midshipman and a wardroom officer was huge. The wardroom, where the commissioned officers messed, was a fair-sized room, aired and lit by a skylight on the upper deck. The officers' sleeping cabins were arranged on each side of it and opened into the wardroom. All of them – a First Lieutenant, a Navigating Lieutenant, three Watchkeeping Lieutenants, an RNR Lieutenant, a Parson (chaplain), a Doctor, a Chief Engineer and a Paymaster – seemed old to us, but in truth the lieutenants were in their twenties. The fact that some of them wore beards added to their ages. They were a good lot, but we didn't mix with them at all.

The Captain needs a few words. He was a curious sort, extraordinarily good-looking, and under 40 years of age. He seemed terribly shy – tall and slim, blue eyes, a red pointed beard and mustachios, and always smartly turned out. He inspired awe rather than fear. He was as aloof with his officers as with the midshipmen. On the other hand, he was not unkind or even taut with us, and regarded midshipmen as a

---

3 Admiral Sir Algernon Heneage, GCB (1833–1915) was known for his immaculate dress and his white-glove inspections of the ships under his command. He was appointed C-in-C, The Nore, in 1892.

4 Gieves began supplying uniforms to the Royal Navy in the mid-19th century. Later, it became Gieves & Hawkes, the Savile Row tailors.

5 Admiral Sir Richard Poore, KCB, CVO, JP, DL (1853–1930) was a Royal Navy officer who in 1911 also went on to be Commander-in-Chief (C-in-C), The Nore.

necessary evil. What he lacked in demonstrative fatherliness was made up for by the very great kindness of his wife, who put herself out to look after us midshipmen with good victuals and a warm welcome to her house whenever we were in Bermuda.

On Tuesday, 25th April 1893 we left Sheerness. After calling at Portsmouth and Plymouth, we shaped course for Madeira. The wind came fair, and I was thrilled. Who wouldn't be at 15 years of age! We made plain sail, and the banging and clanging of the engine ceased. It was gorgeous on deck, damnable in the stuffy gunroom, and the food was filthy. The ports [portholes] were 'barred in' meaning that what little light might have crept in was blocked by bars. That first night I went to bed in my hammock at about 7:30 pm, very tired. At about 8:30 pm I was awakened by a tall Marine with five badges who shoved a huge plateful of apple pie smothered in cream under my nose. My God, did I wolf it! The dear old chap had filched it from the Wardroom Mess, where he was a servant. 'Here ye are. Thought you might like it.' What a kindly thought.

The days on this part of the voyage were very full of every sort of drill, and especially sail drill, as the ship's company was all new. During these 'evolutions' my station was on the poop ready to run messages for the Captain to the officers in charge of the fore and main masts. We made sail, we furled sail, we shifted sails and changed to gallant masts. Every evening at about 5:00 pm we took in the royals and flying jib, and one reef in the topsails. One day was much like another. Our speed was between 5 and 6 knots, and there were no violent excitements. I liked the drills and 'evolutions', not least because they interfered with my schooling, which I detested. And as the Captain's doggie, I soon took a fiendish delight in being vicariously rude to my seniors.

We reached Madeira. One could hardly find a more satisfactory landfall for one's first visit to foreign parts. We sighted the island 70 miles away. It was a riot of colours – gold and rose and imperial purple and flaming flowers. The Portuguese governor, and the virgins at His Excellency's ball, were the other things that impressed me. Flowers were everywhere and indescribably beautiful. The governor was no more than 4 feet 6 inches in his socks and perhaps 5 feet in full dress – perfectly turned out in his tiny Wellingtons [shoes] with 6-inch heels and a uniform which must have been sewn on to him. The girls, too, were perfectly groomed and delightfully round. Magnolia blooms tinted their cheeks and the scarlet of hibiscus their lips. Being only 15, I was much too shy to study them at close quarters. It had never entered my head before that girls could be so feminine.

After a couple of days, we left Madeira, found headwinds veering north-west and made plain sail with one reef in the topsails. As we neared the Tropics, the wind was light but fair. Usually, work began with the morning watch scrubbing decks, coiling ropes and resetting sail. After breakfast and a 'Stand easy' to allow a smoke, a general clearing-up of decks followed. At 9:00 am all hands would fall in for Divisions Inspection and Prayers. We midshipmen then had to 'go to school' in the Captain's fore cabin while the ship's company did gun drill. In the middle forenoon, we had a ten minutes' 'Stand easy' as the bugle sounded 'Cooks to the galley'. At noon, eight bells were struck followed by 'Pipe to dinner'. Food in our Mess consisted of salt horse, sometimes disguised in a pie or as hash, or corned beef known as 'Fanny Adams', named after a factory worker who had disappeared one day leaving bits of her red-flannelled petticoat in numberless tins of corned beef! On Thursdays we got pea soup as an extra. Fresh vegetables soon ran out, and our drink was tepid – fresh water with a little lime juice. There always seemed to be rope yarn in the *Tourmaline* tanks which made the water supply taste of tar. No good!

Instruction was conducted in the afternoon. At 3:30 pm we were free and invaded the gunroom for 'seven bells tea' – usually a ship's biscuit hard as iron, except where the weevils had got in. If we wanted jam, we had to pay for it or steal it. After tea we were free, more or less, until 5:00 pm when Quarters were sounded, followed by General Sail Drill. When the skipper had had enough, we played games like cricket, quoits, boxing and singlesticks [a martial art] until dinner. This was a reproduction of the midday meal with 'figgy duff' [pudding] thrown in on Thursdays.

The engine on *Tourmaline* was a constant problem. It was a bag of tricks.[6] When it was working the fug below was appalling. It was installed on its side and there was a half-inch play so it wheezed and snored and stank. One time a boiler burst. A huge crack appeared above the furnace, so the engineers threw a wet swab over the tear, and steam and water bubbled out. Gunroom lights were supposed to be out at 10:00 pm but if we had watches to keep later in the night we turned in earlier. Often, due to the fug down below, we would drag our blankets on deck and sleep there unless the weather was bad. My hammock was slung just outside the gunroom pantry. Kettlewell[7] slept alongside mine, touching it. We used to talk a bit, and watch the cockroach parade along a beam a few inches above our faces. Kettlewell slept with his mouth open and the roaches would drop into it. One night I awoke at about 3:00 am. Kettlewell was snoring next to me and on his bare chest was a huge rat!

Once I got into a fight with Bill Lee, the AP, who was as tight as a tick and quarrelsome. He was sitting on the settee. I was at the other end of the table. He picked on me and made some disparaging remark, so I rapped out 'Shit on you!' He went a bit cold and nasty, and remarked that he would deal with me later. He did. As soon as the apology for a dinner had been cleared away, he left his place, sat beside me and asked me to repeat what I'd said. I remained silent. He repeated his query. I kept mum. Crash! Bill's elbow hit me in the ribs. I was mad and hit his nose, a very silly thing to do seeing as how he was twice my weight and years older. The next thing I remember is flying through the air out of the gunroom, taking a curtain with me, and landing on my back outside. Bill descended on my chest and knocked the wind out of me. However, on my sudden passage out of the gunroom I had seized one of his ears. Next thing I know I was back in the gunroom. Bill, in a sweaty, half-torn vest with a towel round his loins, was in a corner in a fighting stance, surrounded by seven midshipmen. His starboard ear was three parts detached from his head and his bare chest was covered in blood. Seven midshipmen were too many for Bill. It ended pleasantly with him standing us all a glass of beer. The incident was forgotten.

I was really growing up. We arrived at Bermuda on my 16th birthday. I had gone up to the fore topsail yard for a smoke with a friend (we were not allowed to do this). After 42 days at sea, it was thrilling to see Gibbs Hill lighthouse show up on the horizon. 'Land ho!' we shouted. Next morning, we picked up a pilot and edged into one of the most attractive ports in the world. Everything was so beautiful – the turquoise sea, the pinkish sand, the green hillocks, and 'piff'. I can't recall why this drink was called piff except that it was the noise made when one banged a glass ball in it with a knife or pencil. The steward brought it on board at midday. We paid him threepence a bottle (it cost him a penny). It was only lemonade or ginger beer, but nectar! Madeira had been majestic. Bermuda was pretty with its beautiful blue robin and cardinal birds and the black-and-gold sergeant major fish. The Governor did not impress me; they never did. Governors' wives are much more impressive – invariably kind to midshipmen, providers of good teas, and with daughters who are 'jolly good sorts' – probably more easily forgotten than other sorts of girls when a ship sails.

After Bermuda, we went north to Nova Scotia. One evening, near Halifax, a boy fell out of the fore rigging. We were travelling quite fast at the time under steam with a fair wind – maybe 8½ knots. I was in

---

6 A chief engineer in *Tourmaline* committed suicide because of the engine.

7 Captain William Kettlewell, RN (1877–1969) went on to head the Gibraltar Torpedo Boat Squadron, subsequently commanded by Claude Cumberlege (see Chapter 5). Court-martialled for stranding *TB 91* in 1898, Kettlewell was acquitted. In 1899 he was deemed careless by the Admiralty for grounding *TB 93*. Later he specialised in wireless telegraphy, before retiring from the Navy in 1922.

the poop. Hearing the cry 'Man overboard', I rushed aft to lend a hand with the lifeboats. Both were dropped into the sea immediately, together with patent lifebuoys. Suddenly the lifeline became taut and for a moment it seemed the boy had grabbed it. Given the speed of the ship, he could not possibly hang on for long. Both lifebuoys passed close by him and he might have touched either of them. Similarly, both the cutters passed within a few yards of the lad. By then the ship had been thrown into the wind, with the foretopsail aback and the engine going full speed astern. Once the ship's speed slackened, it was possible to haul away on the patent log line. But the harpoon log, which had somehow caught in the boy's clothing, suddenly disentangled itself. The cutters had been left way behind. Later, it was thought that the poor lad must have been filled up with salt water when dragged through the sea and consequently sank like a stone. We never saw him again.

Then we had another tragedy. The ship's steward died of DTs [delirium tremens]. I could see into the sick bay from the cubby hole where I did my copy of the ship's log. The man was imagining rats with hummingbird feathers instead of fur. And then, quite suddenly, there was peace. I went ashore that afternoon in Halifax, and a man shoved a special edition of a local newspaper into my hand. The loss of HMS *Victoria*[8] led the paper – the flagship of the Mediterranean station. 'Oh well,' we thought, 'that makes the third tragedy'. All of us were greatly affected by the news; a couple of the midshipmen who drowned had been cronies of mine in *Britannia*.

Soon we sailed south to Barbados – a longish trip of 14 days carried out partly under sail and partly in steam. There were no particular adventures, but we saw some of the 'Works of the Lord and his wonders in the Deep' such as a battle between thresher sharks and a huge whale, lunar rainbows, Portuguese men-of-war and flying fish. Sunday forenoon was about the busiest day of the week, as it included the Captain's inspection followed by church. Religion didn't bother us midshipmen much, but going to church was a bore, if less boring than being a conscientious objector. My father was an agnostic – he called himself a 'scoffer'. But he always gave the local curate a fiver at Christmas because he was poor and meant well. I was greatly influenced by my father's attitude. When 'pipe down' came at the end of Divine Service, it was always a great relief. Religion at sea, I found later, was more useful as a disciplinary measure than as an aid to spiritual enlightenment.

Off Barbados we anchored in a bay near a wooden pier called the Engineer's Pier – a wonderful place from which to bathe. We were told there were sharks in the bay and it was dangerous to swim, but did so anyway. Bridgetown Bay was full of movement. Big square riggers came round the point southwards of us to lie up for the anchorage, shortening sail as they approached, backing their topsails and letting go their anchors. At intervals the Royal Mail packet from England came in with longed-for letters. Half a dozen little ships of the same company would meet her before sailing away to other islands having transferred their mail to the larger ship.

During the voyage south I had committed an 'atrocity', which resulted in my leave being stopped for three months – a fierce punishment for a growing lad. I felt some grievance about this because in my erroneous opinion I had done nothing very awful. We had been in school one day and I was bored, drawing pictures of ships in my copy books and not paying attention to the instructor. It was hot and tempers were fraying. 'Pay attention to what I'm saying, Cumberlege!' I paid no attention and continued with my sketching. Round came the padre and I closed the book. 'Give me your book. What have you been drawing there?' He obviously

8 HMS *Victoria* was the lead ship in her class of two battleships. On 22 June 1893 she collided with HMS *Camperdown* near Tripoli, Lebanon, during manoeuvres. She sank quickly, killing 358 crew including the commander of the British Mediterranean Fleet, Vice Admiral Sir George Tryon, who was later blamed for causing the accident.

thought I had been drawing something risqué. I replied, 'Ships,' and sent the book skimming through the open porthole into the sea. Now he was angry, and dragged me then and there before the Captain, citing me for inattention and disobedience and contempt and one thing after another. The result was that I had my leave stopped for three months, commencing on arrival in Barbados. 'Only,' the Captain added, 'he must be allowed to go ashore once a week for exercise.'

I duly chose the day we arrived in Barbados to take my weekly run ashore, put on my best clothes and had a look around and a couple of lovely iced 'green bitters' at the Ice House. Then I called on the local bishop. My mother had told me to do this because his daughter was a family friend. Bishop Bree[9] was charming, and so was his daughter Evie. They lived in a fine house called Bishopscourt with a lovely garden. 'My dear Murray,' said the bishop to his chaplain. 'I think we might have some of that delicious beverage called green bitters.' To me, he said: 'Have you brought your bag? Of course, you're staying here.' I explained my situation. 'Never heard such nonsense,' the bishop responded. Eventually I took my leave, arriving on board by the last boat that evening. Next morning, the senior midshipman said: 'Here you! The First Lieutenant says you're to pack your bag and go up to Bishopscourt and stay there until the ship sails, damn you!' I went. Apparently, just after I left the bishop the previous evening, our chaplain – also our Naval Instructor – arrived to pay his respects. The dear old bishop had little difficulty in pointing out the great spiritual advantages likely to obtain from a small midshipman staying with him – especially a midshipman 'so lost to shame' as this one. Evie told me later that the second 'green bitters' did the trick. Did I enjoy myself! What food! How I chortled away at the thought of my messmates wolfing the Mess fare. Butter would not have melted in my mouth on Sundays when we rolled sedately down to the cathedral.

One day we sailed away from Barbados to British Guiana, and anchored 13 miles offshore and could only spy the top of the palm trees. I got ashore for my one day, and at the only club in town met an awfully decent bloke who asked me to stay. So I told him the whole story. 'Humbug,' he announced. 'Hold on a minute.' Away he went, and I saw him talking to the skipper. The result was that I stayed the whole time with the Colonial Secretary. After that, I heard no more about my stopped leave.

We got to know the West Indies well in our leisurely wanderings. We could easily take a week to sail between, say, Trinidad and Jamaica. And when we got there, we stayed a fortnight. On rare occasions we took in a couple of islands in a day. Once we stopped off at Sombrero Island off Anguilla – so called because whoever found it thought that it looked like a hat. We manned the sea boat and went ashore. There were three men living on this outsized cowpat, two whites and a black: one shaking with suppressed DTs, one most melancholy mad and one (a jolly black man) full of fun; he tended the flickering flames of the other two's existence with quip and quirk and bottled gin, and his jewelled lanthorn (lantern) with pure colza [vegetable] oil.

Later that voyage we coaled at Port Castries, St Lucia. It was in this port that my crony Fitzwilliams and I decided it was high time we had some first-hand knowledge of the thing called Love. We had often discussed the matter; all the ancient mariners in the gunroom seemed to know all there was to know about it. Bill Lee, the AP, had served in the China seas. According to him, there was nobody to touch Japanese girls. Chinese girls, he said, were unique in that they were 'fitted athwartships'. The Americans of Hong Kong were 'too damned expensive'. He said that you signed a chit for them, and a Chinese boy would bring the chits to the ship at the end of the month. Fitz and I raked up five bob apiece and sallied forth into the wilds of St Lucia. We found a few shacks constructed of old paraffin tins and thatch in the shade of forest greenery

9 Herbert Bree (1828–1899) was educated in Bury St Edmunds and at Cambridge University. He was ordained in 1852. He became Bishop of Barbados and the Windward Islands in 1882, and died in post.

and cotton trees. There were two jolly girls, shining and black. We dallied, we trifled, we toyed, we fondled – all very well for a foursome, but terrifying when alone with a laughing young girl in her birthday suit. We did not relate our adventure to the gunroom. Our experience, we decided, was well worth five shillings – and we were still virginal. Everybody pleased!

Port Royal [Jamaica] was a fascinating place. Its old dockyard looked more like a botanical garden. I went to a ball there in a kind of hall. Tina asked me – a very pretty snuff and buttered nursemaid belonging to an official. The brass band was black and functioned on wind and rum. On the left there were rows of girls: on the right, bucks and rum. If the girls were magnificent in their starched cotton frocks with their beautiful breasts overflowing their Victorian corsages, the bucks were superlative in spats and flowered waistcoats and gold-washed watch chains. This was early in the evening. Much later, I found myself sitting with Tina in an upstairs room, on a window seat. We were chaperoned by the Bosun, crooning drunk and swaying on the other side of Tina. She took her chance. Her lovely little hand on its slim wrist slipped into the Boatswain's pocket where silver jangled. The crooning did not cease. But a massive arm shot across Tina's saffron chest, a pair of black silk stockings flew into the air and Tina was gone! I rushed downstairs and found her in the flagged courtyard. She had fallen on her head and blood was all over her face. Bowles,[10] a midshipman, had borrowed a silk pocket handkerchief for the evening. I got hold of him and together we carried the yelling Tina to her shack. Her mother doubled the uproar but we bathed the head and, finding that only the skin had been broken, bandaged it up with the silk handkerchief, tucked her up comfortably and went back to the ball.

By now it was very late. The bucks were getting argumentative, thrusting chins in each other's faces and calling each other 'you damn black man' or 'you damn white trash' according to the shade addressed. The girls were either hysterical or beautifully drunk. Some lay still, 'clothing disarranged', as they say in the police courts, where they had capsized. Bowles and I collected the Boatswain, who called us 'black bastards' for our trouble, but became instantly sober as we stole over the gangway of our ship just as all hands were being called to 'Rise and Shine'. A few days later, I happened to be Midshipman of the Watch on a sultry afternoon with only the Corporal of Marines on the gangway and no one else awake. Tina, in stiff starched cotton and black silk hose, tripped up the gangway and presented me with the white silk handkerchief washed and ironed and folded in tissue paper.

One night in Jamaica we co-operated in a sham attack on the capital. The palisades enclosing the great harbour of Kingston were about 7 miles long. At the end of the sand promontory was the fortified Port Royal with its gunners and sappers and searchlights and guns – impossible to force. At midnight we closed the land about halfway along the palisades. Lights out, and in silence in the calm of the night, we hoisted out our boats and rowed ashore, landing in the deserted sand of the palisades. The landing party jumped ashore, armed to the teeth and furnished with large amounts of tobacco tins labelled 'dynamite' and a polite chit inside 'With our Compliments'. The boats were dragged across the sand by a hundred chuckling tars [seamen]. Now and again a wandering beam of searchlight swept our way; we dropped like dead men among the mangroves until it passed over. Then the boats were launched again within the great harbour. Without seeing a soul, we deposited the tins in all the public buildings. By and by, the weary but successful landing party returned, full of themselves at having 'done in the bloody leathernecks' [gunners and sappers]. Before dawn, our good ship was anchored in the narrow waters of Port Royal.

10 Commander Geoffrey Tatton Bowles, RN (1879-?).

We returned to Halifax, Nova Scotia, and its gorgeous harbour. Days spent at Josh Umlah's[11] the hunter. What food! A turkey at one end of the table and a baron of beef at the other. A gallon of pure cream for breakfast. We picnicked amongst fir trees surrounding the lovely Bedford Basin. From Halifax we went to Quebec and became the first man-of-war to go up to Montreal. In August 1894 we were sent to mark the entrance to the Gut of Canso, so that if fog came down it would be easier for the flagship HMS *Blake* to find it. Fog did come down but we found the mournful bell buoy and anchored near it. All night we lay wrapped in wet fog. Next morning, we fired guns and made our name on the steam siren. Suddenly, at four o'clock in the afternoon the fog lifted, and there was the big black *Blake* with her band playing, brass gleaming and purring along at 20 knots in the sunshine over a calm sea. A few days later we picked up the fleet at anchor somewhere below Quebec and steamed up together to moor off the city. Then we moved up the St Lawrence, touching the riverbed twice as we went.

One fine day we reached Montreal and hoisted the flag of the Commander-in-Chief, Sir John Hopkins.[12] We had a wonderful time at Montreal. *Tourmaline* was the first man-of-war ever to have been so far up the river. After a day or two Fitzwilliams and I decided that we would like to see Niagara Falls. We touched the skipper for £5 apiece, and that evening took the train to Toronto, arriving at the Falls the next day and seeing them the same evening. We had our return tickets, a week's leave and one silver 10-cent bit between us. We returned to Toronto and put up at the best hotel, had supper and went out for a walk. We came across an auction going on. Fitzwilliams made a bid of 10 cents for a white-handled pocket knife taken from a cardboard box. The auctioneer said he couldn't have it. 'I cannot rob you, Sir. You shall have the whole box.' Fitz handed over the coin and the auctioneer handed him the box, empty, amidst roars of laughter. The auctioneer laughingly wished to return the 10 cents to Fitz but he refused to accept it back. So we returned to our hotel to think things out. I had a pair of gold cuff links (borrowed from another midshipman) and Fitz had an iron-cased watch.

Suddenly, there was a rat-a-tat on our door. 'Come in,' we shouted. In walked a waiter carrying a card on a silver tray. 'Mr. Jones, *Toronto Globe*' ran the legend on the card. 'Newspaperman, Sir,' said the waiter. 'Show him up,' we chorused. In walked Mr. Jones with pad and pencil. 'Good evening, gentlemen. I saw your names in the hotel register and thought I would ask you about your lives in the Service and about HMS *Tourmaline* now in Montreal.' We gave him lots, and went to bed without a care in the world. Next morning, breakfast in bed, baths, best clothes – and another knock on the door. In walked a venerable man of great age (remember, we were only 17). Tapping a newspaper, he said that he was Mr. Walker and hoped that we would let him do the honours for the city of Toronto. His carriage and pair were at the door. We went.

The forenoon ended by our new friend introducing us to his daughters. We were in clover! Ice cream sodas by the thousand, lunch, racing, a garden party at Government House; dancing and dinner followed. What a time! Our train left the following evening after we had squared the hotel manager to await our return to the ship for his money (borrowed from the chaplain). The platform was crowded with our new friends as we climbed aboard the Montreal express at half past ten at night. I only remember one thing about the crowd – the lovely face and corn-coloured hair of Maisie. I have never forgotten her.

We stayed in Montreal for three happy weeks, which included a great ball given at the Chateau Frontenac. The midshipmen on *Tourmaline* were a good lot. Lord Aberdeen Crawford had social style. Kettlewell was a damned good artist. Coppinger[13] was called 'Holy Ghost' and was known as 'godly Coppinger'. Charlie

11 George Joshua Umlah (1873–1922).

12 Admiral Sir John Ommaney Hopkins, GCB (1834–1916) went on to be C-in-C, Mediterranean Fleet, in 1897.

13 Rear Admiral Robert Henry Coppinger, CBE (1877–) commanded the battleship *Dreadnought* in 1919. He retired in 1922.

White,[14] a great friend of mine, had the biggest nose I have ever seen and a droll sense of humour. Laurence Oliphant[15] – 'Polyjuice', our only gentleman – and Wilfred Tomkinson[16] joined us later, as did John Bray, a fine addition to the ship's cricket eleven. I was known as 'Bloody Eye-balls' which contracted to 'Balls'. We got on wonderfully well – all nearly of the same age, all poverty-stricken, all living cheek-by-jowl day and night sharing victuals, clothes and money. There are few secrets in a gunroom.

Ulises Heureaux (Britannica)

After Montreal we moved back to Halifax and November gales *en route* to the Windward Isles. The great ship steamed ahead in the teeth of a gale. Then we wandered south round our friendly islands again – St Vincent, Grenada, Barbados, Antigua, Trinidad, San Juan de Puerto Rico. In San Domingo the guard turned out with equipment for every third man; one had a shirt but no trousers, one had trousers but no upper tunic, the third had nothing but a gun and an arse clout [cloth]. Ulises,[17] the coal-black magnifico of a president, was togged out in a blue-and-gold outfit much as you see in paintings in London clubs of old admirals.

Suddenly we were ordered to return to St John's, Newfoundland, where the banks had gone bust and riots were imminent. We stayed there from December until early May. The harbour froze over and we roofed in the ship with timber and canvas and wove hot water pipes everywhere. Our Marines looked like Cossacks in bearskins, overcoats and sea boots. We enjoyed ourselves, sending to Canada for toboggans (nobody had heard of skis), fishing for trout through the ice, ice-sailing on Lake Quidi Vidi and meeting some polar explorers. We rigged up soup kitchens. Two American opera companies spent evenings with us, lapping up unlimited stout and spitting on the deck. They hadn't a cent, having lost all their money when the banks went bust. In return, they would do stunts. On March 10th 1895 we watched the Sealing Fleet leave. Each ship had crews of hundreds, all apparently bottled [drunk]. A couple of steam tugs followed to pick up the ones who toppled overboard. The first ship to return, about a fortnight later, had 40,000 seals (for blubber, not fur) in her hold and in the cabins. As soon as she discharged, the vessel sailed again.

On May 3rd, *Tourmaline* finally left Newfoundland. Some of us had sore hearts but I was still fancy-free. As we sailed back to the West Indies, we had well passed the halfway mark of our three-year commission. Christmas 1895 found us on the north coast of Jamaica. I fell in love with an American at Morant Bay on the south-east of the island; I forget her name. Then it was 1896, and soon we were homeward bound. The old fiddler on board scraped away as one island after another was left in our wake – always playing the 'Girl I Left Behind Me'. Bermuda was our last port of call. Cheered to the echo, we set sail for England on April 30th, 1896.

---

14 Commander Charles White (1876–). Retired 1918.

15 Captain Henry Gerard Laurence Oliphant, MVO, DSO (1879–1955). He was mentioned in despatches for his role in the blocking operations at Zeebrugge and Ostend in 1918 and a second time for similar operations at Ostend in 1918. In 1919 Vice Admiral Dampier described Oliphant as 'a dashing officer (who) spent 793 nights on the bridge of a ship during the war'.

16 Vice Admiral Wilfred Tomkinson, CB, MVO (1877–1971) commanded HMS *Hood* in 1920.

17 Ulises Heureaux (1845–1899) was president of the Dominican Republic 1882–1884 and effectively from 1887 to his assassination in 1899. After his death it was discovered that he had taken secret loans from foreign banks for his personal use. The government declared bankruptcy, the economy crumbled and US military intervention followed.

CHAPTER 4

Learning the ropes

Between 1896 and 1902 Cumberlege served in four ships. He was promoted to lieutenant, enjoyed life ashore, swindled supplies for his ship, watched an execution, and fell foul of a senior officer.

Three years out of England – let it blow! We parted [hoisted] every sail we had in *Tourmaline* and were homeward bound. The Wolf Rock hove in sight, Land's End, the Dodman Peak. Our anchor dropped in glorious Plymouth Sound, 19 days out of Bermuda. I was the first of the crew to set foot on English soil, as it was my cutter that was called to take the Marine postman ashore to get the mail. As soon as he landed and left for the post office, I divided the cutter's crew of 12 into two watches, fell one of them in on the wharf, and solemnly marched them in bare feet to the nearest pub 500 yards up the street. Having stood each man a couple of pints, we marched back to the boat. Then I took the other six up to the pub and treated them likewise. By this admirable method I managed to stow away two quarts of lovely beer. Rather flushed, I got back to the ship. Here there was some backchat over the time I had taken from the First Lieutenant, who was anxiously awaiting letters from his wife. No matter – we were HOME.

From Plymouth we went to Sheerness to pay off. That night, some of us went ashore and walked into the Criterion, an old-fashioned music hall attached to a pub of that name. We took a box for a shilling. The hall below was full of 'Stormies' ['Stormy' was the pet name for *Tourmaline*]. One of the songs, sung by a certain Miss Tessy Vandeane wearing a green plush waistcoat from which her ample bosom overflowed, raised the roof – 'Blow ye winds softly over the sea/Send back the *Tourmaline* sife 'ome again/Free from all danger across the wide main/'Eaven send the *Tourmaline* sife 'ome again!!!' Later, I found myself sitting on the kerb outside the pub with Rourke, captain of the main top, weeping drunk.

The Criterion pub and music hall in Sheerness in 1896 (PD)

'The young gentlemen may proceed on leave' ran a message from the Captain. I sent a wire to my father and caught the first train. I got out at Hassocks – nobody to meet me – and started walking the 3 miles to my home, leaving my gear at the station. How lovely is the Sussex countryside! At Clayton Hill I suddenly saw a high-wheeled dogcart coming all-out down the slope. It was my mother and Noonie,[1] my sister. I really was home. I must have learnt a lot during three solid years at sea, but now I knew I was still a boy. Yet I had commanded men.

1 Mary Natalie Cumberlege, 1879–1916. In 1906 she married George Barrow at Steyning, Sussex.

Jolly days fled by on the South Downs until I found myself appointed to the battleship *Royal Sovereign*. I joined her in Portsmouth, early in August, a few months before I became an Acting Sub-Lieutenant. How different a modern battleship was to my dear old corvette. I enjoyed it – comfortable, with a huge gunroom and a fine crowd of officers. The Gunnery and Torpedo Lieutenants especially took a lot of trouble with us midshipmen. We went off to Leith with the fleet and did the honours during a visit by the Czar of Russia. Then we sailed to Galicia. In Vigo I looked a bull firmly in the eye in the bullring and walked slowly towards him. He charged. I took to my heels and ran, shinning up a big post in the far corner as the baffled brute turned away. By Christmastime we were back at Spithead. I went home briefly but had to go back to the ship to pass an exam for Lieutenant. Which I did, but to my utter disgust only got a 'second class'. It didn't matter a damn to me; I was never likely to be a 'five-one-er' (an officer with five first-class certificates).

Early in '97, I started my courses as Acting Sub-Lieutenant in Gunnery, Torpedo and Pilotage – hard work, with hideous examinations looming. Suffice to say that I scraped through Greenwich with a second in Gunnery, a third in Torpedo with 13 marks after some illicit help from a friend, and a pass in Pilotage. We had to go to London for the Pilotage exam. My turn came just after my friend Fitzwilliams. He emerged from the exam room, furious. 'The blighters failed me.' 'On what question?' I asked. 'So and so and so and so.' I dashed for the book, looked up the answer, memorised it – and it was the first question I was asked. But then my initial success rapidly dissolved. Something drastic had to be done. So I said, 'You've got me all tied up. Whatever you ask me now, I shall make a mess of – even though I know the correct answers.' I was summoned to the Charts table. Here I was quite comfortable, almost glib, so much so that I nearly queered the whole pitch by tilting back my chair and stabbing holes in the chart with a compass point. 'Get out,' they said. I went.

There were lucid intervals. We were allowed out once a week until 1:00 am, and I discovered the Savoy Theatre and all that Gilbert & Sullivan meant. Often, I went with a friend night after night; I forget how we squared the lynx-eyed corporal on our return, but I recall climbing the railings. This passion for music came suddenly to me and has stood me in good stead. If it had not been for that Savoy magnet, I wonder what devilment I might have tried. I also played rugby football (I was a fast wing three-quarter) until I tried for the Navy XV and dislocated a knee, which put me in hospital for three months. If it hadn't been for this, I might have anticipated my namesake's success in international rugby. Now, all I get when I am introduced is 'Cumberlege! Are you any relation to Barry Cumberlege?'[2] I enjoy the reflected glory. Cumberlege is an uncommon name of Huguenot origin, and we carry the fleur de lys as a crest. Nobody else in England does.

To Whale Island and Gunnery. They hated Acting Subs at that institution and seemed especially venomous to our section. First Lieutenant Leveson[3] – 'Levi' – was in charge. For some reason he chose me and Joe Shuter,[4] an Australian, to be his doggies for the weekly battalion drill. He worked us to the bone with Levitical cunning, and got rid of us without ever inviting us up to the Mess for a glass of beer during the stand-easy half-time, as was the invariable time-honoured custom. We celebrated the end of our Gunnery course by putting black gaiters on the hind legs of the stone lion on top of one of the buildings and painting the testicles vermilion. Next day, the section was fallen-in. Never have I had to listen to such abuse and obloquy that poured from Levi's lips: 'Not one of you deserves to receive a certificate,' he concluded, 'except

2 Barry Cumberlege (1891–1970) won eight caps for the England XV 1920–22 as a full back, and also played cricket for Cambridge University and Kent. He was a Lloyd's underwriter.

3 Admiral Sir Arthur Leveson GCB (1868–1929) commanded the Royal Australian Navy 1917–1918 during a time when Cumberlege was also serving in the RAN. He became Commander in Chief China Station 1922–25.

4 Commander Joseph Shuter MVO (1876–1915) died aged 41 from disease of the liver.

perhaps my two runners, who perhaps ...' We heard no more. As one, Joe and I stepped out of the ranks and shook each other warmly by the hand! Levi burst out laughing and hurried away, human after all.

A notable interlude in our studies occurred because of the 1897 Jubilee Review. I was appointed to an old-fashioned, two-funnelled cruiser called *Medea*, which was hauled out of a berth in Southampton to swell the serried ranks of Britain's sea power on parade at Spithead. It was a fine show, and we had a rare party on board. The only trouble was that accommodation for the ladies left much to be desired. The one toilet on board was well forrard. We overcame this difficulty by buying 12 large jerry cans that we ranged in line across the Captain's sleeping cabin, which had been appropriated for the ladies as a retiring room. We needed at least 13!

1897 drifted along. I found myself a full-blown Lieutenant. No more examinations. I had seen some of the new destroyers.[5] Politely, I indicated to the Secretary of the Admiralty that I would like to be a second-in-command in one of them. I was appointed to HMS *Decoy*. A Lieutenant Vivian[6] was in command, a delightful fellow. How I loved it all! The chief engineer and the steward were always drunk; I am afraid (I was still very young) that we hid their delinquencies from the skipper. It was in this fine little ship that I developed the art of swindling the dockyard out of such essentials as white enamel paint, brass tubes and so on – solely, of course, for the benefit of the Service and the particular unit in which I was serving. My methods were as follows: two destroyers would find themselves in dry dock together. About 11:30 am one or other of the Subs would stroll ashore and find the master painter of the yard who, by this time of day, was pretty certain to be thirsty. He would be asked on board, taken to one of the wardrooms and regaled with Plymouth gin. Meantime the other Sub would excuse himself, go straight to the paint store and help himself to whatever was going – gold leaf, sandpaper and so on; anything that was fairly easy to conceal on his person.

In Devonport I had a great friend in the dockyard called Ham. He was the dockyard rat-catcher and adored whisky. One of his duties was to take 25 wooden buckets on board a battleship; somehow or other he brought five to my ship. On another occasion we had been lent a dockyard cutter when we were lying out at the buoys, and had left it at a buoy temporarily when we came into dock. A gale blew up and my cutter no longer existed. 'Ham,' I said, 'my cutter is missing. What are you going to do about it?' 'Get another,' said he, and did so. Nobody missed it, but a couple of days later my original cutter was discovered miles up the river and there was quite a difficulty about it. The only way to suppress the matter was to neglect to answer correspondence on the subject. After all, the British Empire was unlikely to go up in a blue flame because one cutter happened to be missing.

I had a bit of leave in 1898 and had a wonderful time hunting with the Southdown foxhounds. Father produced a mare with the strange name of W.H.T.J.; the damn thing had been out at grass for ages, threw me into a ditch and tried to stamp on me. Once I recovered her, W.H.T.J. took complete charge when a fox went away.

I also fell in love. She was quite eligible, but I was young [21] and she was a bit older. My parents became worried. Eventually, my father tackled me. 'Look here, old boy. I don't know what your idea is, but may I remind you that if you mean to marry the girl, then you damned well have to sleep with her for years. *Have* her, by all means.' That was really *all* I wanted, and the prospect of sleeping with the same person for the next 50 years seemed so absurd that I hauled off [backed off]. Fortunately, just then I was transferred from *Decoy* and sent as executive officer in a ship shortly sailing for the Mediterranean.

---

5 By the early 1890s torpedo boat speeds as high as 25 knots were achieved. As a defence, the UK deployed large torpedo boats, capable of outrunning and outgunning regular torpedo boats. They were called destroyers.

6 Captain Gerald William Vivian, CMG (1869–1921).

I joined *Halcyon* at Plymouth. The skipper was a bearded Scot, Commander W.H.A. Gray. I liked him at once. I think he liked me, but he was a lot older and at times I was a bit of a trial. The Navigator was a hungry hundred [RNR] lieutenant. My crony was Nicholls, but he died young and was relieved by 'Lummy' Lumsden,[7] a fine fellow from Watson's[8] *Halcyon* was a cheerful little ship with a couple of 4.7-inch guns and torpedo tubes – a torpedo gunboat. There were half a dozen of the same class in the Mediterranean, and we relieved each other at out-of-the-way places but usually managed to put in at Malta at some point.

One day in Malta I paid a visit to the dockyard, taking Jack, a perfect fox-terrier, with me. I told my skiffman to lay off the steps just inside the dockyard and wait for me. I called in at the joiner's shop and came away with about a foot of 2-inch square box wood wrapped in a newspaper. Jack and I, very well pleased, returned to the steps and I hailed my skiff, which was 100 yards off. Just then, up walked a dockyard policeman who politely asked me what I had in my parcel. Immediately, I made a diversion, calling Jack to jump in the water – he played up wonderfully.[9] Then I said: 'I beg your pardon, officer, what did you say?' My boat was approaching rapidly. The cold-hearted slop insisted on his rights. I pretended not to pay attention but when the boat was 20 yards away flung the lathe into the water and Jack plunged after it. The parcel sank like a stone. While I was still shouting to Jack and trying to gain time, the boat came alongside. Then I made myself very busy hauling Jack out of the water, jumped into the boat and shoved off. It was a very close shave.

On another occasion we were in dry dock at Malta. Nosing around, I found a pile of brass tubes – just what I wanted to split and make into running streaks around the skipper's whaler. I organised a plan involving a reel of twine and enlisted a crony [an Able Seaman]. Six times we slid the solid brass tubes surreptitiously from the store, over the flagstones towards the dock, over the edge of the dock and into a skiff. We also stole a lot of paint from dockyard painters when they were working on our ship. A tot of whisky was good for a gallon of white enamel to be left behind. The pattern-maker's shop was useful too. Such things as crowns for the tops of ensign staffs could easily be exchanged for 'hospitality'. Gold leaf was difficult and much sought after, but one day, by a stroke of luck, we met the royal yacht *Osborne* in Suda Bay in Crete. Queen Alexandra was on board, on a Mediterranean cruise. I went on board and, of all the people in the world, met Mr. Morgan, the carpenter on *Tourmaline* for three years. I came away with a couple of hundredweight of white zinc paint and enough gold leaf to embellish the Albert Memorial. This villainy was carried out solely for the good of the Service. We were never allowed enough paint to keep the ship really chic. Those days, round about the 'Naughty Nineties', were peak days of smartness in Royal Navy ships. In *Tourmaline* the stream anchor was burnished like silver. I saw white ensigns made out of pure silk. Malta was always a grand place for getting everything in order.

Malta! The Union Club, the lower bar. *Viva* Malta, *viva* Gozo! A sea of Dypsos [alcohol] and a land of *carozze* [horse-drawn cabs] and the elite. There was a Marquis this and a Baron that round every corner, some perfectly charming. Most naval officers didn't have much to do with the Maltese except for those who kept them in food and drink and out of difficulty with the police. But I got to know some of them. P.J. Saliba knew to a half-pound weight which pony was likely to win a race at the horse track. Anthony Tabona was a superb bumboatman. Michael Borg, another bumboatman, sent me bouquets of flowers on the basis that one day I might command a battleship, and then it would be a question of whether he or Tabona 'got' the ship. I did meet some of the Maltese nobility, who bored me, but I also got to know quite a few 'ordinary,'

---

7 Rear Admiral Walter Lumsden (1865–1947). In 1907 he assumed command of the cruiser *Gladiator*. From 1909 to 1917 he was Flag Officer Commanding the Royal Indian Marine.

8 Almost certainly George Watson's College in Edinburgh.

9 From his interaction we can infer that he had come by the lathe illegally.

The opera house in Malta (PD)

well-to-do Maltese. The opera meant a great deal. It was in Malta that I had a complete education in grand opera for the price of a 1/6d seat in the stalls. The chorus was old and fat and ugly, but I heard some of the most famous stars. I also went in for light opera and was roped into the chorus in a production of *HMS Pinafore*. I fell for several of the girls – Marie and Gwen especially.

All of us were great dancers in Malta. There were a dozen dances during the season at the Club. At one of them I was with Cerise – much older than me, but so lovely – and ran into Jackie Fisher.[10] I was in seventh heaven in Cerise's arms in a mazy waltz, when suddenly a black-vised old tough pushed his way into the middle of the dance floor and stopped us. I recognised the villain as my Commander-in-Chief. 'You will dance now with me!' he said to the fair lady, ignoring me. 'I will do nothing of the sort,' she replied. 'I am already engaged for this dance.' Fisher gave me a vicious look and said: 'Never mind *that*. I tell you that you are going to dance with me!' 'Certainly not!' she said gallantly. 'Very well,' said Jackie, 'I am going now, but tomorrow morning at 10:30 am I shall call on you at your flat, and you shall give me a dance *then*.' Directing another malevolent glance at me, he strode off. Cerise told me later that the old devil turned up at precisely 10:30 next morning and, after shifting the furniture himself, made her dance in her room without any music.

I fell for other girls too. Anne Ingraham was an American – she thought I was 'terribly cute'. I also had real affection for Georgina. She was swivel-eyed and taught me a lot, but we sailed for the Red Sea and that was that.

Port Said! What a place in those days – business mainly in the hands of English firms, utterly French in culture, and filthily Egyptian in the streets. One was never bored here. All ships bound to and from the East passed this way. It was so interesting, but hard to explain why; one first must be a sailor to understand, and

10 Admiral Sir John Fisher, 1st Baron Fisher, GCB, OM, GCVO (1841–1920). Known as Jackie. Appointed First Sea Lord in 1904, he removed 150 obsolete ships from active service, instead developing a modern oil-fired fleet. He retired in 1910, but became First Sea Lord again in 1914 before resigning seven months later over the ill-fated Gallipoli campaign. At the time of his encounter with Cumberlege, Fisher was C-in-C, Mediterranean Fleet.

one must have a lot of imagination. I found an old 'half-rater' [small sailing boat] laid up by a Pando [P&O] captain. She leaked like a sieve, but our carpenter patched her up, and I spent days and weeks in her sailing about the harbour, taking note of every ship that came and went. In a café on land where they performed French operettas, I fell for one of the Viennese girls in the chorus. She had glorious red hair. Unfortunately, as soon as each performance ended, the girls were fallen-in two deep and marched off to their lodgings. Apparently the impresario had to guarantee to return his flock to Vienna intact or married. I wasn't marrying anybody just then. Instead, we all went to the whore shops where there was every nationality available except English.

It was a rum sort of life in Port Said – a sort of Surbiton dumped into Montparnasse. One rubbed shoulders with all sorts of quaint persons. The most interesting to me was a gentleman by the name of Donald Andreas Cameron[11] – a 'senior wrangler', whatever that may be, and an Egyptologist. He looked like Svengali. He hated a friend of mine called Cobb, who was second-in-command of the local Egyptian police.

I got on well with our skipper; he did not worry me overmuch, and I was happy in *Halcyon*, though I do not pretend I was a howling success. I was young and always hard up, and so was the skipper, and we were unable to buy the expensive paints and enamel needed to beautify the little craft. We did envy the appearance of a sister ship, HMS *Hardy*, which boasted a rich skipper and a streetwise First Lieutenant, Freddy Noble.[12]

Our wardroom was a quaint collection. Looking back, my best friend was Smith, my loyal old Marine servant. The Navigator was much older than me and religious, and would stand on his dignity; how he irritated me! He used to run me to the skipper for the funniest things – once because I called him a 'God-damned son of a bitch' during dinner. The Chief Engineer and Assistant Engineer hurriedly left the table. Only the saturnine doctor remained. Until then he had assumed complete aloofness and never uttered a word. Now he burst into a roar of laughter and said, 'Serves you right, you psalm-singing bastard,' – his first words in the Mess for three months.

From Port Said we slid silently south through the canal. I always felt that an unseen curtain rolled down behind us on arrival at Suez. The actual passage along the canal always had a thrill for me. From Suez we wandered down the Red Sea. Once, we came across a 10,000-ton tramp hard and fast on the rocks under the Ras Carib lighthouse. She had got stuck here on her old skipper's birthday – he was 77. We laid out two bower anchors over our stern on slips and went ahead while the chain was paid out. When the chair was out of the clinch, we knocked off the slips, and after a spring tide and jettisoning a lot of cargo the tramp got off. Next we went to Suakin (north-east Sudan) where I made friends with the Mahdi's right-hand man – a good sport. We used to go shooting quail and sand grouse and gazelle. He gave me a silver-gilted Sudanese sword; when I cleaned up the blade I found Templars' marks bit into the steel, and the legend '*Honi soi qui mal y pense*'. It was a Crusader's sword.

Back through the canal to Crete, where there was a war on – Christian Cretans rebelling once more against their Turkish Mohammedan conquerors. The matter came very much to a head after a terrific massacre in 1898 of Christians at Candia [Heraklion]. There happened to be a detachment of the Highlight Light Infantry in Candia. The Mohammedan Cretans thought it would be fun to have a go at the H.L.I. after murdering and raping the Christian Cretans. Things would have gone very badly for this small unit (130 men) but the news got through to Malta, and within a few days the entire Mediterranean Fleet was lying at

11 Donald Andreas Cameron, CMG (1856–1936). Consul General in Eastern Sudan, Benghazi, Port Said and Alexandria.

12 Frederick Burnaby Noble, Captain, RN (1876–1946).

anchor off Candia. We arrived on the scene led by Jerry Noel[13] – 'a stern unbending soul'. In *Halcyon* our duties mainly consisted in running between Candia and Suda Bay, a great and beautiful bay some 70 miles to the west, as mail boat, beef boat and passenger steamer.

All sorts of international courts were set up following the massacre to try the most blatant murderers, and on one of our trips to Suda Bay we had a witness on board to give evidence. She was a Cretan girl, about 20 years of age and very pretty. Without any *arrière-pensée* [ulterior motive], I offered her my cabin for accommodation, but the skipper had her stowed in his after-cabin behind a screen. While we were waiting in Suda Bay for the mail boat, she gave me her story. She had seen the whole of her family sliced up with *yatagans* [Ottoman knives]. She had hidden in the bread oven in the kitchen and so saved her life. A little later, thanks partly to the evidence from this Cretan girl, seven 'Bashibazoukas' [irregular Turkish soldiers] were hanged from the same beam, each man without doubt guilty of atrocious killings. And yet, I felt somehow sorry as I saw them twisting and un-twisting on their ropes, their slippers just hanging on a big toe. They stayed up on the beam all day. In the evening I saw them cut down. Only six coffins had been provided by their relatives, so one poor negro, who presumably had no relatives in Crete, was stuffed in with one of the others. They looked calm enough in death, except that their eyes were sticking out of their sockets, their tongues were out, and they had big green and black bruises under their left ears where the knots had been.

The execution of seven Turkish rebels in Crete 1898 (PD)

We gave up hanging people after that, but I have snapshots of the execution of two more. The men are sat down and tied to stools. In front of them is a five-man firing squad – one man each from Italy, France, Russia and Austria, and a British 'Tommy' on the right. The photo was snapped at the instant the order to Fire was given. The two poor wretches are sagging off their stools, a spurt of smoke is coming from the rifles. I noticed there was something strange about these spurts of smoke. With the aid of a reading glass, I discerned that every rifle in each squad was pointing straight at the poor devils except that of the Englishman; in both squads his rifle is pointing at an angle of 45 degrees in the air.

And so, back to Malta and the old round – Port Said, Suez, the Red Sea. Plague was reported in Alexandria the day after we arrived there. If we had left, we would have had to do a long quarantine, so we were ordered to stay. It was most enjoyable. Polo with the soldiers, 5:00 am chariot racing followed by early morning bathes, weekly sailing races, the casino. Then suddenly, after a few weeks I was relieved; all Sub-Lieutenants and First Lieutenants of gunboats had been relieved.

13 Admiral of the Fleet Sir Gerard Noel, GCB, KCMG (1845–1918) was Second-in-Command of the Mediterranean Fleet in 1898. After that he became C-in-C, Home Fleet, C-in-C, China Station, and C-in-C, The Nore.

After a spell of leave, without more ado I found myself appointed as a Watchkeeping Lieutenant in HMS *Furious*, an old cruiser lying in Chatham and part of the Channel Fleet. Captain Foley[14] and Frankie Melvill[15] were the senior officers. Berwick Curtis[16] was the Senior Watchkeeper. How I hated watchkeeping in harbour wearing a frock coat and a sword belt and a telescope under my arm. Foley had a hideous reputation and was said to be a terror to evil-doers. He seemed charming to me, but was shortly after relieved by F.T. Hamilton[17] who had the opposite reputation. The Paymaster was always drunk; he consumed 24 glasses of Marsala [strong Sicilian red wine] every day. The *Furious* had a new type of water-tube boiler. This meant that the water, which had to be boiled to make steam to turn the engines, was contained in tubes – a reverse process of the old-fashioned boiler where water was contained in a sort of big kettle and the heat was passed through tubes that were part of the boiler. Our first Chief Engineer was carried out of the ship a complete wreck after battling this contraption. A fine fellow called Cant was sent in his place; he must have had nerves of steel. *Furious* was called a Fleet Ram. It sounds exciting, but as far as I could gather it meant only that she had a specially reinforced stern and that most of her cannons were disposed to be able to fire ahead.

In 1901 *Furious* went to the Mediterranean for combined Home–Mediterranean Fleet manoeuvres. All went well until something happened in the engine department and we were unable to work our evaporators to make drinking water. Lord Charles Beresford[18] signalled: '*Furious* is to proceed to Nauplin (Nafplion, in Greece) as she is unable to contain her water'! The great Bay of Nauplin is fed by one sweet water stream. We anchored as close as we could get to this stream, and the arrangements for getting water on board were put in the hands of Berwick, and me as his assistant. What fun we had! There was a wide sandy beach and pure water ran down in a stream about 12 feet wide before losing itself on the foreshore. Only one building was in sight – a sort of Martello tower[19] with the top knocked off. We anchored our pinnaces as close to the shore as possible and hauled their sterns towards the strand. Then we used ordinary fire hoses to siphon the water into the boats, which were filled to the gunwales, towed to the ship and pumped out. One afternoon, with all the sailors rather naked and enjoying this unusual activity, a couple of distinguished gentlemen appeared. They had landed from one of the ships of the fleet. Immediately I recognised one of them, Prince Louis of Battenberg[20] with his black beard. Berwick, in a white tunic finishing just below his navel and wearing nothing else, had no notion who P.L. was.

To have served in *Furious* and not to mention Glengariff in Ireland would be more than absurd. In those days the Home Fleet used to go to Berehaven [Castletown] for weeks, if not months, on end. Every man who

14 Vice Admiral Francis Foley (1855–1911) was captain of HMS *Furious* for a year in 1900–01.

15 Commander Francis Melvill (1867–1904). He drowned when taking a steam pinnace in company with Cdr Hodges and Miller from Weymouth back to HMS *Illustrious* off Portland in heavy seas. After Melvill had taken the wheel and sent the coxswain forward, a sudden lurch of the pinnace caused him to slip and go overboard. Hodges leapt overboard to try to help but Melvill was dragged under by his heavy coat.

16 Vice Admiral Berwick Curtis, CB, CMG, DSO & Bar (1876–1965) took part in the 1916 Battle of Jutland and the 1918–20 Russian Civil War. He commanded the Gibraltar Dockyard 1929–31 and retired from the RN in 1932. In the Second World War he returned to service as a commodore of convoys.

17 Admiral Sir Frederick Tower Hamilton, GCVO, KCB (1856–1917). In 1916 he was appointed C-in-C on the Coast of Scotland. He died from heart failure at Rosyth on 4 October 1917, aged 61.

18 Although Beresford, a baron, would normally have been called 'Lord Beresford', Cumberlege added 'Charles'.

19 A small defensive fort, a series of which were built across the British Empire during the 19th century. Most were sited on the coast. They stand up to 40 feet high, have thick walls and typically had a garrison of one officer and 15–25 men.

20 Admiral of the Fleet Louis Alexander Mountbatten, 1st Marquess of Milford Haven, GCB, GCVO, KCMG, PC (1854–1921), formerly Prince Louis Alexander of Battenberg, was a German prince related to the royal family. He enrolled in the Royal Navy aged 14. In 1912 he became First Sea Lord. His origins forced his retirement in 1914. In 1917 he relinquished his German titles.

Roche's Royal Hotel, Ireland (PD)

went ashore spent at least £1,[21] to say nothing of the amount expended by wardroom and captains' stewards – a gold mine lost to the locals after Irish independence. We had great fun, bicycling or taking a horse-and-cart 18 miles over a wild pass to Roche's Royal Hotel in Glengariff. At Roche's we had the purest honest fun that I ever had. One day Sandy, our Royal Marine officer, was discovered by Father Roche, the head of the family, dallying with one of his many daughters. He went to fetch a gun. 'Ah, for God's sake, Cumber, get Sandy out of it. Father's gone for his gun,' said Mrs. Roche. Quickly, we got Sandy out of the hotel and into a Shandrydan[22] which was stationed in the back yard. When things quietened down a bit, we took whiskies and soda out to Sandy, still dallying with the girl in the old four-wheeler. One night I crept downstairs to where the daughters were sleeping and plunged into a big bed only to find three friends already there. I had to hop out and find a water jug and pour it over myself to cool things off a bit.

Although I disliked the somewhat constrained, in my opinion, life as a watchkeeper in *Furious*, we did have some thrilling times. During manoeuvres I was on board when the whole of the Channel Fleet was brought to anchor in St Mary's Sound in the Scilly Isles during a dense fog. After the fog cleared, we saw that not a single ship had to shift its berth for being out of station – a wonderful example of navigation and seamanship. Masts and flags by then had gone, for all practical purposes in the Navy. This is not to imply that seamanship was dead; in many ways, the need for it had increased, as vast fleets slam-banged about in narrow seas already crowded with merchant shipping.

The destroyer had also arrived to stay, and something fresh was required in their handling. Young officers found themselves in command of delicate little craft stuffed full of as much horsepower as a battleship. From the moment I passed a few months in *Decoy* as second-in-command, I set my heart on getting command of a destroyer as soon as possible. I dreamt of tearing about the ocean in a sort of super speedboat, all white paint and yellow funnels [destroyers at the time were painted black].

Meantime, I felt cribbed, cabined and confined in *Furious*. Nevertheless, we were a contented crowd on board and, if we liked to play, we had no objections to work such as the 'evolutions',[23] which were always interesting and often very funny. The flagship used to order by signal individual actions such as 'Send a bower

21 Around £130 in 2020.

22 A two-wheeled cart or chaise, usually with a hood.

23 Any seamanship task that requires special effort or co-ordination. A replenishment at sea or taking another ship under tow are considered evolutions.

anchor to the flagship' (always a very awkward task), or 'Fire Stations', or 'Clear Ship for Action,' or 'Away All Boats. Pull Round the Fleet' and many others. At an Admiral's Inspection, every mortal thing supposed to be carried on board had to be ready to be demonstrated. All sorts of tricks were resorted to by commanders and lieutenants to get away with a good 'evolution', especially where other ships were involved, and an element of competition got in. 'Coaling Ship' always made a tremendous evolution. However much everybody loathed the idea of coaling, when it came to the point all hands and the cook worked like tigers to get the stuff on board in record time. After a short 'Stand Easy', the seemingly impossible task of cleaning the ship followed. Somehow this was done. In this business, our ships seemed to be miles ahead of foreign men-of-war. Some simply gave up the task of getting 1,000 tons of coal on board and paid coal-heavers to do it for them.

As a matter of fact, though, it was the same with all evolutions. No foreign ship could compete with the Royal Navy in any sort of general exercise. It might take a French vessel a whole forenoon to lay out a bower anchor, weighing several tons; we could do it easily in a few minutes, without fuss. Most of the foreign warships I saw did not seem to have much team spirit. Possibly they had a larger view, for in every French ship I noticed that the legend in brass, stuck up across their quarterdecks, read: '*Honneur et Patrie*'. Nigel Bartellot's[24] ship *Liberty* had one too – 'One More Won't Hurt Us' – when she went into action and he got his head taken off by a shell. As for their seamanship, it was amateurish. Even the rising young German fleet, the Kaiser's pet arm, made a poor show. I once saw a couple of their cruisers make a complete balz [*sic*] of entering and securing in Gibraltar when escorting the Kaiser's yacht, *Hohenzollern*.

Back in Gibraltar I had a tiff with my Commander, Frankie Melvill. It was to do with my inspection of liberty men,[25] many of whom I regret to say were as drunk as Chloe.[26] By dint of being propped up by their mates, most at least were able to stand. Just as I dismissed them to go and turn in to their hammocks, Melvill arrived on the scene and gave me a sound ticking off. I answered back – always a stupid thing to do. Melvill was always inclined to sarcasm. He replied to me with an undoubtedly sarcastic grin: 'In your opinion, then, these men are fit to go over the royal yard?' I responded, certainly uppishly: 'There are no royal yards in this hooker [anchorage] to start with. And in any case, if a man has the sense to come on board when his leave is up instead of breaking it—' 'Mr. Cumberlege,' he broke in, 'in future, I do not wish to speak to you except on service.' Of course, I nursed a grievance; I may have been correct in my judgment but utterly wrong in airing my opinions to my commander. Melvill, it's true, seemed to be looking for trouble. And his manner to an inferior officer was most irritating. Luckily, the next day was my day off. I went ashore early having forgotten the incident. So, probably, had the Commander.

---

24 Nigel Kenneth Walter Bartellot (1883–1914) was a Lt Commander in the Royal Navy. He commanded the destroyer HMS *Liberty* during the Battle of Heligoland 28 August 1914, when he was killed along with seven other crewmen.

25 Crewmen who had leave to go ashore for recreation.

26 The phrase means 'very drunk'. Its origin is thought to be poetry by Matthew Prior (1664–1721) in which Chloe is described as someone who had 'a great propensity for strong drinks'.

CHAPTER 5

Gibraltar 1902–1905

Lt Cumberlege describes his time in Gibraltar commanding nine torpedo boats, being invited to lunch with Kaiser Wilhelm II, and meeting the Russian fleet in 1905. At some point in 1904 he married Laetitia.

On Main Street early the next day I saw young Nestor Diggle,[1] who had been a junior midshipman with me in *Royal Sovereign*. He was in a *carrozza*. He said: 'Jump in. I have just received a wire telling me I have been dug out of this wonderful job [command of the Gibraltar Torpedo Boats] and I am going to telegraph my father to ask him to try and get me reappointed. But I'm afraid it will be no good. Now is your chance, if you want, to put in for it.' I went along, and while he was at a desk making out his telegram I was at one alongside. My telegram was addressed to the Secretary of the Admiralty, Whitehall, London, and read simply: 'Volunteer Gibraltar Torpedo Boats'. I was not aware of any Queen's Regulations making it a criminal offence to ask for something I wanted. I don't recall ever having opened that prolific tome portentously described as being intended for the 'Guidance of a Naval Officer', which essentially explains that if one carried out Regulation 3560 one could easily be court-martialled for having done so by Regulation 3561. I did hear later that My Lords Commissioners of the Admiralty were very seriously upset by this casual communication. However, the Secretary to the Second Sea Lord, being both a sportsman and a humourist, promptly telegraphed my appointment to this delightful job.

Everybody was pleased. Berwick Curtis called me a lucky bugger. Frankie Melvill was charming – was he just pleased to get rid of me? Perish the thought! He put a cutter at my disposal, and I transferred my gear from the old cruiser *Furious* to the little ship of my dreams, Torpedo Boat *TB 99*. And she was painted in white enamel and had two yellow funnels, just as I had dreamt. The year of our Lord was 1902.

From the day I joined that perfect little vessel until the day (in 1922) that I was invited to quit His Majesty's Active Service, except for a few weeks on gunnery and torpedo courses, I was continuously in command of Her/His Majesty's ships of war. I grew no corns on my backside through sitting on an office stool, and I suppose that is why I am not now C-in-C of the Home Fleet – or is it? I had 21 men of a crew. *TB 99* was good for about 23 knots, with a single screw. I divided my affection between her and *TB 93*, a dear little craft with powerful twin-screw engines, built by Yarrows.[2] I had nine of these craft, but all except one or two were kept in reserve. We lay at moorings in the old Torpedo Boat camber down by the Ragged Staff[3] in

---

1 Captain Neston William Diggle, CMG, RN (1881–1963) became Naval Attaché in the British Embassy, Rome 1919–1922.

2 A leading shipbuilding firm based on the River Clyde. Alfred Yarrow, its owner, was an inventive naval engineer and responsible for the development of increasingly fast warships. The company built the first naval vessel globally to exceed 40 knots.

3 A cave/tunnel under the Rock, used as a magazine.

Claude Cumberlege, Lt, RN, in 1902–05 (Family collection)

Gibraltar. I was employed primarily as a special means of communication between Gibraltar and the [British] Legation at Tangier, inhabited then by Sir Arthur Nicholson.[4] Carrier pigeons were kept in those days at Gibraltar. One of my duties was to take out a couple of crates of the birds and release them at anything up to 100 miles distance from the Rock for training purposes. The pigeons were a godsend; if I wanted to go to a race meeting or a bullfight at Seville or Malaga, all I had to do was to take a few pigeons along for training. We treated Spain as a sort of extension of Gibraltar, and used it for its fine anchorages and for sporting purposes. I wonder how much good English gold rolled into the country; the Dons [Spaniards] certainly had no objection.

So here I am, in an independent command. My nearest boss was the elderly Admiral Sir William Acland,[5] who always said 'Why?' as in 'I'm going to Tangier tomorrow, Sir.' 'Why?' 'Well, Sir, I've received your signal ordering me to be ready to sail on arrival of the mail steamer.' 'Why?' 'I understand I have to give passage to Sir Harry Maclean.'[6] 'Why?' 'Well, Sir, he wants to get back to Morocco.' 'Why?' 'I shall return the same evening, Sir.' 'Why?'

I felt that a new chapter in my life had started when I got this command. I don't think that I looked forward at all, but I certainly closed my book on the past. I had done with watchkeeping. For the moment I was supremely contented. By ancient custom, as skipper of my own ship, I would even be piped on board the flagship! At sea in my little craft, there was never a question as to who should keep the morning watch – it was a case of 'Watch and Step on' all the time for this proud skipper. A Spanish friend once gave me an admirable proverb: 'It is better to have the head of a rat in your hand than the tail of a lion.'

In my inner heart, though, it was the ships of the service, not the Royal Navy itself, that really mattered to me. I appreciated the superiority of my superiors and mostly liked them, and even played up to some of them; a little 'chocolate', gently applied, does no harm in any walk of life. And, funnily enough, I always felt they liked me. I even got on with my contemporaries. At this time, 1902, I was just a youngster of a rather adventurous nature. Probably I expected to rise to exalted rank, but I never dreamt of it. All I wanted was lovely ships to play with – and one in particular. To my amazement, I had got her.

My second-in-command was the gunner, Mr. Burgess – one of the best-looking and quite one of nicest men I ever met. Like all warrant officers of those days (and still today), he was a vertebra of the backbone of the Service. Blue eyes and a golden beard, humorous by nature, very strict yet not above losing something overboard 'by accident' when occasion required. HM *TB 99* was his darling. He may have had a house or a wife stored away at Stonehouse or Devonport, but in harbour at Gib. he slept and fed on board the local depot ship, leaving the one little cabin on the torpedo boat free for me and my harmless misdemeanours. The crew consisted of 21 men headed by the coxswain, a first-class petty officer and an absolute jewel of a

4 Arthur Nicholson, 1st Baron Carnock, GCB, GCMG, GCVO, KCIE, PC (1849–1928), was a British diplomat. He was British Minister at Tangiers 1895–1904 before becoming British Ambassador to Spain 1904–05. From 1906 to 1910 he was the British Ambassador to Russia in Saint Petersburg. He then became Permanent Under-Secretary 1910–16 in the Foreign Office.

5 Admiral Sir William Alison Dyke Acland, 2nd Baronet, CVO, JP, DL (1847–1924) was Admiral Superintendent of the Gibraltar Dockyard in 1902. He lived in some style at the official residence, The Mount, 1902–04.

6 General (Kaïd) Sir Harry Aubrey de Vere Maclean, KCMG (1845–1920) was a well-known Scottish soldier, and official Instructor to the Moroccan Army.

Chief Engine Room Artificer. The rest were seamen and stokers. My Navigator was a fine man called Able Seaman Hall. I also had another eight of these boats in reserve, each with a skeleton crew, secured in the little camber, or basin, off the Rock. Was I proud of my command!

From a service point of view, life was easy. On board, everybody knew they had 'picked a good number'. Socially, ashore in Gibraltar, I was a freelance. I had no mess to live in, but was made an honorary member of all the soldiers' messes and used the Royal Artillery Service Corps Mess quite a lot because it had better and cheaper food. I could well have messed at the Club[7] but the senior Army Medical Colonel who presided there always wore a tail coat and white tie, combed his moustache with his fork and snipped [flicked] the olive stones over his shoulder! I felt I could not live up to such rococo heights. We often had to run over to Tangier with despatches for the Legation headed by Sir Arthur Nicholson, the so-called *Bashdoor* [a de facto 'Ambassador'] There was always a square meal and good company. In addition, His Excellency Sir George White, VC[8] told me 'There's always a knife and fork, my boy, for you whenever you like to come' to the Convent [the old name for Government House].

Outside ordinary jobs, such as running torpedoes and firing off little 3-pounder guns at target practice, all sorts of interesting duties fell my way. I would receive a signal – 'The Admiral Superintendent wishes to see you at 9:30 am.' Normally in those days one had to buckle on a frock coat and sword when going to attend on the Admiral, but through his Flag Lieutenant, Kerr Pearce, I knew that in my case this was not necessary; I was treated as one of the staff, or perhaps as the coxswain of his barge. Pearce, a droll character, would greet me: 'Good morning, my boy. The Admiral has sent for you. I don't know what you've been up to, but step this way – he wants to see you immediately. So, mind your Ps and Qs, and don't laugh if he says "Why?" ' We would go into the Admiral's office. He, sitting at his desk, would glance at us as we enter without raising his head and look up over his gold-rimmed *pince nez*.

The Flag Lieutenant presents me. 'You have sent for the Captain of the Torpedo Boat, Sir.' 'Why?' responds the Admiral. The Flag Lieutenant fades away with a chuckle. 'How soon can you raise steam?' 'Three hours, Sir.' 'Why?' 'It takes three hours to raise steam, Sir.' 'Why?' 'Because the fires are not lit, Sir.' 'Why?' 'Oh, er, because you approved my signal requesting permission to let fires die out the day before yesterday on my return to harbour, Sir.' 'Have steam ready for full speed on the arrival of the mail steamer tomorrow. I want you to etc etc.' 'Aye, aye, Sir.' 'Will you come to lunch at 1:15 at The Mount [the residence of the Senior Naval Officer on Gibraltar]?' 'Thank you very much, Sir.' 'Why?'

One day I went alongside a P&O mailboat and, after a lot of huge packing cases had been hoisted out and placed on board my ship, over the side came a personage in plain clothes and sporting a great beard – a jolly, big man of about 60. Kaid[9] Sir Harry Maclean was returning to his job as the uncrowned king of Morocco after receiving a knighthood for his great services to England in Morocco. In a few moments we were purling [speeding] along at 20 knots *en route* for Tangier. Kaid Maclean asked if he might have some place to change into uniform for his arrival,

Sir Harry Maclean in full uniform (Wikipedia)

7 Not clear which club this might be.

8 Field Marshal Sir George Stuart White, VC, GCB, OM, GCSI, GCMG, GCIE, GCVO (1835–1912) won his VC during the Second Anglo-Afghan war. He also took part in the Boer war and commanded the garrison at the siege of Ladysmith. He finished his illustrious career as Governor of Gibraltar and then as Governor of the Royal Hospital Chelsea.

9 Arabic for 'Commander' or 'Leader'.

so I showed him my small ward room and left him to it with his valet. In a few minutes he was back, looking like the Caliph himself – magnificent in a red cap surrounded by a white turban, with a gorgeously-worked Zouave[10] jacket and Arabian *bumbaches* [pantaloons] finished off with immaculately polished brown boots, silver spurs and a flowing white woollen cape. Under his arm he was carrying a set of bagpipes which he began to pump up. For the rest of our voyage, he gave us selections of native music.

On arrival in Tangier, Maclean had to go ashore, surrounded by austere Moors who had come to meet him. He asked me to come up [to his residence] to lunch, saying that he would send down a horse. I landed at one o'clock in white uniform and found a most beautiful barb [Berber horse] waiting for me, with gorgeous trappings and huge silver stirrups, and a posse of cavorting Moorish cavalry as an escort. This imposing cavalcade galloped at speed up the narrow, cobbled streets of Tangier as ringleted Jews and less picturesque Gentiles fled into dark doorways.

Kaid Maclean's homecoming had an oriental rather than Scottish flavour about it. Shortly, we pulled up at Sir Harry's home where I was welcomed by the whole of his family. What a feast followed! What lashings of food! The lunch was served mostly by girls, probably Spanish. Doubtless, the masses left over were distributed later to innumerable servants and hangers-on. Half way through lunch, the wooden packing cases were lugged into the dining room and prized [*sic*] open by Moorish men servants. The jolly old Kaid stripped off his Zouave jacket and, getting down on his hands and knees, started pulling out presents brought from England for his family. Lady Maclean was presented with a fine diamond ring. 'Do you like it, Cissie?' said Sir Harry. 'Cost me £300.[11] Not too vulgar-looking, Cissie?' 'Oh no, Chummie – it's lovely.' Maclean's daughters each got a charming gift from Aspreys. Then it was the turn of the servants; each male servant received a lovely cloth Moorish costume made in Savile Row, each female servant a complete dress with underclothing thrown in.

The Rock [Gibraltar] mobilised on a war footing from time to time. It was my business during these episodes to make night attacks with my torpedo boats. I had a free hand to do what I liked, and we tried all sorts of stunts to hoodwink the sleepless soldiers. It was not easy. Once we got the huge lateen mainsail of a Spanish *falucho* [felucca] and hoisted it up, hoping that the sweeping searchlights on the Rock would see the sail and pass on in search of more dangerous prey. That didn't work. Sometimes we hid behind coal hulks and sent a dinghy-load of men to sneak ashore with bombs made out of tobacco tins to blow up Government House. [This was] partially successful. Once, I lay over at Campo [de Gibraltar], out of sight on a dirty night. Half a dozen of my men towed a torpedo for hours against a headwind, got through the viaduct on the commercial mole on the Rock and carefully aimed the torpedo at the flagship. The damned thing sank the ship's diving bell!

I tried sending a detachment of my vessels right round the Bay to attack from the north while I raced across from the south-west, hoping attention would be concentrated on the others. Closer and closer we came, unseen. The entrance lights had been put out, but that didn't worry me. At full speed, I could soon see the loom of the Rock. Suddenly, a searchlight flashed dead ahead, right in my eyes. I knew it was one put up recently at the south end of the detached mole. Immediately, others flashed on us. A searchlight looked devilishly close, shining straight at us. However, I knew where I was and the guns had not fired. Then I saw a clean-cut wall to starboard, and beyond it a battleship which was evidently the flagship, lying at No. 1 buoy. 'Hard-a-port, Coxswain,' I ordered, and added 'Get the wheel over quick or we shall be too near that detached mole.' Round we came. 'Stand by to fire, Mr. Burgess. Steady! Steer straight for that ship. All right, Mr. Burgess,

10 A short open-fronted jacket with long sleeves.

11 About £3,800 today.

fire!' The green Verey[12] light shot into the air, representing the discharge of our bow torpedo tube. It descended in a gentle curve 50 yards ahead of us, and broke into emerald fragments on dry land. 'Full speed astern.' I crashed over the engine room telegraph myself. But the bow of my ship rolled up like a carpet to my nose. The clean-cut wall I had seen was the end of the coal sheds and they stopped 80 yards from the end of the mole. The ships' masts I had seen were those of the battleship lying alongside on the other side of the mole!

We came off the mole immediately. I stopped, guessing that my ship would sink, then went slow ahead and rested our battered nose against the wall, so that at any rate we could walk ashore in comfort. Then I went below and found that no water was coming in abaft the foremost bulkhead. So I knew that she wouldn't sink and that nobody was a penny the worse. We paddled into harbour and secured alongside, and no one seemed to realise until the next day that there had very nearly been a tragedy.

Imagine my feelings. Right at the outset, I had smashed up my first command. A Court of Inquiry was ordered. It was held on board the battleship. Two Post Captains[13] were sitting in it. I went on board, miserable, in frock coat and sword. A paymaster acted as Secretary of the Court. 'Hullo, young fellow. Sit down. Tell us all about it,' a jolly-looking Captain said. I told him the simple truth. 'Very interesting. Nobody hurt?' 'No, Sir.' 'Do you want to ask any questions, old chap?' one of the officers said to the other.' 'No, but why don't we go over and see the spot he hit?' 'Good idea. Call away my galley.' We went to the mole and I found the spot about 40 yards from the end. Then we went back to the battleship and I was given a glass of port wine. 'That's all right, my lad. Don't worry.' A few weeks later Admiral Acland sent for me and handed me a letter which he had received from the Admiralty. It requested that he convey to Lt Cumberlege their Lordships' desire 'that after consideration of the findings of the Court of Enquiry Lt Cumberlege should be informed that my Lords attach no blame to Lt Cumberlege and also desire that the commendation of My Lords be conveyed to this officer for the remarkable qualities he demonstrated in taking care to minimise the possibility of more serious consequences of the accident.'

So I went out to Campo and played polo. I had had to give up football as there was no one to play with at Gibraltar. I learnt to play polo there, mainly thanks to the Larios[14] family who now and again took me on as an extra and mounted me on one of their ponies. I acquired three horses – one too big for polo, which I used for hunting in winter. We few sailors ran our own stables , a ramshackle place made out of odd bits of timber with room for eight horses, inside the dockyard. I was the Hon. Sec. and Hon. Treasurer, but I kept no accounts and issued no statements. I used to stick up a notice in the stables: 'Bills this month – £1 a horse and no questions.'

On my visits to Tangier, I would buy barley at half the price charged in Gibraltar. It was interesting bargaining with the Moors. One just sat and talked for an hour about anything other than buying grain. Only on getting up to leave did one deign to notice the heaps of grain piled on mats. Then, 'For the love of Allah, give me $2 the sack, and this gift from God is yours,' they would say. 'To hell with you and to hell with Allah,' I would reply. 'The bloody stuff is half brickbats [rocks].' Quite a change after the peaceful conversation over coffee the previous hour! In the end, a string of donkeys, each with a sack of barley over its back, would amble down to the pier headed by 'El Reiss' (as the Captain of the Torpedo Boat was known) and his immaculate gunner, and loaded on to the quarterdeck of my little command. Gibraltar would be made after

12 A Verey, or Very, gun is a single-shot breech-loading snub-nosed pistol that fired flares, and it is normally used to send a distress signal. It is named after Edward Wilson Very (1847–1910), a US naval officer who developed it.

13 RN captain of a vessel. In this case Captain Barnardiston and Captain Tothill.

14 The Larios family 'Anglicised' the Gibraltar region by introducing social and sporting practices previously unknown in the rest of Spain, such as polo and fox hunting. It also built spectacular luxury mansions with landscaped gardens, some of which survive.

nightfall so as not to offend the susceptibilities of more orthodox senior officers. Indeed, the small vessel might have been taken for a Rochester hay barge. But it cut down our polo expenses tremendously.

One day I had three crates of pigeons to fly. A good friend of mine, 'Croppy' Benet, a Major in the Lancashire Fusiliers, came out for a trip. Somewhere off Cadiz I released the birds, but before doing so I asked Croppy if he would like to send a message to his wife in Gibraltar. This was just after the kidnapping in 1904 of Mr. Ion Pericaris, a rich Greek-American, by Raisuli, a famous Rif [mountain] bandit. Raisuli wanted £30,000[15] for Pericaris, a gentle man of 64 who lived in Tangier. Croppy wrote the same message to his wife on six slips of paper: 'Just off to lunch with Raisuli. Wish you were here' and signed it 'Benet'. Most of the slips reached Gibraltar. A week later I picked up a copy of the *Daily Mail* – it would be the *Daily Mail* – and on top was a scare headline: 'Naval Officer lunches with Raisuli'. The story went on to state that Raisuli had 'entertained at lunch Lt. Cumberlege who is in command of the Gibraltar torpedo-boat flotilla. Additional interest is lent to this incident by the fact that Lt. Cumberlege was accompanied by a Mr. Benet who, we understand, is the chief of police in Gibraltar.' Apparently one of the goddamn pigeons had lost its way and been shot by a Tangier sportsman who, on discovering that it was a carrier pigeon with a message, had taken it to the Havana News Agency in Tangier who immediately passed it on to the *Daily Mail*. As it happened, the chief of police in Gibraltar was called Bennett but was no relation to my friend Benet.

In those days we regarded Spain as a sort of English playground. The Dons used to do us awfully well whenever we happened to put into their ports, and sometimes it was rather difficult to boot off would-be passengers who thought they would rather like a nice little trip in the torpedo boat to Seville or Malaga. Some disgruntled swine who had tried to cadge a passage and been refused wrote to the *Truth* newspaper claiming that it was customary for the local torpedo boat to take parties to Seville, spending taxpayers' money and all that sort of thing. Labby[16] put a paragraph in his paper about it: 'We don't know much about torpedo boats,' went the story, 'but we imagine that it is necessary for them to go to sea from time to time for exercise. We rather think a torpedo boat is like a race horse, and we know that race horses have to be trained and money spent on providing proper food and so on. Money must also be spent on fuel if a torpedo boat has to go to sea, instead of food, so if a torpedo boat has to go to sea, why *not* go to Seville?' What a sell for the blighter!

In truth, there was nothing I liked better than nosing about the African shore, that almost unknown strip of territory opposite Gibraltar on the other side of the Straits, between Tangier and Ceuta; 30 or 40 years ago[17] no one ever went there, and even nowadays (mid-1930s) I doubt if anybody ever lands there. All day, year in year out, ships pass in and out between the Pillars of Hercules – called Gibel Tarik and Gibel Musa in Moorish (Gibraltar and Apes Hill to us). Mysterious Africa. There are some wonderfully beautiful sandy bays, with green valleys running back into the mountains, along this coast. Once, I found a vast old Portuguese fort called Alcazar, long since deserted by the original builders. I had to go on my hands and knees through a sort of tunnel in the walls to enter it. I could find no other land entrance, but there was a ruined stone 'sea port' running into the water to which galleys came long ago.

There is also a little island over there, 200–300 feet high and a few acres in size, right under Apes Hill. In Spring, it is covered in large white narcissi, and countless sea fowl have their nests in great caves. There are Roman baths hewn in the solid rock. A lovely osprey had its three houses on this island too – great structures of

15 Nearly £1 million in today's values.

16 *Truth* was a British periodical founded by the diplomat and Liberal politician Henry Labouchère. *Truth* was known for its exposures of frauds.

17 At the end of the 19th century.

piled branches and twigs. I took old Willoughby Verner,[18] the ornithologist, over there once; he was thrilled. The Moors[19] used to come down to the waterside and fire their rifles – not *at* us, I think, but by way of scaring us off. I soon got round them by paddling ashore in a dinghy, unarmed of course, and inviting them on board. They came with brand-new German Mausers, so when I got them on the ship I laid out a target and lent them some of our rifles and opened a case of ammunition. As long as they could let off a gun, they were perfectly happy.

Ceuta, at that time, was a great Spanish prison. The captives were more or less free to roam during the day; guards were not necessary. It was impossible for anyone to escape by sea, and it was certain death for anyone who might wander into the Rif. I met an English prisoner there – he told me a story which I believed, and reported to the authorities in Gibraltar. He said that 18 years previously he had been a seaman in a sailing ship in Havana in Cuba. While ashore with his mates, a row broke out in a whore shop and a Spaniard was killed. The Englishman and his mates were taken and condemned. Two were hanged and he was given life imprisonment. He swore to me that he knew nothing of the killing and begged me to do something for him. All I could do was to take his name. I knew that later enquiries were made in Madrid, but this happened shortly before I left Gibraltar and I never heard anything more. What a life! The man was aged about 40, so he could not have been more than 20 when he started his time in a lousy Spanish prison.

In my capacity as Captain of the Torpedo Boats I had the opportunity of meeting, on more or less equal terms, the captains of the big naval ships in Gibraltar in spite of my lowly rank and youth. Consequently, I made a lot of friends amongst these tolerant people. It was very interesting to study their manners and customs. I recall a number of names such as Kit Cradock,[20] George Warrender[21] and others. And it was here that I met, and loved for ever, Lord Charles Beresford[22] and Prince Louis.

One day, the *Hohenzollern*,[23] with the Prussian Emperor on board, turned up escorted by a couple of cruisers. It was painful to see the mess

Lord Charles Beresford in *Vanity Fair* in 1903 (Mauritius Images)

Prince Louis of Battenberg (PD)

18 Colonel William Willoughby Cole Verner (22 October 1852 – 25 January 1922) was a British soldier, writer and ornithologist, and inventor of a compass. He is remembered for bringing Cueva de la Pileta, a cave filled with prehistoric paintings, to international attention.

19 The term 'Moor' was first used by Christian Europeans in the Middle Ages to designate the Muslim inhabitants of the Maghreb plus the Iberian peninsula, Sicily and Malta. Initially, the Moors were indigenous Berbers. The name was later applied to some Arabs.

20 Rear Admiral Sir Christopher 'Kit' George Francis Maurice Cradock, KCVO, CB, SGM (1862–1914), earned a reputation for great gallantry. Appointed C-in-C of the North America and West Indies Station before the First World War, his mission was to protect Allied merchant shipping by hunting down German commerce raiders. In November 1914 he was tasked with destroying the East Asia Squadron of the German Navy as it headed home around the tip of South America. Despite numerical and tactical inferiority, he engaged the enemy in the Battle of Coronel off the coast of Chile, but was killed when his flagship was sunk.

21 Vice Admiral Sir George John Scott Warrender of Lochend, 7th Baronet, KCB, KCVO (1860–1917) was a senior officer in the Royal Navy during the First World War.

22 Lord Charles William de la Poer Beresford, 1st Baron Beresford, GCB, GCVO, FRSGS (1846–1919 was a British admiral and Member of Parliament who combined the two careers. A popular figure in the RN who courted publicity, his career was marked by a bitter dispute with Admiral of the Fleet Sir John Fisher over reforms championed by Fisher introducing new technology and modernising traditional RN practices. Beresford rose to the most senior sea commands in the RN but failed to become First Sea Lord.

23 SMY *Hohenzollern* was used as the German Imperial Yacht from 1893 to July 1914.

At the Kaiser lunch in Gibraltar, March 1905 – CLC, aged 28, front row centre (Gibraltar National Museum)

they made of going alongside the mole. Next day the Admiral [Sir William Acland] sent for me and asked me to come up to the house to act as extra Flag Lieutenant for a luncheon party at The Mount. I went. Just before lunch Sir William thrust into my hands a big leather case and said: 'Here, Cumberlege, see that His Majesty gets one of these for every course at lunch.' I opened the case and found a dozen sort-of forks, each with a knife edge on the outside prong. I turned them over to the chief steward with the same instruction. This weapon was necessary to the Kaiser because his left arm was too short and anyhow useless, and his left hand – white and fat and decorated with lovely rings – was attached to his sword belt. He only used his right hand, and sawed away at the roast Spanish cow with the knife edge and then picked up the bit with the fork, all with the same hand. He talked all the time in good, if guttural, English, flourishing the fork with a bit of beef on it in the most dangerous fashion. Once he damned nearly stuck it through Lady Acland's ear.

After lunch the Kaiser and Lord Charles took a stroll around the garden. Meanwhile chairs were arranged and a local photographer set up his machine to take a picture of the party. On returning from his walk the Kaiser, arm in arm with Lord Charles, on seeing the preparations, noticed that the ladies seemed a bit diffident about taking their places. So he said: 'We will arrange these matters. The ladies will sit down in the chairs. The young officers will sit down on the ground in front. And we will stand behind.' So the ladies sat down in the chairs. We sat cross-legged on the ground, and all the tosspots[24]stood at the back with the Kaiser in the middle and Sir William beside him, with a couple of German admirals and Lord Charles Beresford at the end of the line. The moment came when the photographer, having manipulated his cloth and clapped in the slides, stood ready to remove the cap of the lens, when a hell of a riot broke out in the hen roost behind The Mount. 'Shtop!' said the Kaiser, raising his working hand. 'It sounds as if one dog vos killing some hens.' A deadly silence followed, broken by the still small voice of Lord Charles Beresford from the end of the back row. 'It sounds to me,' he said, 'as if that little hen was most probably having her trousseau pulled about a bit.' Click went the photographer. For once, an

24 A rather derogatory term much misused in the book by Cumberlege. He intended to mean 'the high and mighty' or 'the bosses.'

official photograph emerged with a smile from here to Halifax. I simply had to send the story to the 'Pink 'un.'[25] They wrote back to say they did not think they could use it because it involved too many distinguished names.

Lord Charles had arrived in Gibraltar after a stupid panic induced by the Russians on the Dogger Bank.[26] The excitement in England was intense, and public opinion was all for retaliation. Lord Charles knew that the Russian fleet was proceeding south across the Bay of Biscay and heard a bit later that it had anchored in Vigo Bay off north-west Spain. A fire-eater by birth and education, he urged the Admiralty to give the Russians a lesson. The cables got busy and the Admiralty, all but the First Sea Lord – 'sick' in a nursing home – seemed in favour of Lord Charles' plan. However, at the Admiralty Board meeting one man felt that the First Sea Lord should know exactly what was happening. That man was Charles Carter Drury[27] who afterwards told me the story. Drury, as much in favour of beating up the Russians as the rest, stole out of the boardroom and rushed to the nursing home where he pitched his tale of the trend events were taking at the Board to his chief, Jackie Fisher, 'ill' in bed. In an instant Fisher jumped out of bed, slung on some clothes, taxied with Drury to the Admiralty and walked into the boardroom. 'What's all this talk of beating up the Russians?' he asked. 'Stop it!' There was no war.

One morning around this time I left Gibraltar with my little flotilla with a view, as usual, to making a night attack after dark. To get away, I turned west and steamed along the Spanish side of the Straits. Once out of sight, I nipped across the Straits towards Tangier and then steamed slowly along the African shore to the east and anchored in a sheltered little nook I knew. Here I sent for the captain of my other boats, and the gunners and sub-lieutenants and unfolded my plan of attack. As soon as darkness fell (about 7:30 pm) one boat was to steam to a point 2 miles south of Europa Point, arrive there and make a violent demonstration with a view to decoying away the defending flotilla. To attract attention, the boat was to tow a long grass hawser tied to it at intervals along the boat's length with Holmes lights [patent distress lights] that would burn in water. If this didn't do the trick, the captain of the boat was to let off his pop-guns, fire Verey lights, flash his searchlight and chase his tail. As soon as he was attacked, he was to leg it for all he was worth towards the Levant to indicate to me that the coast was clear for my attack with the rest of the flotilla.

I had the boats paint a broad white stripe on their sterns (they were painted a very dark grey) and impressed on all their commanders that as soon as I had decided to attack I would order the flotilla to weigh [anchor] by word of mouth. Their orders were to keep close up to each other once we started, and do their utmost to conform to my changes in speed without my having to signal by lamp. Meanwhile my crew spent all afternoon painting my ship black all over instead of white. At dusk my decoy, without signal, weighed anchor and was soon out of sight. It turned out to be a very dark night with no moon. Suddenly, over by Europa Point, I saw a terrific battle in progress. My moment had arrived. Silently, we started off, slowly at first, increasing to full speed as we approached Carnero Point on the Spanish side of Gibraltar Bay. My plan was to creep at speed right round the Spanish side of the bay, as I knew the searchlights would not make me out over there.

By now terrific volumes of smoke were rolling out of my ship's funnels, trailing astern and completely hiding my consorts. I hoped they were close astern. We skimmed past Algeciras and a shaft of one searchlight wandered across, but I had no fear of them picking us up. No blank guns were fired from the Rock, either. After rounding the head of the Bay, we found ourselves amongst a huddle of big coal hulks moored off the Spanish

---

25 Later the *Financial Times*.

26 The Dogger Bank Incident occurred on 21/22 October 1904, when the Baltic Fleet of the Russian Navy mistook a British trawler fleet for Japanese vessels and fired on them. One British trawler was sunk, two British fishermen died and two Russians were killed.

27 Admiral Sir Charles Carter Drury, GCB, GCVO, KCSI, (27 August 1846 – 18 May 1914) was a Canadian Royal Navy Admiral who became Second Sea Lord and Chief of Naval Personnel in 1908 before retiring in 1911.

Campo. I eased down for a moment to see if my mates were close up, but saw no sign of them. Committed to the attack, I could not wait and we opened up. My objective [target] was the collection of large cruisers anchored outside the moles when I left Gibraltar that morning. They were no longer there! Nor was the rest of the fleet.

Suddenly, another wandering searchlight showed up the masts of a ship within the moles. The fleet was there all right, but blacked out. I rushed along, closer to and parallel with the long-detached mole, and was blazing away with our pop-guns when I caught the note of a bugle playing 'Action'. 'Hullo! What's the game?' Some instinct made me shut down our gunnery and stop engines as we ran into the beam of another searchlight. 'Odd,' I thought, 'not a gun fired.' Usually, the Rock was a *feu de joie* [rifle salute] during my attacks. I waited a bit and then, going slow ahead, turned to enter the south entrance between the moles. Fifty yards short of the entrance my coxswain spun the wheel and said, 'Look out, Sir, the boom's across.' We just avoided it. I turned and headed for the northern entrance, where I found a gate, entered, and steered silently among the great black shapes of the battleships and cruisers all cleared for action.

Slowly, I got close to the stern of the flagship. I could make out a knot of officers on her quarterdeck and heard a hail in a staccato voice. 'What *are* you?' 'Number *93 TB*, Sir, leading the night attack,' I replied. A relieved 'Ohhhhh!' went up from the group. There was a short pause while I lay up, engines stopped. Then I was hailed again. 'Number 93, go out and collect all TBs and send them inside [the mole] forthwith.' 'Aye, aye, Sir,' and off I went to find the others except for the gallant *Battler* which, off Europa Point, eventually turned up. Next morning at daylight I returned to Gibraltar and saw the big cruisers going out. They were off, by Lord Charles's orders, to scout and shadow the Russian fleet if and when it left Vigo.

I came inside the moles again and secured to my buoys. I was still in complete ignorance of the happenings in my absence. Shortly after, I got a signal from the flagship: 'Repair on board.' I went. I was instantly taken down to Charlie B's [Lord Beresford's] cabin by the Flag Lieutenant. 'And what the dickens d'you think you were up to last night?' the great man said. I told him, more or less, what I have written here. He at once savvied the situation. 'But Cumberlege, a couple of hours after you left I received certain information and sent out the defending flotilla to get in touch with you and order you back to Gibraltar.' 'Yes, Sir, but they didn't find me. For all I know they are still chasing one of my torpedo boats in the direction of the Levant.'

Lord Charles smiled genially. 'I don't mind telling you, my lad, you had the narrowest escape of being blown out of the water that you will probably ever have. At one o'clock yesterday I received a report that Russian torpedo boats had vanished from Vigo Bay. I said to myself that they [the Russians] are mad enough to attack by night the fleet lying peacefully at anchor outside the moles. So I took the precaution of sending all ships inside. The Rock was immediately mobilised for war, ships cleared for action and all ships darkened. At 8:00 pm I was having a conference at Government House with the Governor and Army Chiefs when the Flag Lieutenant rushed into the room, his face chalky with excitement. 'Russian torpedo boats attacking the boom defences!' he blurted out. I ordered him to make a general signal to open fire on Russian torpedo boats. You see, we knew that there were no torpedo boats in the whole Royal Navy painted black, and we also knew that Russian torpedo boats *were* painted that colour. Luckily, you stopped your engines in full beam of a searchlight from the *Mars*.[28] You'd better go and ask Captain Marks why he didn't open fire. Well, run along now and keep steam for full speed at half an hour's notice. All's well that ends well.'

I left the flagship and went over to the *Mars*. 'My dear boy,' said Captain Marks. 'Let me tell you that the fingers of every captain of a gun that would bear on you were on the trigger. I would have given the order to

28 HMS *Mars* was a battleship of the Majestic class, the seventh member of a class of nine ships. It was commissioned into the fleet in June 1897.

fire in another second. But when, for some reason, you went full speed astern in the beam of the light and stopped, something told me to hang on, black as you [the ship] were – and, knowing there were no black TBs in the Mediterranean, it struck me in an instant that there had to be some explanation. And anyhow the damned thing [a torpedo boat] can't do any harm. And I thought of those Russians in the North Sea falling into a panic at the sight of a collection of fishing boats. Had I fired and blown you out of the water, what a complete answer to our charge of panic against the Russians. In another instant a lynx-eyed signalman shouted, "It's *TB 93*, Sir. I can see her number on the funnel boards." '

I went back on board *No. 93* and told Mr. Burgess to screw the warheads on the torpedoes.

The next thing we heard was that the Russian fleet had left Vigo and was proceeding south. The C-in-C sent for me and my other captains. 'I want you to go out and get in touch with the Russian fleet. If you sight them, keep well out of range; you are merely to keep in touch if possible and report their movements. We must not have any incidents. Should they open fire, you are to clear out at once. I say this particularly because you haven't even got your warheads on your torpedoes, and I'm not going to ask you to go into action like that. It would be like asking a man to fight another with one arm tied behind his back. Now, you all understand what I want you to do? Anybody got any questions? Anybody got anything to say? Very well, cut along and let me know as soon as you're ready to proceed.' My skippers turned to go. 'I screwed on my warheads on arrival yesterday, Sir,' I murmured. 'Oh, you did, did you? Well, jolly well hurry up and unscrew them,' replied Charlie B. But there was an unmistakable twinkle in his jolly eyes.

Laetitia Couldwell in 1903 before her marriage to Claude (Family collection)

That was the end of it with the Russian fleet – an amazing collection of old crocks. It anchored in Tangier Bay and then left for its long voyage for Japan where it was comfortably mopped up by Admiral Togo – which saved us the trouble. Japan at the time was a great friend of ours. Years later I made friends with a Prince Levin, who was signal officer on board Rozhestvensky's[29] flagship. I asked him if he had seen any [British] destroyers in the North Sea the night they sank the trawlers. He replied: 'No, I did not, but other officers gave me their word of honour that *they* had seen destroyers without a shadow of doubt.' I have always wondered if any Home Fleet destroyer officer, bound to secrecy, *could* tell a tale.

Back in Gibraltar, I fell in love, got married[30] and lived happily ever afterwards. Only the Man with the Scythe put an all-too-early end to a union which otherwise would have been indissoluble except for the temporary vagaries and 'exigencies' normal to a naval career.

Laetitia Cumberlege, Claude's first wife, in 1904–05 (Family collection)

29 Zinovy Petrovich Rozhestvensky (1848–1909) was an admiral of the Imperial Russian Navy. He was wounded while commanding the 2nd Pacific Squadron during its disastrous defeat by the Japanese at the Battle of Tsushima in the 1905 Russo-Japanese War.

30 In Gibraltar, to Sarah Laetitia Crossley Couldwell aged 21 in 1904 (no marriage certificate survives). Laetitia had two children by Claude: Michael (b 1905) and Diana (b 1910). In 1918 Laetitia joined the Women's Royal Air Force. The next year she sailed with Diana to Australia to join Claude, returning to England after a year. She died of cancer in the American hospital in Paris in 1930.

CHAPTER 6

Malta Commands

For five years from mid-1905, Cumberlege was based in Malta. Here he commanded three destroyers and the Commander-in-Chief Mediterranean's gunboat 'yacht'. He was promoted Lt Commander in June 1907.

Time flew. Suddenly my happy years in command of the Gibraltar torpedo boats were finished, and we took a P&O ship home for a month's leave. Then a telegram from the Admiralty reached me: 'You are to proceed forthwith to Malta by the overland route and take command of HMS *Banshee*.' I went. With my wife we had a look round Paris and all went well until our arrival in Messina. I had booked our luggage through from Sicily to Malta but knowing a certain amount of Italian had kept my eye on it. As our train south was leaving, I discovered that the bags had not been loaded.

Lt Claude Cumberlege RN in about 1905 (Family collection)

Claude Cumberlege in civilian dress as a young man in 1906 (Family collection)

Telling my wife to stand at a first-class compartment with one foot on the platform and the other on the train's running board, I rushed back to the left luggage office, shouldered a Saratoga[1] and hove it into the carriage before rushing back for the next. Meanwhile, the whole of Italy was blowing trumpets and waving flags and shrieking '*partenza*' as bag number two hurtled through the door of the compartment and landed on the lap of the only passenger sitting there. Again and again I made my hurried pilgrimage while Italians yelled, the army gathered and the racket went on. At last, sweating like a bull, I hurled the final piece into the carriage and I shoved my young wife in after it to a chorus of *maladettos* [damn you]. The train pulled out ten minutes late. But we had our luggage. It was quite a time before we could disinter the respectable-looking gentleman in the corner, but eventually he came to life and all was well after I found a wicker basket and knocked the head off a bottle of champagne. What a country!

1 Saratoga trunks were the premium trunks in the late 19th century. They contained many compartments and trays, and were strongly made.

HMS *Albatross* (IWM)

Early in 1905 in Malta I took over *Banshee* from John Lindsay.[2] The *Banshee* was one of the earliest destroyers (built 1894), not much bigger than one of my torpedo boats and already *passé*. The early days are rather hazy now; perhaps I was more interested in my home life? I enjoyed destroyer life well enough, but we carried out the ordinary routine of a flotilla and it seemed to me a lot less interesting than the imminent arrival that October of a son and heir.[3] Shortly before the birth, I had to change ships; from the *Banshee* I moved to the *Locust* for four months and then to the lovely *Albatross* at the start of 1906. Our Captain D [of destroyers] was Mike Seymour,[4] a jewel. My immediate boss was Arthur Waistell,[5] a really charming fellow. And there were many others in the flotilla.

However much I liked home life at this time, I was keen on the Service. I never thought of the future, only that I loved 'destroying'. In destroyers, from the word Go I had a thorough understanding with my chief engineers and rather cultivated them. I always liked them and they knew much that I didn't, professionally. But I put my approach plainly to them: 'We must be *always* ready to go to sea. Don't ask for 48 hours to screw up your high-pressure cylinder. Just screw it up, and if you have one engine on the floor make sure the other one is fit to heave around.' My policy paid off, and no Lieutenant or Commander Engineer ever let me down.

[William Walter] White had dismantled one engine for quite urgent reasons. When the damn thing was on the floor, there came an urgent signal: 'How soon can you raise steam?' The duty destroyer had broken down and my ship had been requested. Reply from White: 'One hour and a half.' I was told to report to Admiralty House, where I wasted 20 minutes with the Secretary. Then I went in to see the Flag Lieutenant and conversed for a quarter of an hour. 'Here, damn it, the C-in-C wants to see you.' 'Quite so,' I replied. 'But first I should like to make water. Where's the W.C.?' I drew out this operation as long as I dared, and then

2 Captain John Colin Howard Lindsay, RN (1877–1954).

3 Lieutenant Commander Claude Michael Bulstrode Cumberlege, DSO & Bar, RD (1905–1945) was an RNR officer and Special Operations Executive agent in the Second World War. He was tortured by the SS after being captured during Operation Locksmith in Greece, and executed in Sachsenhausen concentration camp early in 1945.

4 Vice Admiral Sir Michael Culme-Seymour, KCB (1867–1925). He commanded a ship at the Battle of Jutland in 1916, then served as C-in-C of the Mediterranean Fleet and as Second Sea Lord.

5 Admiral Sir Arthur Kipling Waistell, KCB (1873–1953) became C-in-C, Portsmouth.

was shown into the presence of that great and good man, Lord Charles Beresford. 'Oh, it's you, Cumberlege. I want you to get away to Bizerte [in northern Tunisia] as soon as possible. It appears that our Gallic friends have lost [sunk] a submarine. I want you to tell the French admiral that the whole of our resources here in the dockyard are at his disposal. How soon can you get away?' I replied that I had already ordered for full speed, and by the time I got back to my ship we should be ready to sail. 'Very well, my boy. Cut along and give my message.' 'Aye, aye, Sir.' Of course, I spent more time with the Secretary and Flag Lieutenant before getting to the ship. By then, steam was up. We slipped our buoys and proceeded with one engine. As we left harbour, we received the following signal: 'C-in-C wishes to convey to Captain, officers and ship's company of HMS *Albatross* his appreciation of their smartness in carrying out his orders.' Little did he know that we were wandering off to Tunisia on one engine. By the time we were off Gozo, however, we were going at 33 knots, biffing into a westerly gale. We got to Bizerte the same evening and I delivered the message.

It was early days for destroyers in the Royal Navy, so that we young skippers were sort of tolerated. Naturally, we considered ourselves a cut above our contemporaries in big ships who we rather pitied as 'dogsbodies'. The big pots [potentates] rather liked us; the destroyer service was a new arm of the Navy and they gave us rope. And there *were* big pots in those days – Beresford, Seymour, Hedworth Lambton,[6] Kit Cradock, David Beatty.[7] Our particular boss was Mike Seymour – one of God's own noblemen. He liked us because we enjoyed 'destroying' and also because we raised a darned good polo team out of the flotilla.

Life wasn't just one continual round of pleasure; we really worked, and enjoyed it. Some of the sardonic type of captains certainly 'misunderstood' us – Luigi Bailey, the Captain of HMS *Glory*, was one. Once, he borrowed our flotilla for a night attack. It was a full moon and we had to go out and attack his single battleship. He could see us from 5 miles away so that if we tried to torpedo him, all he had to do was to turn *Glory*'s stern to us so that we could not possibly hit her. I was at the rear of the destroyer line. When everybody else had fired at *Glory* and missed, I jammed my telegraphs to full speed, chased *Glory*, overtook her and let my torpedo go at 150 yards' range. I actually had Bailey yelling at me from the bridge: 'If you lose your torpedo, you damned well ought to pay for it!' I said nothing and pulled the string. My torpedo hit *Glory* plumb amidships. Its collapsible head caved in, came off, turned round and hit the ship again! I made a pretence of looking for the torpedo, stopped engines, stayed out all night and went to bed. Next morning, I reported that I had sunk the *Glory*. The result of this little episode was that Luigi had us all on board to dinner; before we went, we arranged that the word 'torpedo' should not be mentioned. He gave us a good dinner.

From time to time, we left Malta as a flotilla and went as far east as the Aegean. Days and nights were taken up by exercises which were, if strenuous, full of excitements. At Corfu I was designated to embark Admiral Hedworth Lambton, who appreciated female society but had temporarily turned his attention to mythology. We sat on some rocks at the island of Fano and discussed Homer while his coxswain collected pebbles from a famous grotto for him to give as wedding presents! Another place I found attractive was Smyrna [now İzmir]. We used to dine at the club and then set out to view the Turkish underworld under

---

6 Admiral of the Fleet Sir Hedworth Meux, GCB, KCVO (né Lambton; 1856–1929). In 1899, during the Second Boer War, Lambton stopped at Mauritius and picked up a battalion of soldiers stationed there. Knowing that the British forces at Ladysmith urgently needed more powerful guns, Lambton led a naval brigade to the rescue with four 12-pounders and two other guns. The enthusiastic response in Britain made Hedworth Lambton a well-known public figure. He went on to be C-in-C of the China Station. During the First World War Meux, as he was then known, served as C-in-C, Portsmouth.

7 Admiral of the Fleet David Beatty, 1st Earl Beatty, GCB, OM, GCVO, DSO, PC (1876–1936) commanded the 1st Battlecruiser Squadron at the 1916 Battle of Jutland. In 1918 as C-in-C of the Grand Fleet he received the surrender of the German High Seas Fleet. Later he became First Sea Lord and took part in negotiations surrounding the 1922 Washington Naval Treaty.

the guidance of an enormous pimp called Adolf. The little ladies would perch on my knee and do their best to seduce me, but I was extremely pure and took pains to explain that while I was good for unlimited beer there was nothing doing in more intricate matters. They didn't mind. Sometimes we even went westward for manoeuvres out in the Atlantic. Once, I shook 100 rivets from the bottom of *Albatross* by hurtling at full speed into a Portuguese trawler while being chased by a cruiser. I got away, but down in my cabin found water halfway up to my bunk and my full-dress coat drifting under the bunk.

Around Christmas time, I was sent up to Naples alone at sunset, for some reason I forget. We banged on north overnight through a terrific gale and snow squalls, and sighted Capri at 3:00 pm. Then my signalman reported a ship in distress a couple of miles away on our port bow. She was a three-masted sailing ship, under bare poles. I altered course to see if we could do any good, and spotted that she had been towed by a very small tug which had cleared out and left her to her fate when the hawser parted. The only thing we could do was to take her in tow. We tried to attach a hawser twice and failed. By then we had drifted dangerously close to the Capri cliffs on which the seas were breaking in 100-foot spurts of foam. As a last resort I turned our stern to the gale, and we managed to get within a few yards of the ship, to windward of her jib-boom. A line was tossed on board, immediately bent [tied] onto a new hawser, and I managed to get my own ship round and face to the sea. Ever so gently, we edged away. The hawser held. By 4:30 pm I knew she was safe. Six hours later we had covered 18 of the 20 miles to Naples. A pilot boat came up and asked if we wanted a pilot. 'Pilot, my foot! Go and take a line from that blighter astern and tie him up.' With that I let go the hawser, found a berth, anchored and tied up to the wall, and all hands went to bed tired out. Nobody went ashore.

About noon the next day I got a signal from *Bacchante*, the flagship of Admiral Barry[8] which had also got into Naples harbour overnight. 'Captain, Repair on Board.' 'Oh hell,' I thought. 'What have I done now?' I fished out my frock coat, buckled my sword and was met at the gangway by Harry Oliphant, the Flag Lieutenant. 'What's the game, Harry?' I asked. 'Damned if I know, but the old man's as mad as harps.' The Admiral had just returned from paying official visits to the Governor and the Duke of Aosta and other tosspots. 'What's all this?' he fumed, pointing to some Italian newspapers. 'I go ashore and hear a cock-and-bull story from the authorities, and I know nothing whatever about it. Made me look a damned fool. What's all this tomfoolery about being kissed by the ladies of Naples? What have you been doing?' I responded: 'I think there must be some mistake, Sir. Not a soul left my ship last night.' Barry told me to write an immediate report. 'Get out.' I went. Shortly after, I sent him a letter explaining what had happened. A few weeks later, I received a charming letter from the Admiral enclosing one from My Lords Commissioners of the Admiralty requesting that he convey their appreciation to Lt. Cumberlege for his 'tara tara tara ...'

Before we left Naples Harry O and I were bidden to some very swagger parties and met some very elegant women. [But] all that nonsense about a sailor having a wife in every port is just that, nonsense; a sailor never stays long enough in one port to regulate matters. Any fool can go ashore and pay for a girl, and many do. I may have missed a lot of fun but, because of some early Victorian kink, I just didn't like the idea. The fact is that it is really dangerous to one's health to take a girl whose medical history sheet is unknown. In most continental places one is advised not to drink the local water or ginger beer or to eat ice cream. As you cannot depend on either the women or the ginger beer, they are best left alone. Love at first sight so rarely happens. But perhaps it was just as well that our visits to foreign ports never lasted more than a few days.

Malta was a bit different. Society was much the same as in any provincial town, but with the naval and

8 Vice Admiral Sir Henry Deacon Barry, KCVO (1849–1908) was later Director of Naval Ordnance and Admiral Superintendent at Portsmouth Dockyard.

military element predominating. One spent months on end there and one loved, of course. Personally, I loved 'purely', but I certainly loved. There were two women I admired from a distance, but I was happy in my home life. My young wife and I had a nice little house in Sliema.[9] We were always a bit hard up, but managed to have a great deal of fun and somehow managed to keep within our income. Pay was not bad, and we had about £400[10] a year of private means. I also made £200 a year racing as I had some good ponies, One, called Kangaroo, won me seven races out of nine. Beeswing won both the races I entered her for, and paid for my polo. Certainly, we destroyer officers were always regarded as a bit extravagant, but polo was actually cheaper than golf or tennis, which were all pay-out and nothing back. We used to go home after polo and have a hot bath.

Ernest Troubridge in 1908 (NPG)

HMS Hussar (PD)

Time flew by. I had done three years commanding destroyers, and my assignment was up. One evening I was having a drink in the club when the Flag Captain, Ernest Troubridge,[11] came up to me. 'Hullo, Claudie, who is that man just going out there?' he said. 'I haven't the faintest idea,' I replied. 'Oh well, if neither of us know him, he couldn't be of any consequence,' Troubridge said, and ran his fingers through his curled and silver hair. 'By the way, Claudie, they tell me you want to go home. But how would you like to take on the *Hussar*?' – the C-in-C's yacht, a lovely little ship, all tessellated marble bathroom and chic saloons. 'Good Lord, Sir, d'you mean it? I'm your man.' 'Well,' said Troubridge, 'as a matter of fact the C-in-C has already applied for you to be appointed to *Hussar*.' A few days later I received the appointment, and a few days after that *Hussar* arrived back in Malta from some cruise. It didn't take me long to jump into a *daighso*[12] and go alongside. It was a bit of a shock to David Hamilton,[13] who commanded her, when I told him about the new arrangement – but no one had been more surprised than me. The fact was that David had just been promoted to Commander and the *Hussar* job really was for a Lieut. Commander. I had just got my half stripe as a Lieutenant of eight years' seniority when I took over command of this fine little ship.

Life for me then became very different to that of a destroyer skipper. We had no torpedoes and just one gun. I bunged a baulk of timber in each end of the cannon and enamelled it white; if you have a yacht, I thought, it may as well be a yacht. *Hussar* in fact had once been a gunboat, but the accommodation had been altered to make her fit for the C-in-C and his family and any guests. She was about 1,000 tons displacement and could shove along at 11 knots. A new wardroom had been built amidships where the torpedo tubes had been, and cabins and bathrooms put in. There was also a big deck house in the poop in place of the 4.7-inch

9 A resort town on the north-east coast of Malta.

10 £400 in 1907 is worth about £50,000 today.

11 Admiral Sir Ernest Troubridge, KCMG, CB (1862–1926) became Chief of Staff to Admiral Sir Charles Drury in 1907. As commander of the First Cruiser Squadron in 1914, he inexplicably failed to bring his ships into action in the Mediterranean, resulting in his court martial. He was acquitted, but his reputation never recovered. He was promoted Vice Admiral in mid-1916 and Admiral in 1919. A biography, *The Coward? The Rise and Fall of the Silver King*, by Steve Dunn was published in 2014.

12 Or dysar, a sort of water taxi used in Malta.

13 Captain David Monteith Hamilton, CMG (1874–1942). He was admitted to Plymouth Hospital in 1910 for treatment of facial paralysis. In 1912 he retired from the Navy.

guns. I had a roomy cabin and bathroom to myself under the poop. The old wardroom formed our dining room, and the old captain's cabin was a downstairs saloon. There were two or three guest cabins under the poop in addition to the admiral's sleeping quarters.

I had a rare collection of officers – Arthur Brown, the chief; Bradley with his eye glass; and Maguire[14] from *Albatross* as my First Lieutenant. Hensman was Navigator. They all had the right idea and we were a very happy crowd – and, for me, it was a very delightful experience. Wherever we went, the C-in-C often had to entertain foreign dignitaries on board in places such as Venice, when the fleet had to lie 8 miles offshore while we were comfortably tied up to the tail of St Mark's Lion in the Grand Canal. I found myself on quite equal terms with the big ships' captains, some of whom regarded destroyer captains as pirates – but for me, as skipper of the C-in-C's yacht, it was a quite different matter; we hobnobbed. When the fleet went for a cruise, we dodged about lovely places with the C-in-C's wife, going where we pleased and keeping a date later to meet the fleet at some location. How we got out of some of the delightful holes and corners we got into, I don't know. Lady Drury was a delightful person to have on board. She knew nothing about the sea but enjoyed herself. Our Dalmatian cruise is one of the pleasantest memories of my entire seafaring career.

Emperor Franz Josef I in a photo taken in 1908 (PD)

We went to Trieste and Fiume, and here I had lunch with old Franz Josef.[15] His butler was formerly a sailor and when the Imperial Tokay [wine] came round it was a glass apiece for the locals and half a bottle for me. On a visit to Montenegro *en route* to Corfu to rendezvous with the fleet, the old king[16] there sent us the latest newspapers and asked us up to play bridge. Corfu is one of many lovely places in the world with its fortresses, the 'cypress for death', age-old olives, the shaft of pale blue sea and the copper-and-gold of far-off Albanian mountains. While we were in Corfu a P&O tourist vessel came into port. I got hold of the passenger list, and found Sir W.S. Gilbert[17] and family were on board. I told the Admiral who was with us, and he at once sent a message inviting the Gilberts over for a cup of tea. As W.S. came on to the ship, I hoped he would break into *HMS Pinafore*'s 'My gallant crew, good morning.' He didn't, but as he stepped on board I could not help murmuring, 'Sir, good morning, I hope you are quite well!' He was charming – and so were his nieces.

Admiral Sir Charles Carter Drury (PD)

Admiral Sir Curzon Howe (RM Greenwich)

14 Commander Owen Hugh Knox Maguire, DSO (1885–1924).

15 Franz Joseph I (1830–1916) was Emperor of Austria and other states of the Austro-Hungarian Empire 1848–1916, and President of the German Confederation 1850–1866. He became the sixth longest-ruling monarch of any country in modern history.

16 Nikola I Petrović-Njegoš (1841–1921) was the ruler of Montenegro from 1860 to 1918, reigning as prince from 1860 to 1910 and as the country's first and only king from 1910 to 1918.

17 Sir William Schwenck Gilbert (1836–1911) was a dramatist, librettist, poet and illustrator best known for his collaboration with composer Arthur Sullivan, which produced 14 comic operas.

Near the end of 1908 Admiral Drury was relieved by Sir Assheton Curzon Howe.[18] Before that, Drury had gone to Constantinople to acquire his Order of the Osmanieh.[19] Dorothy Fisher, daughter of the great Jackie, had accompanied the family. 'How did you get on up at Constant?' I asked her one day. 'Fine,' she said. 'The old man got his Osmanieh and Lady D. got the Order of Chastity set in brilliants.'[20] 'And you, Dorothy, what did you make of it?' 'Oh, I got it too ... fourth class!' Her Uncle Bill,[21] Jackie's brother, was Dockyard Admiral at Malta at the time. He said to me one day: 'I can't understand why that decent-looking fellow Eric Fullerton[22] wants to marry that ugly niece of mine.' Little did he know that there were other points worth consideration. It was Dorothy herself who told me how she was having a bath while staying on *Hussar* (before my time) when a couple of bluejackets painting the ship's side found themselves alongside the bathroom portholes. Most discreetly, they immediately shifted the painting stage. 'Bill,' said one to his mate, 'that there Dorothy may not have a pretty dial [face] but, cripes, she's got a darn fine backside.'

Admiral Drury left, and Curzon Howe reigned in his stead. I had been very fond of old Carter Drury – not a very great naval officer, but a man with any amount of shrewdness and a most useful C-in-C in peacetime. Curzon Howe, however, was one of the most loveable men I have ever known – and the most extraordinary. From an actual seafaring point of view, it is hard to judge his capabilities – the times were the piping times of peace. Drury was often querulous with his Flag Lieutenant. Curzon Howe would have felled him with a blow if he had been quicker on his feet. But his manners were always too perfect to believe. I saw him once come down to the Custom House in Malta where his barge was waiting to take him on board the flagship. Just before stepping into the boat, he saw a young ordinary seaman standing quite correctly to attention on the wharf. Curzon Howe stepped up to him and, in his rather indistinct voice, said: 'You are waiting for a boat to go on board your ship, I assume. May I offer you a passage?' The wretched youth, utterly flabbergasted, blurted out something to the effect that he was in no hurry. 'Pouff! My barge! No hurry! Pouff! Damned impertinence! Pouff!' One just never knew what he was driving at; if the sailor had accepted the offer, I think Curzon Howe would have had him keel-hauled there and then. One evening at dinner, his Flag Lieutenant grieved him. 'I shall have to change my staff,' he told the Flag Captain. 'Mr. Hardman Jones[23] will leave for England tomorrow.' And he did. Before he left, the Admiral sent for him. 'Enjoy your leave,' the old chap said, 'and as soon as you've finished it, I trust you will do me the honour of returning to my staff.'

At one of Curzon Howe's dinners another young officer was unmistakably tight – so much so, that the Flag Captain convinced himself that serious notice be taken of the episode. Next morning he informed the Admiral, and was cut short. 'Do you mean to suggest that the officer would have dared to arrive at my table intoxicated?' 'Impossible, Sir, impossible.' 'Whose fault is it, then, if he leaves my table drunk?' 'Mine, Sir, mine. If anybody ought to be court-martialled, it should be me.' He always obscured kindness with dignity,

18 Admiral Sir Assheton Gore Curzon-Howe, KCB, CMG, CVO (1850–1911) served as C-in-C, Mediterranean Fleet from 1908 to 1910. He died aged 61 while serving as C-in-C, Portsmouth in 1911.

19 The Order of Osmanieh was an important civil and military decoration of the Ottoman Empire.

20 A brilliant is a diamond or gemstone cut in a particular form that gives it exceptional brilliance. Its shape resembles that of a cone and provides maximized light return through the top of the diamond.

21 Sir Frederic William Fisher, KCVO (1851–1943), younger brother of Jackie Fisher, became Superintendent of Malta Dockyard in 1907 and President of the Royal Naval College, Greenwich, in 1911 before retiring in 1914.

22 Admiral Sir Eric Fullerton, KCB, DSO (1878–1962) commanded a squadron which completed the destruction of the German cruiser *Königsberg* in the Rufiji river in German East Africa in the First World War. For this action he was awarded the DSO. In 1932 he became C-in-C, Plymouth and held the post until 1935.

23 Vice Admiral Everard Hardman-Jones, CB, OBE (1881–1962) became C-in-C, Coast of Scotland.

Captain William Packenham (PD)

and it took a Hardman Jones to raise his ire to such a pitch that on one occasion he started chasing him on the flagship quarterdeck, unbuttoning his coat and blurting out 'By gad, Sir, by gad, Sir, if I were younger, I'd I'd …' It was the anger of a parent for a mischievous son.

Another character in the fleet at this time was William Pakenham,[24] Commander of one of the fleet battleships. Curzon Howe was a big man – a Georgian portrait. Pakenham was a Velasquez – tall and thin and neatly bearded. They were the two politest men in the world. On one occasion, when Pakenham went on board the C-in-C's ship, it took 25 minutes for the pair to get from the gangway to the Admiral's cabin, bowing and scraping to each other every two paces: 'Please, Captain Pakenham.' Bows. 'After you, if you please, Sir.' 'No, I beg of you.' Bows. It took minutes to arrange who should go down the ladder first and there was, of course, more trouble on arrival at the cabin door, and much more when they got inside as to who should sit in which chair. Pakenham always spoke in a very low voice. I got to know him pretty well, as he came on a trip with me in *Hussar.* I asked him why he chose to speak like that and he told me he had schooled himself into this way of speaking because, as a young officer, he found that if he raised his voice, he lost control of it and 'shocked myself at the terrible expletives that, ah, rolled from my lips'.

Pakenham was invariably well turned out. On *Hussar* I heard him admonish his valet for polishing only one of his shoes. He was also a bachelor. One day a fellow Captain congratulated him on a report that he had become engaged. He thanked the man and said: 'One of the happiest days of my life was that on which I became engaged to a most charming woman. But, if I may say so, a far happier day was when I managed to disentangle myself from the, ah, alliance.' Perhaps the best story about Pakenham was when he was on board *Mikasa*, the Japanese flagship, at the battle of Tsushima in 1905. He asked if he might have a chair and table placed on the top of the fore turrets to get a perfect view. There he sat in his beautifully cut white uniform until a Russian 12-inch shell hit the *Mikasa,* just under the bridge, killing 25 men. When the smoke cleared, table, chair and cigarettes had gone to blazes. Pakenham, in his white suit now slopped with blood and brains, picked himself up, went below to change into another white uniform and was quickly back in his turret with a new chair, table and fresh box of cigarettes. He had a curious habit with cigarettes, cutting them in two. 'I find my method more economical,' he told me.

Our duties on the *Hussar* were not entirely confined to ambling about the ocean with the C-in-C or his guests or family on board. Once, the Mediterranean Fleet went home to join up with the Home Fleet. The Admiral told me that he would not be taking the *Hussar* with the fleet and asked me where I should like to

24 Admiral Sir William Christopher Pakenham, GCB, KCMG, KCVO (1861–1933) served as a British observer with the Imperial Japanese Navy during the 1905 Russo-Japanese War. In the First World War he commanded the 2nd Battle Cruiser Squadron at the Battle of Jutland. From end 1916 he was C-in-C of the Battle Cruiser Fleet.

go in his absence. I plumped for the Levant, which I found of great interest. 'Very well, my boy, then I leave the Mediterranean in your hands.' We had a really wonderful cruise for months, visiting many quaint and out-of-the-way places.

For a young skipper, a very great benefit of such an independent cruise was being entirely on one's own. All sorts of delicate little matters had to be dealt with on the spot, without reference to higher authority. Once, inside the port of Beirut, I was having dinner on board at about 8:00 pm when my First Lieutenant came in and reported a serious-looking blaze in the centre of the city. I might have gone ashore and called on the British Consul or gone with him to see the Turkish Governor and offered the services of my ship's company to help quash the blaze. Instead, I cleared the lower deck, hoisted out the fire engine, formed demolition parties, landed every available man and went off at the double to the scene of the fire. We had a grand evening, and managed to make an extensive gap between the main fire and the rest of the city. It was a very dirty but happy crowd that returned to the ship early in the morning to a whacking good supper and unlimited beer. Next morning, I sneaked off early with my Turk dragoman [guide/interpreter] and took the road to Damascus – which thrilled me – and stayed there for several days, thus avoiding a number of deputations from the authorities and the almost inevitable decoration.

Near Antioch, I came across a very handsome tribe of nomads. At Alexandretta [İskenderun] I made friends with a charming group of young people. The girls were not wearing veils and were not Muslims. Nor were they Christians, nor Druze, nor Jewish. They turned out to be good honest pagans who practised the ancient 'Mysteries of Eleusis'.[25] I walked on the Plain of Issus (southern Turkey) and saw the devilry of the Turk in the beautiful burnt villages of the Armenians. I bathed in the Cydnus [Berdan] river near Tarsus; did not Cleopatra sail that way?

Eventually, we turned up at Smyrna to rendezvous with our fleet. Before it arrived, we found the new Turkish fleet there, a collection of wallowing water buffaloes. The British Admiral Gamble[26] told me that he had received a few hundred champagne corks through the post when his appointment appeared in the *Gazette*. I was lunching on the flagship one day when Gamble ordered one of his ships, the *Hamidieh*, to shift berth. No notice was taken of the order. So he repeated it and was ignored again. This time he summoned the Turkish captain to repair on board. He came – and explained that the entire ship's company was at dinner when the first signal arrived and when the second turned up he had not finished his coffee. He was relieved of his command.

Gamble once had to dig out his [Turkish] second-in-command from a comfortable harem in Constantinople. On remonstrating with the fellow, he was informed that the man had been given the rank of Admiral in lieu of payment for installing electric systems in the Yildiz Palace on the orders of Sultan Abdülhamid II. 'You are an Admiral now,' the Sultan had told him. 'Go along and draw the pay, and don't be a fool.' Another time Gamble found that one of his captains had hired out the whole of his crew to a contractor engaged on the building of a railway, going 50:50 with the contractor on the deal. One of his captains fell out with his fellow officers because of his penchant for little boys and was reported to the Admiral. Not that this conduct worried the officers, but it was felt that the honour of the Turkish Navy was at stake and a line had to be drawn somewhere. Gamble had his hands full one way and another.

---

25 The best-known of the secret religious beliefs of ancient Greece. Worship included rites centred on the beginning of life. A young girl is said to be chosen each year to take the place of a goddess.

26 Admiral Sir Douglas Gamble, KCVO (1856–1934). He resigned as head of the Ottoman Navy in 1910. In the First World War he commanded the 4th Battle Squadron 1914–15.

CHAPTER 7

Destroyer Commander

After serving abroad for five years, Claude Cumberlege was posted back to the UK and went on a gunnery course. He was promoted to commander, and became captain of an old torpedo gunboat and three destroyers.

Following two years in command of *Hussar*, my time being up, I was sent home in the Spring of 1910. Having been on foreign service for something like five years, I had about three months' full-pay leave due, and set about enjoying the same. The three months passed quickly – mainly in visiting parts of the land of my fathers hitherto unknown to me – and uneventfully, except in one important particular. The 'important particular' was a woman a year or so younger than myself[1] called Lenore, the mistress of a City magnate. She said she was the daughter of a king. Lenore seduced me – I, who had been married for nearly seven years and who never, never once looked outside my wedding ring. Well, there it was, and there was nothing to be done about it until the cash petered out and my leave with it.[2]

I had applied to the Admiralty for a gunnery course at Whale Island [Portsmouth] and found myself appointed at the termination of my leave. I went there, living in the Portsmouth naval barracks and found myself attached to a class of naval reserve officers and one or two senior lieutenants like myself. Captain Tupper,[3] whose nickname was Shovie, was the boss of this establishment, and a charming fellow. The staff (who wore ordinary uniform with the addition of black gaiters whereas we outsiders had to wear white flannel trousers and rather sloppy-looking scarves round our necks), were actually, apart from Tupper, junior to me, but I was there to learn things. I had no objection to the rig as it was comfortable enough and had a touch of informality about it, and I had no intention of getting into a muck sweat over a little peaceful instruction in modern gunnery.

---

1 Cumberlege was 33 at this point.

2 Cumberlege is being economical with the *actualité*. During his leave his wife Laetitia, residing at 93 Ashley Gate, Westminster, gave birth on 7 August 1910 to the couple's second child, a daughter named Diana. CLC, selected for a gunnery course at Whale Island, Portsmouth, had begun the training on 2 August 1910. On 21 November 1910 he was granted 'Leave to continent. Urgent private affairs.' On 8 December 1910 a fellow RN officer, Lt Cdr Oscar Valentin de Satges, aged 27, the son of a French *vicomte*, filed for divorce in London. He cited his wife Sallie's adultery with CLC on 21 November 1910 at the Charing Cross Hotel, London, and on 22–28 November at the Hotel Cambon in Paris. Oscar de Satges had retired from the RN at his own request on 28 October 1910. Sallie Alexandrine de Satges, the daughter of a major general, was 29 at the time of the alleged adultery and had married Oscar aged 16 in 1897. The petition was 'Dismissed on Summons' on 7 May 1914, by which time CLC was serving in the Royal Australian Navy on the other side of the world. Before 1914 divorce was rare, caused a scandal and required proof of adultery or violence. Divorce of a woman by a man for her adultery was even rarer. There was just one divorce for every 450 marriages. It is believed that the de Satges marriage endured.

3 Admiral Sir Reginald Tupper, GBE, KCB, CVO (1859–1945) was appointed to command HMS *Excellent*, the Whale Island gunnery training depot, in 1907. In 1912–13 he commanded the Portsmouth Division, aboard the battleship HMS *Revenge*.

'Class, fall in!' a smart petty officer barked in my ear after Divisions [a formal parade] and prayers had taken place in a huge enclosed drill shed on the first morning after my arrival. Wishing to make sure this order was intended for our class of nondescripts, I addressed the young man in kindly fashion and invited him, if he had anything to say to me, to do so moderately – reminding him that the usual marks of respect due to officers of my rank were in no way obliterated by a pair of flannel trousers. He saw my point – and there and then I submitted to the absurdity of being retaught the manual exercise with a rifle. 'It's these acting sub-lieutenants what comes down here knowing nothing and not wanting to learn, Sir, what makes one have to shout at 'em or they won't listen to nobody,' he said. 'I know,' I said. 'A loathsome tribe. I was one myself.' We got on famously after that. Later we were even asked by 'Fizzer' Sinclair[4] (in charge of our studies) if there was any particular line on which we should like extra time.

One morning I was walking across the parade ground towards the drill shed to attend Divisions and noticed that the captain, Shovie Tupper, and the whole of his staff were wending their way in the same direction. Suddenly, to my amazement, I saw the most rampageous beast, quite evidently out of control of two herdsmen, about 100 yards away on my starboard beam. Having on one solitary occasion, as a midshipman, been chased out of a Spanish bull ring by a similar monster, I took to my heels and gained the shelter of the drill shed. Not so the staff. The monster, at full gallop, was about a few yards away from them when, at the last moment, dignity was thrown to the wind and the glittering array was scattered in all directions. Even the ranks of Tuscany could scarce forbear to cheer! Who the perpetrators of this dark deed were I never heard. But that they belonged to that happy band of 'untouchables' known as Royal Navy sub-lieutenants can safely be guessed.

After a few weeks 'rub up' in gunnery, My Lords had the neck to invite me to go as a 'Bob-a-Day' gunnery officer of a biggish cruiser. There must have been a temporary shortage of gunnery lieutenants. The job meant doing the work of an officer who had 'specialised' in gunnery and having all the extra responsibility normal to that job, and getting a miserable shilling-a-day more for one's trouble. 'No thank you,' I replied, while glad to note that even a 'salt horse' officer was considered by My Lords to be quite capable of turning his hand to such simple, if mysterious, duties embodied in the hieroglyphic G for Gunnery.[5] Was it a smack in the eye to Whale Island? Or was it a compliment to the efficiency of its instruction, which still included a short discourse on the properties of the sea service cutlass, once described as 'the most awkward weapon for the purposes of attack or defence'? Well, thank goodness I had only been 'invited', not appointed, to take up this job. To refuse an appointment without some extraordinarily good reason at that time was tantamount to asking to be put on the shelf.

However, the authorities were determined to do something with me in the gunnery line. Damn it if I didn't find myself appointed to the staff of the Admiral Inspector of Target Practice![6] As such, I joined the old *Hogue* cruiser where I and about half a dozen other lieutenants lived as passengers, together with an Admiral and his tribe of real gunnery experts. From this hospitable base we went on board one or other of

4 Admiral Sir Edwyn Alexander-Sinclair, GCB, MVO (1865–1945) was notable for firing the first shots of the Battle of Jutland in 1916 and for leading a squadron of light cruisers in the Baltic to support the independence of Estonia and Latvia in 1918–19.

5 Prior to 1918 responsibility for RN ordnance and gunnery training had lain with the Naval Ordnance Department. In 1918 the Naval Artillery and Torpedoes Division was set up. In 1920 it was split into the Gunnery Division and the Torpedo Division.

6 Naval gunnery in the pre-First World War era saw the Admiralty at its most resistant to change. Sir Percy Scott (1853–1924), appointed Inspector of Target Practice in 1905, pioneered many innovations but was deeply unpopular with the RN elite which managed to stymie his most important ideas, notably the introduction of directed firing, until war broke out and Churchill and Fisher took charge in the Admiralty.

every ship in the Home Fleet more or less daily when it was carrying out gunnery practice – quite one of the most thrilling and amusing jobs I ever had. One of the most interesting aspects was to note the different 'atmospheres' evident in the many ships, all more or less alike in their geographical surroundings and in the human way – just sailors and officers. But temperamentally, what a difference. Some showed a sort of nervousness. Maybe a former 'Shoot' had not gone well, or perhaps the preparations were unavoidably hurried, but one felt the atmosphere on board. Another perhaps had a high reputation for good gunnery to keep up and were confident, but anxious.

All the ships regarded us, quite erroneously, as spies who could make or mar their reputations. All showered hospitality on us which would have been embarrassing to anybody but naval officers – even turning out of their cabins to allow us to pass the night in comfort. Some ships rigged temporary canvas cabins for our convenience. Only in one ship were we treated with a certain coolness. I put this down to the Commander of that ship, who not only knew all there was to know about gunnery but also, having been the first man to organise this system of outside supervision and being perfectly satisfied that we could teach him nothing, was also fully aware of our limitations. On this vessel there were no shelters rigged up for our sleeping accommodation, no officer gave up his cabin, and we were allocated a row of hammocks slung in one of the flats [passageways].

I unhooked my hammock from the beams at bedtime on this ship and laid it on the polished floor and spent a comfortable night. No arrangements had been made for our morning ablutions. So I took a stroll round the flats in search of a wardroom bathroom and found a most palatial affair, all nickel plate and porcelain and mosaiced floor with a huge Turkish bath towel draped over a white enamelled chair, a sponge about 2 feet in diameter and a bath filled to the brim with crystal hot water. Over the entrance to the door was a brass plaque with the legend 'Commander' inscribed on it. This will do me, I thought, and walked in, slammed the door, bolted it, hopped into the bath and stayed there the best part of an hour.

We had Saturdays and Sundays off, and on these days Malcolm Goldsmith[7] and I would go off for long walks. From Weymouth we walked to Bridport one Saturday – quite a step [22 miles] – and put up at a little pub for the night, walking back on Sunday. Later on, we found ourselves at Lamlash in the Isle of Arran on the Firth of Clyde. We marched right round the coast of that island to the opposite side, put up for the night, and marched back in a beeline right across Goatfell in a howling gale with rain dead in our faces. I had often heard tell of terrific stalks of wild red deer in Scotland, or getting up before dawn and toiling all day and seeing nothing until the ghillie in charge of operations takes pity on the worn and puzzled Sassenach in his charge and lets him have a long shot at a stag just before it gets too dark – and pocketing a fiver for his troubles. All I can say is that plodding blindly on through driving rain and gale force wind with Malcolm, I suddenly heard a noise behind me. Turning around, there we were, face to face, at no more than ten paces, with a magnificent

Malcolm Goldsmith (IWM)

7 Vice Admiral Malcolm Goldsmith, KBE, DSO (1880–1955). With CLC and other lieutenants, Goldsmith was appointed for duty under the Inspector of Target Practice in 1910. He commanded the destroyer HMS *Lydiard* at the Battle of Jutland. Having retired from the RN in 1934, in September 1939 he was appointed to HMS *Cormorant* as Commodore, Second Class, RNR, for Convoys. Later, he was shifted to HMS *Eaglet II* for the Liverpool Convoy Pool. He was Mentioned in Dispatches for 'outstanding devotion to duty during three years arduous service as Cdre of Ocean Convoys' on 1 January 1943.

stag. Not a bull! I had no idea what to do with a really vast and extraordinarily surprised be-antlered wild red deer. We did the right thing. Without a word, we both rushed straight at him. With a snort, if stags do snort, the noble beast whipped round and I just failed to make contact on his rump with the boot of my foot. I doubt if the stag got over the episode. I imagine he had been sheltering from the gale and as we were walking upwind in the driving rain he had not winded us until we passed within a few feet. We saw several more stags, long before they saw us, probably solely on account of the weather. In my mind, I registered that if ever I was asked to go deer stalking I would save my fiver.

HMS *Speedy* (Wiki)

HMS Kale (PD)

We finished off the fleet's firing in Scotland, and I left *Hogue* up there, landed at Ardrossan and, with a terrific German motorbike, rode to London through the night.[8] To my intense delight I was offered, and accepted immediately, command of *Speedy*, a torpedo gunboat then lying at Sheerness and unattached to any particular fleet. *Speedy* had been fitted to work with other torpedo gunboats in minesweeping, an operation that only recently had been introduced into the Service. She was detailed to take the place of one of the Fishery Protection gunboats, and the duties involved pleased me very well. Essentially, they consisted in ambling about the Channel, keeping an eye on foreign fishing craft, going to any part of the coast one cared to and anchoring where and when one pleased.

However, this job didn't last very long. I had reached the seniority when I might expect to be promoted. But I was not part of any particular fleet and I had no reason to expect anyone's recommendation. I had not realised that Prince Louis of Battenberg, as the local Admiral at Sheerness, might have a say in the matter. He had. I found myself promoted to Commander, aged 34. I had known the prince well over many years in my Mediterranean days, and he never forgot anyone who had once served him.

8 A letter (undated) by Claude to his wife Laetitia survives from this period. Written from the Arts Club in London, it suggests that the couple were already living apart most of the time. 'Claudie' hopes that the two can meet in London soon, having previously 'had a nice time at Littlestone'. It ends: 'With much love dear Tishie which you could so easily improve on as you wished.'

The result was that seven months after arriving at *Speedy*, in August 1911, I was dug out of the ship (a Senior Lieutenant's command) and sent to command *Kale*, a River class destroyer lying at Harwich and part of the Nucleus Crew Flotilla,[9] with Captain Wilfred Henderson[10] in charge and with the amazingly tough Richard Halton Sterling Lecky[11] as his second. Lecky was a hundred years after his time. When I think of him W.S. Gilbert's ballad about HMS *Mantelpiece* springs to mind: 'Sir Berkley was a martinet, A stern unyielding soul, Who ruled his ship by dint of whip, And horrible black-hole ... A sailor who was overcome, From having freely dined, And chanced to reel when at the wheel, He instantly confined! ... In short, the happy *Mantelpiece*, Where all had gone so well, Beneath that fool Sir Berkley's rule, Became a floating hell.' Lecky, however, was no fool; no more energetic, more hardworking officer ever trod a quarter deck, and the awful thing about him was that he was always right.

Wilfrid Henderson, although physically not very strong, almost beat Lecky for energy. That flotilla certainly worked. Wilfrid had one obsession – the certainty that war was bound to come with Germany at no very distant date. He acted accordingly. Every hour, day, week and month was mapped out to a millimetre. The boats, all rather *passé*, fairly rattled off their legs and so did the nucleus crews, about two-thirds their proper complements. I found something rather fine in all this, and if I found a certain 'tiredness' apparent in the flotilla when I arrived, I understood it. The younger fellows had not quite realised our Captain D's extraordinary mentality.

Work, to Henderson, was a passion and directed to one end – the supremacy of British destroyers. Most of our work was done around Harwich, and we saw a good deal more of the Outer Gabbard light vessel than we did of our home town. Wilfrid never took weather into consideration. Blow high, blow low – the work went on night and day. Nobody cracked up, and I don't recall a single accident. Still, it was not long before some of us challenged him. At conference, which before had been entirely one-sided, we organised a sort of 'Question Time'. Arthur Marsden[12] of the *Erne* and one or two toughs like de la Poer[13] got in a few shafts but, instead of being shut up as they had expected, they were on the contrary encouraged: 'Now that's a very

9 In 1911–12 *Kale* was part of the 3rd Destroyer Flotilla on the Nore. In October 1911 two of its crew were charged with stealing a cruet and five bottles from the Norfolk Hotel and Dining Rooms at Harwich. Both were found guilty, and fined (paid by an officer from the ship). On 4 February 1912 a collier dragged its moorings in a snowstorm at Sheerness and drifted into *Kale*, pulling off its propeller guard.

10 Vice Admiral Wilfred Henderson (1873–1930). Born in Italy, Henderson could speak French, German and Italian. When war broke out in 1914 he was serving as Royal Naval Attaché to Germany. He was appointed to command the 1,500-strong First Royal Naval Brigade tasked with trying to help defend Antwerp, but the brigade was cut off. Rather than surrender and become prisoners of war, Henderson took his men over the border into Holland. Here they were interned for the duration, in accordance with international law. Henderson was instructed not to attempt escape. In 1920 he applied for reparation for the loss of career that resulted from his internment and an Admiralty order to him that he should not attempt escape. He was informed that a statement in Parliament and his being placed on General Service Pension was all that the Admiralty could do to inoculate him from possible stigma. He was promoted to the rank of Rear Admiral on 29 July 1920, placed on the Retired List the following day and promoted to Vice Admiral in 1925.

11 Captain Halton Lecky, CB (1878–1940). Two of his evaluations noted that he was tactless. His naval career was rocky. In March 1914 his character upended his career when he was found responsible for insubordination among stokers in HMS *Zealandia*. This prompted a switch to half pay, effective 30 March 1914. The First World War arrived just in time to offer him professional salvation. In 1917, when commanding the cruiser HMS *Southampton*, he was court-martialled for failing to take 'reasonable and seamanlike' precautions to protect a work party. The charge was proved. Lecky was reprimanded. His final evaluation stated that Lecky was 'extremely capable & fearless', but 'not fit for high command'. He retired from the RN in 1925.

12 Sir Arthur Marsden (1883–1960) was a Royal Navy officer who became a Conservative Party politician. He was an MP 1931–35 and 1937–50. He took part in the Battle of Jutland in 1916, commanding a destroyer, HMS *Ardent*, which was sunk by a German battleship. He retired from the RN in 1920 and began his political career in 1929.

13 Edmond de la Poer (1883–1965). In May 1912 Captain Wilfrid Henderson noted that de la Poer was 'Energetic keen & somewhat impetuous'. In the First World War he served in the battleship HMS *Monarch*. In 1924 he retired from the RN with the rank of commander.

interesting point. I hadn't thought of it. Let's go into the matter.' We finished up like a lot of snakes in a basket. When Henderson was transferred to the 4th Flotilla (in May 1912) he said at his farewell dinner: 'Whenever a vacancy arrives at my new flotilla, if any of you care to come along for it, I shall see to the matter.'

To add to the racket, these boats were coal-burning, so coaling the ship was all too frequent. Once I had to go into the Tyne to take on fuel from a collier moored upriver. Another flotilla was already there, commanded by a captain who was thoroughly disliked – one of the fault-finding brigade. Watching other boats go up and turn to go alongside the collier, I noticed that they had a good deal of difficulty in turning such long boats in the swiftly-running tide. When my turn came, instead of turning my ship with the propellers I merely let go an anchor, allowed the ship to swing to her anchor, raised it and paddled peacefully alongside the collier. Why this perfectly seamanlike operation should have raised the ire of this captain, heaven alone knows. Evidently he thought I had made a mess of the manoeuvre and been obliged to anchor to minimise damage. Noticing a slight kink at the top of my stern-piece, he made a signal which was couched in language that indicated '*Now* I've got you! … How the – why the – what the … ?' Butter would not have melted in my mouth; I was able to reply, oh so skilfully, to the effect that the kink had already been there when I had taken command months previously. Perhaps 'Mind your own business' would have been a more suitable response.

Just before this episode, I was working a patrol line with three other boats during annual manoeuvres off Flamborough Head about 50 miles seaward, right across the track of ships bound up and down the North Sea. Fog came on with a hard, cold north-easter wind. We verified our position by means of getting our echo back from Flamborough Head with the fog siren when we thought we might be close to it. I did not leave the bridge, except to conduct normal evacuation operations, for four days and nights. An hour or so after the gale had brought down the fog, we heard the sound of a steamer's fog horn apparently to port of us. We were travelling at 12 knots; the other boats were close up astern but out of sight. Suddenly, the steamer came right at our stern out of the gloom. Later, Jock Wullie Forbes, my Chief Engineer, swore he could have smacked her plating with a walking stick. Being right aft, he said, he had seen her passing not more than an inch and a half off our rudder. The piper had anticipated my order for full speed, and the fact that I then gave the helm the order to alter course towards the steamer, thereby swinging my stern, saved us. But in those few seconds, when I felt she had just missed us, did I have anything to say to that old cock on the bridge [the helmsman] with his walrus moustache, other than bug-eyed amazement? I won't repeat what I said, but I included his progenitors even unto the third and fourth generations in my appreciative discourse!

A time came in this blasted fog when it became necessary to quit the patrol line and proceed to the Tyne for fuel. We headed off in the supposed direction, observing that our starting point was only hazily known, and steamed on, with the lead going, until we thought we were at the entrance to the port. Not a sound. Not a sign. Five fathoms of water by the lead, so we must be close inshore. Stop engines. Four fathoms. Then, suddenly, children's laughter! A nursemaid cries: 'Come out of the water, you little blighter! Didn't I warn you not to get your feet wet?' Full speed astern. We were off a bathing beach a few miles north of the Tyne. Lionel Dawson[14] once claimed that in a similar predicament he hoisted out his dinghy and sent his gunner ashore to ask the name of the town at the first pub he saw. That is Dawson's story; personally, I believe he went himself.

It was not all work, of course, but we all got a great kick out of the whole business. I did pity our poor engineers. Jock Wullie Forbes was the dourest old rascal of a Scot that ever I met. He came from a manse in the Orkney Islands. His mortal enemy was a colleague hailing from Glasgow who sometimes came

14 Captain Lionel George Dawson (1885–1968) served in the Navy in both world wars. He wrote several books about his destroyer years including *Flotillas: A Hard-Lying Story* and *Mediterranean Medley*.

to consult him about a recalcitrant blow-off valve or some such engineering problem. Their last words on parting were always the same: 'Here's to ye, swine of a highlandman.' 'Here's to ye, dirty lowlander.'

Now and again we found ourselves in harbour for a few days. Arthur Marsden came over once from the *Erne* to see me. 'What about going up to town for 48 hours, Claude?' 'Right you are, but we've only got a quarter of an hour to catch the train.' We caught it as it was steaming out of the station, and flung ourselves into a first-class compartment. In the corner sat Wilfrid Henderson, our Captain D. We hadn't had time to ask for leave, personally or by signal. Arthur was spokesman. 'Good morning, Sir.' 'Ah, good morning, Marsden. Good morning, Cumberlege. Going up to town?' 'Yes, Sir. I'm afraid time was so short that we've omitted to ask for leave.' 'Good gracious, why should you? Really, you knew we're not going to sea until next week. Only too glad to think that you know yourselves when you can be spared. Don't give the matter another thought.'

There was a second great man whose flotilla was based in Harwich - Sir Robert Arbuthnot[15] - another of those terrors to the evil doer. As Commander of *Royal Sovereign* when I was second-in-command of a potty little gunboat, he gave my lower deck rugby team their first game against the crack officers' team of the Mediterranean Fleet. We beat them 42–0! Sir Robert was inclined to indicate the course of conduct to be pursued by his officers when in port. He considered, for instance, that every officer should walk to Mistley or Manningtree at least every other day when their ship was in harbour in Harwich. He did it himself. One of his orders was that commanding officers should sleep on board their ships in harbour if a south-westerly gale seemed possible. Many of these men had their wives living in Dovercourt [Harwich], but if the barometer was falling it was more than their job was worth to go ashore. Arbuthnot once thought he had caught out a couple of officers who he met at a pier carrying suitcases as he set off on his 20-mile saunter. On his return, he ordered them to his ship. The signal was sent, and responded to at once; the scoundrels had returned to their ships well before they knew Sir Robert would return.

At that time, I had rooms at Number 4, King Street in Covent Garden, in a house kept by one George Seymour. There were other flats, one of which was retained by George Palmer,[16] baronet of the United Kingdom and uncrowned king of Genoa. I had met George in my *Hussar* days - a delightful character. When I knew him, he was getting on for 60, very *distingué*, a good liver - a bon vivant, with a terrific knowledge of the opposite sex. The port of Genoa came to him for advice on all matters. He was teetotal for 12 years because, he told me, he had had DTs three times and was the only man to have had that complaint so often and lived. He gave the very best dinner parties, and would ask to scent the wine in one's glass but he never touched it with his lips. Well, it was to 4 King Street that Arthur and I dashed. I was a member of several clubs including the United Empire in Piccadilly. Arthur and I were coming out of the hall at this club one day when the porter at the telephone was saying ' 'ang on a moment, lady. I'll make enquiries.' Then, putting his hand over the mouthpiece, he said, 'She's rung again, Mr. Marsden. Same one. Shall I tell her you're 'ere?' Marsden replied: 'No, I'm not here.' 'Are you there, lady? No, lady, the valet just told me that Mr. Marsden went away and won't be back for a fortnight. Didn't leave no address. Can I take a message?'

Another of my clubs was the Cosmopolitan at 3 Rupert Street, kept by the American Jack May.[17] It was intended for use by music hall and theatre artists, and the police regarded it with a friendly eye as

15 Rear Admiral Sir Robert Keith Arbuthnot, KCB, MVO (1864–1916) commanded the 1st Destroyer Flotilla 1910–12. He was killed at the Battle of Jutland when the cruiser squadron he led came under heavy fire after a bold but ill-judged attack on the German battle fleet.

16 Probably Sir George Hudson Palmer, 5th Baronet of Wanlip Hall, Leicestershire (1841–1919).

17 Jack May is often credited with introducing morphine and cocaine to the London club scene. He is unlikely to have been a lone innovator, but for at least 20 years at this time was one of the main local sources of recreational drugs in the London clubland scene.

its members generally did not finish work until around eleven o'clock. It was also wonderfully cheap. The company was free and easy, and often very pretty, and one could hobnob with all sorts of quaint birds unlikely to be met elsewhere. One night I strolled in for a glass of beer about 2:00 am and sat down alone at one of the marble-topped tables when a man came in and sat down at the same table. He was a music hall artist and told me his life story; he claimed he was known throughout the world as the 'uman bird. He said that the Emperor of Austria had wanted once to hang him up in a cage. Eventually he petered out and asked me how business was with me – 'Looks like you might be a juvenile lead?' I explained that I had just come from the Outer Gabbard and was taking a bit of a rest.

I also went to a club in Arlington Street. 'Ten bob' Nield ran it, and it had port and starboard lights at each side of the entrance. Anybody was eligible as long as he had some connection with nautical affairs. It didn't last long. I saw a notice in the paper one day. It ran: 'The Mariners Club went down with all hands last night.'

But the Outer Gabbard was calling. I arranged to meet my First Lieutenant [John Francis Williams] to ride back on our motor bikes in late May. At the pier, we caught the steam boat full of liberty men returning to their ships at half past midnight and shoved off into the dark, swift tide of the river. A dirty night, raining and blowing. Suddenly, a cry 'Man overboard!' Instantly, young Williams was over the side after him. I thought I might as well have a swim too. Our quarry was a totally inebriated stoker who, when we got to him, was intent on swimming down instead of up. Luckily, he collapsed and we manoeuvred with the tide and reached one of the destroyers. With my free hand, as we scrabbled along her side, I got a couple of fingers in some inlet hole, just above the water line, and stayed our progress. The Watch on the destroyer, followed by the rest of the crew, aroused by fresh cries of 'Man overboard,' made every endeavour to spear us with boathooks and brain us with lifebuoys in a praiseworthy but disorganised passion to rescue us. At length we were able to assure them that we were quite all right but would they kindly pass us a line that we would attach to the 'apparently drowned' crewman and they could haul him on board. This was done.

The 1912 Royal Humane Society Silver Medal (Family collection)

HMS *Fury* (IWM)

Leaving the corpse to be revived, we once more boarded the steam boat which had come alongside and in a few minutes were back in *Kale* and downing a good glass of grog, nobody a penny the worse. The story, of course, got about. Damn my eyes if we didn't both get a medal from the Royal Humane Society.[18] Not that I care too much for medals, but this one is more special than most because you wear it on your starboard side instead of port, and it is for saving life instead of for destroying it. It had never entered my head that we were in the faintest danger. Nor were we; one can swim just as well at 1:00 am as at 1:00 pm. On the other

18 The 1912 Royal Humane Society's Silver medal, its oldest and most prestigious. *For saving life in the river Stour off Parkeston 28.5.1912.*

hand, if nobody had gone in the man most certainly would have been drowned, as it was highly improbable that the steam boat would have found him in the dark.

That August [1912] I got a line from Wilfrid Henderson asking me if I would like to join his new flotilla[19] where there was a vacancy. I jumped at the chance, turned over *Kale* to Berwick Curtis at Queensferry, and joined the beautiful little *Fury*, which had been designed by a professor who built royal yachts. In many ways *Fury* had had 'yacht practice' put into her extras. All her canvas screens were beautifully finished and down below, wherever possible, machinery was nickel-plated rather than polished steel, which requires continuous polishing. This was also a 'running' flotilla, using oil fuel.

Mention of oil recalls a droll episode soon after I joined. Our flotilla had been carrying out gunnery and torpedo exercises from Lamlash on the island of Arran, and was looking forward to the annual fleet manoeuvres which were imminent. Another running flotilla had assembled off Troon on the east side of the Firth of Clyde about a dozen miles away. Orders for oil fuel for our flotilla had somehow miscarried. Henderson was very anxious. One morning he sent for me and, closeted in his after-cabin, explained the position. 'Cumberlege, we must have our fuel and at once. The N flotilla is at anchor off Troon, ready to complete with fuel there as soon as it arrives by train. Do you think you could go over there and find out, most discreetly, how the land lies? Of course, we mustn't take anybody else's fuel ... but ... well, if the fuel has arrived and nobody else is taking it, I don't see why ...' etc. 'Leave the matter to me, Sir,' I replied. 'If there's any fuel over there, it will be ours.' 'How soon can you get steam?' 'I daresay my chief has a drop in one of the kettles,' I answered. 'All right, away you go, but mind – *discretion*.'

It was one of those lovely, steely-calm days as I moved across. Getting close, sure enough, there was the N flotilla lying peacefully at anchor off the harbour. To my disgust, I suddenly realised that the inquisitive little man who had tried to be nasty that time in the Tyne was the Captain D in charge of this flotilla. Up goes a semaphore signal – 'What are you doing here?' I felt he meant 'What the devil are you doing here!' I responded: 'I have come to pick up my steward.' Stopped engines, turned out the whalers [whaling boats], stowed the steward in the bottom of the boat under pieces of canvas, and sent him ashore with orders to come back sitting in the stern sheets, having first asked the railway people if the fuel train had arrived. While the inquisitive one was about, I knew nothing further could be done. By and by, back came the whaler with my man sitting up smugly in the stern sheet. Hoisting up the boat, I made a polite signal asking 'Permission to proceed' and slipped into the blue. The steward brought information that no fuel had arrived but was expected hourly and certainly by evening.

Now, there is a first-class golf links at Troon and I knew that the Captain D was a passionate golfer. I calculated that he would play that day and land about 3:00 pm. By 5:00 pm he should be involved in a bunker. I hoped that he had taken his signal officer along with him. We passed a quiet afternoon out of sight, with engines stopped. Timing my arrival on my calculations, we slipped through the N flotilla lines at that peaceful hour in the dog watches when the men are smoking on the forecastle and work is temporarily chucked for innocent recreation. Nobody paid the slightest attention to us, and we slipped unobtrusively into the little walled harbour of Troon and secured up alongside just as a trainload of tank trucks was being shunted right alongside. Without a moment's delay, the hoses were rigged. In a few minutes the priceless fluid was pouring into my bunkers. Simultaneously, a stencil party was formed which plastered every truck with the legend 'Oil Fuel Fourth Flotilla.' Then I wirelessed Henderson as pre-arranged, telling him that the

19 The Fourth Destroyer Flotilla.

fuel for the Fourth Flotilla had arrived and it was convenient for his destroyers to come over at intervals to fill up during the night as there was only one berth available. I proposed to remain in possession of the berth pending the arrivals. This suggestion was carried out at intervals during the night.

At daylight one of the N flotilla entered the harbour and steamed close to us. There was a Commander in charge who I didn't know. 'Hullo,' he rang out. 'Where's our oil fuel?' 'Haven't a notion,' I answered. 'I see all this lot is marked for the Fourth Flotilla. We won't be long; only a couple more boats to fill up.' He hung around for a few minutes and then cleared outside. The Fourth Flotilla got its fuel. What sort of a riot took place over the wireless between the two Captains D was none of my business.

About now I got wind of a new destroyer being completed at Messrs. Yarrows' yard up the Clyde. From all accounts, she was a super craft. A short time previously the Argentine government had called for tenders from Great Britain and Germany to construct half a dozen destroyers. Our builders refused to look at the price being offered, but Germany took up the offer to build three of them. The other three eventually were taken up by an English firm after pressure from the government. The German boats were knots faster. Ours were heavier. But Mr. Yarrow knew he could build a better boat than anybody in the world and was upset by the poor British showing. Just then New Zealand decided to have three destroyers built, and offered the contract to Yarrows. He accepted, provided he had carte blanche to construct them to his own specifications. Then New Zealand changed its mind about the order. The Admiralty stepped in and took over the order even though these boats were not being built to its specifications. *Firedrake*, *Oak* and *Lurcher* were the names of the three – all a couple of knots faster than anything else. *Lurcher* actually reeled off 37 knots on her trials, all weights aboard. Mr. Yarrow, later knighted, and his chief constructor, Mr. Mariner, had put their souls into *Lurcher.*

Finding myself on 48 hours' general leave in London, I visited the Admiralty and, palming a half-a-crown into the attendant's fist, was shown into the Second Sea Lord's enclosure. 'Hullo, Cumberlege, what are you after?' said Jerry Phillpotts[20] who knew me from Mediterranean days. 'The *Lurcher*, Sir,' I replied. 'The devil you are. Look at that list' – and he showed me a list with 20 or more names on it. 'Possibly, Sir, but I want her, and she's going to my flotilla, and she is a new boat – and somebody from our flotilla should get her …' etc etc. I got her, and rushed off to Glasgow on the night mail train. Next day I found my way in pitiless Glasgow rain to Yarrows. What a yard! Outside all mud and dirt, inside wonderful neatness. I had never imagined a ship or a dockyard could look that way.

I met Mr. Yarrow, white-bearded, patriarchal, and Mr. Mariner and all his department heads. I was taken to a great closed-in shed. There *Lurcher* lay, a gladdening sight, finished, perfect. 'Lurcher' – the dog that can see like a greyhound, scent like a foxhound, and hear like a dingo, with the speed of an express train and the grace of a glamour girl. She was mine! Did I not sign a receipt for her? 'To one destroyer complete.' Then we went to luncheon with Mr. Yarrow at the head of his mahogany table with all the heads of his departments around him. Water was the tipple for everybody but me; behind my chair, a butler stood with a quart of 'pop.' But if water was the general beverage, it had no dampening effect on that easy company and the most jovial host. I did enjoy the lunch and mentally registered a vow that someday I would contrive to level things up.

My opportunity came 12 months later. We were up at Lamlash again and there were a few odd days when no 'exercises' were taking place. I wrote to Mr. Yarrow and asked him to come on board with any of his

20 Admiral Edward Phillpotts, CB (1871–1952) became Naval Assistant to the Second Sea Lord in 1912. In the First World War he was court-martialled after grounding his ship, HMS *Warspite*, when it collided with another ship during a night-firing exercise. He became a full admiral and retired in 1927.

Sir Alfred Yarrow (NPG)

HMS *Lurcher* (historyofwar.org)

team and have a look at their ship after a year in commission. He answered that he would be delighted if he might send his son and daughter-in-law and Mr. Mariner but very much regretted that he could not come himself. It gave us all the very greatest pleasure to receive these important and charming representatives of Yarrows one perfect summer's day. Mr. Mariner, who was mainly responsible for the design of the ship, showed great interest in small alterations and additions that we had made – additions more in the way of embellishment than use. We had, for instance, put a sort of vallance [decorative drapery] made by one of the bluejackets out of new scrubbed canvas with the bottom edge teased out into little tassels about a foot deep, around the wardroom at the height of the eave, apparently obscuring an ugly angle iron. He thought this a good idea and made a note of it for future guidance.

In fact, there was another reason for that vallance. During many a long evening, far from any shore-going attractions, we all used to most carefully cut out those really alluring pictures in the *La Vie Parisienne* magazine. These were formed into a sort of Grecian frieze of the jolliest ladies mostly in their birthday suits all the way round the Mess. A time came when the fat, rich aunt of First Lieutenant Farquhar[21] indicated her intention of descending on her nephew. Auntie must not be shocked. The quartermaster of the Middle watch therefore put on the canvas job, and the visit was an unqualified success.

Now, as we were leaving the wardroom after luncheon, it was pretty Mrs. Yarrow who said to me, *sotto voce*, 'May I look behind the curtain?' 'Of course,' I said, and rolled it up. The laugh was on Mr. Mariner. We had a grand run after lunch at full speed over the calm waters of the Firth, doing 37 knots as if the lovely ship had just come off the stocks. On parting, Mr. Yarrow (son) told me that it was the first time in the history of the firm that any member of it had been on board one of their own-built ships after she had left their hands.

When I took over the ship, I sailed south for Plymouth the following day, making the passage at an easy 24 knots with only a steaming crew, picking up our full complement on arrival. Manoeuvres that year [1912] took us as far north as the Orkneys, and there were some fairly hair-raising moments at times with 60 torpedo boat destroyers rampaging about at full speed amongst stately battleships and cruisers. Once, a fog-like blanket of cloud came down just as three flotillas [some 20 or so boats] converged on the narrow

21 Captain Arthur Farquhar, DSC (1888–) was promoted to lieutenant on 1 October 1910. He was mentioned for his role in the bombardment of the aerodrome at Prosecco (near Trieste) on 29 May 1917. He retired from the RN in 1934 but in 1939 was reappointed, as Senior Officer, Second Minesweeping Flotilla.

entrance leading to Long Hope by Scapa Flow with a sluicing tide running right across the entrance. We all got into Long Hope without accident, mainly by back chat from bridge to bridge as destroyers, yards apart, loomed up alongside each other. Then, when we did get in, a glorious sun came out over the still waters and we jig-sawed into our pre-arranged berths.

The Commodore of these flotillas was one Cecil Foley Lambert[22] with the blackest reputation - another of those scourges of the evil doer. A heavily-built, sardonic-looking character (known as 'Black' in the Service), he seemed to find that *Lurcher* had a curious fascination for him. It was his custom to nose about in his steam boat looking for trouble. He could seldom pass *Lurcher* without coming on board. Once, I had been on another boat for an aperitif when, on returning, I found him lounging in the engine room chatting amiably with my Chief, Railton. Descending the polished steel ladder I said brightly, 'Sorry I was not on board to receive you, Sir!' 'Didn't come to see *you*, Cumberlege. Came to see the ship,' he responded. Personally, I found Lambert what an American might call a 'regular guy'.

Rear Admiral Cecil Foley Lambert in 1917 (IWM)

A collection of ships like this gave great opportunities to look up old friends, and in our hours of ease the motor boats of the flotillas were chugging about the waters of Long Hope until all hours. One delightful evening was on board *Lurcher* with our stoker (the son of a pipe-major of the Black Watch) going full bore on his pipes and all hands dancing reels until 4:00 am when eggs and bacon made in the galley were served and the skipper of *Lurcher* was the cook. A little later that early morning, I saw *Ardent* leaving with the fleet mail. Arthur Marsden, her skipper, was in his proper place on the bridge, wearing Mess Kit.

One evening in 1913 my First Lieutenant, having opened the official mail and glanced at the Admiralty weekly orders, pushed them across the table with the remark 'Sir, this might suit you.' I read that the Australian government was looking for an RN Commander to go out and organise its destroyer flotilla. 'Only Commanders with destroyer experience need apply.' I applied by telegram immediately. Others applied by letter and wasted 48 hours. My reasons for my decision were not confined to the fact that in my opinion I had had quite enough experience in Home Fleet destroyers, nor to the fact that in this vast organisation I was just one of a mob, nor to my desire to see a bit more of the world.[23] But all these reasons certainly counted. I got the job.

22 Admiral Sir Cecil Foley Lambert, KCB (1864–1928) became Commander of the Destroyer Flotillas in the First Fleet in July 1912, and Fourth Sea Lord in 1913. He served in that role in the First World War. In 1919 he was seconded to the recently established Royal Air Force, where he served as Director of Personnel. He was promoted to full admiral on the Retired List 1 March 1926.

23 CLC makes no mention of his domestic arrangements. Yet it is clear from this chapter that following the events of 1910 his marriage effectively was over and he led a bachelor existence. In 1919 Laetitia was to spend a year in Sydney with her young daughter, but returned to the UK in 1920 before CLC left Australia. The couple never lived together again. Daughter Diana claimed that they divorced, but no record has been found.

CHAPTER 8

Australian Secondment

Commander Claude Cumberlege sailed to Australia in late 1913. On arrival he encountered problems relating to his command. He took every chance to explore the country and to meet its inhabitants.

November 1913. I was 36 and quite a lot of things had happened to make my life interesting. If sail had gone out of the Royal Navy, submarines had come in. The Dreadnought[1] had arrived, and it had taken Jackie Fisher to do that even if it had been Cuniberti[2] who had thought of the idea many years previously. The gramophone, wireless, moving pictures, motor cars, appendicitis, suffragettes (there was one real beauty on board the ship that took me to Australia; her father had embarked her to avoid Wormwood Scrubs), flying machines and Lord knows what else had arrived, and I had tried most of them except for appendicitis and suffragettes. Now, here I was, off to the Antipodes for a three-year secondment, and I dare say my feelings were not very different to those of the pioneers 100 years before. I looked forward, and did not regret the past.

Chrysis[3] saw me off. I was sailing in the old *Orontes*[4] of the Orient Line. I was disgusted to find that I had another man in my cabin – an intolerable nuisance for a sailor who had always before had a 'bug walk' to himself at sea. However, this chap proved to be tip-top company. What amazing stories he told me. He was a mining engineer by the name of Kelly, only going as far as Gibraltar to report on a copper mine situated under the snows of the Sierra Nevada range in Spain. Or so he said.

RMS *Orontes* (State Library of Queensland)

---

1 The dreadnought was the main battleship in the early 20th century. The first was built by the RN in 1906 and renewed the naval arms race with Germany. There was one battle between dreadnought fleets; at Jutland in 1916 British and German navies clashed, with no decisive result.

2 Vittorio Emilio Cuniberti (1854–1913), an Italian military officer and naval engineer who envisioned the concept of large gun-ships. He is best known for an article he wrote for *Jane's Fighting Ships* in 1903, advocating a concept known as the 'all-big-gun' fighting ship.

3 Not mentioned again in the book. No reference to Laetitia, his wife, or two children. His father, Colonel Alexander Bulstrode Cumberlege, had died at the age of 80 in 1911. His mother, Emily Florence Cumberlege, died in 1937 aged 85.

4 The 9,000-ton RMS *Orontes* was a steam ocean liner belonging to the Orient Steam Navigation Company, launched in 1902 and scrapped in 1925. In the First World War it acted as a troopship.

The following day I happened to look in at the lounge and saw my new friend playing a game of patience with two packs of cards, one against the other. The only card game I know is poker, which I have played rarely. Kelly looked up at me standing beside his table and said, 'Oh, damn the thing, I can't get it out. Sit down there, old boy, and play that pack against mine – we might get it out between us.' I said: 'Sorry, I'm a perfect fool at cards and can't even play patience.' 'Oh well,' he said, 'I'll have one more shot at it.' I went out on the deck for a saunter. Ten minutes later I returned and saw my friend still at his patience and a young man looking on, just as I had. He repeated what he had said to me. The youth sat down. Kelly sent out the barman for a couple of new packs – 'These cards are bewitched,' he claimed – from which he took off the wrappers when the cards arrived and handed one pack to his new friend. 'We don't need the joker, do we,' the lad said while dealing out his cards. On coming to the end, he said: 'Well, that's a rum thing. Only 49 cards in this pack.' 'Impossible,' said Kelly, reaching over and raking in the cards. 'Brand-new pack. Perhaps two or three cards got stuck together,' and proceeded to count them out for himself. '48, 49, 50, 51, 52,' and handed the pack over to his partner. 'I tell you what,' said Kelly. 'Let's have a penny a pip on the result. It will change the luck!' In 15 minutes he won £20.[5] Don't ask me how or why the penny-a-pip totted up to such a sum, but I imagine the rules of this particular game embodied some patent way of multiplication scoring similar to the result of factorial ten or whatever the numbers left over were.

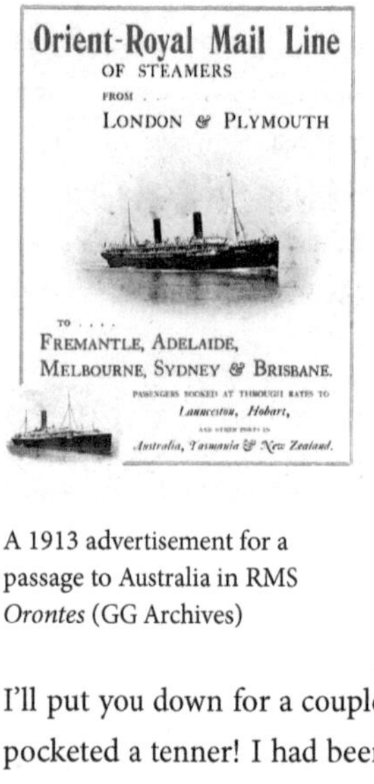

A 1913 advertisement for a passage to Australia in RMS *Orontes* (GG Archives)

What with Kelly, and the extraordinary comfort of the ship, and the fact that I had no responsibilities whatever, I found the life of a passenger at sea quite delightful. I turned out at a reasonable hour, about nine, and found a bath of pure water waiting for me thanks to an agreeable attendant into whose palm I had introduced a gold piece on the evening of the day I arrived on board. I had explained that on board men-of-war we always used fresh water, never salt, and that I couldn't really alter the habits of a lifetime. This was followed by a terrific breakfast at about ten which led to a long chair in the sunshine with my feet on the rails and an adamantine back to the games and fun.

The day before we arrived at Gib. my friend Kelly and another man came round with a sweepstake list and asked me to take a ticket. 'No thanks,' I said, 'I'm no gambler unless I run up against a certainty.' 'Oh, come on,' said Kelly, 'this is as near a certainty as you're ever likely to see. I'll put you down for a couple of tickets.' So to save argument I handed over ten bob. I won the sweep and pocketed a tenner! I had been ashore in Gibraltar on arrival there and returned to the ship just in time to see Kelly boarding the last tender for the shore. He was in a furious rage about something, but on sighting me he came back to say goodbye. 'What's bitten you, Kelly?' I said. 'Don't ask me,' he answered. 'There are a lot of bastards aboard this ship. Not a gentleman among them except for yourself. Goodbye and good luck.'

That night, at sea, in the smoking room after dinner, a few very respectable-looking passengers were talking about forming a party for bridge. 'I'm a bit off bridge,' one said. 'Lost 50 quid last night.' 'Did you?' said another. 'I lost 170. Never saw such cards. I felt sorry for my partner.' At that moment, the bar tender arrived with drinks. He chipped in. 'Not my place to say anything gentlemen, but they're all gone now. All five of them got off at Gib. And you needn't be sorry for your partner, Sir, he was one of them!' I need hardly

5 Worth £2,460 today.

add that my excellent friend Kelly was the leader of the band, an expert at legerdemain – not a low-down sneak thief, but a man who had spent half a lifetime perfecting the art of manipulation. I asked the bar tender if he could shed any light on Kelly's ill temper. He laughed. 'It was because they had only touched the saloon for a miserable three hundred pounds. They reckoned they'd had a very poor trip.' I still don't know why Kelly had called me a gentleman, and I seriously considered returning the subscriptions for the sweepstake that I had won, but better counsels prevailed and I did nothing of the sort.

At Toulon the ship filled up with Australian passengers. I had never met any Australians before. I found their accent awful. The so-called Oxford accent is pretty bloody, but just the ordinary English that I talk hurts no one. The Australian accent is like their blasted gum trees. One gum tree, especially in Tasmania, is a thing of beauty. And a pretty Australian girl, as I was to find out, is the loveliest girl in the world. One can get used to gum trees. Australian girls are different in that way, and their accent is like the trees – you soon get used to it.

The first Aussie I met was called Munroe. I thought he was a 'tough guy' and, having a fellow feeling for tough guys, I took to him. Charming? Certainly not, but manly. He knew more about merino sheep than I did about merino socks, and five minutes after meeting him he had warned me off his girlfriend, who I had not even met! We became good friends. We reached Naples and that meant a trip to Pompeii, which I knew of old. I took a few men friends along there in a deluge of rain. We hired a guide and sloshed through the downpour, the wretched guide doing his best. We saw the 'funny' bits, of course. It was clear to me that the people who lived a couple of thousand years ago had no material differences in outlook to those who live today. There *is* no difference. Pliny tied a pillow on his head to keep off the falling ash; he could have used an umbrella if anybody had thought of making one. As for love affairs, as illustrated – they seemed pretty ordinary practice and natural enough. Unlike us, the honest Pompeiian knew what he wanted and was not afraid to ask for it. Today your respectable sugar broker hides his whatsisname under a bushel and gets the same thing.

The good ship *Orontes* wandered into Port Said and passed that invisible curtain that seems to drop behind one with a click as the ship steams out into Suez roads. T'other side of the Canal you are in a new, yet older, world; the ship takes on a new atmosphere, the passengers a new motley. We knew each other better by then. There is more sitting around late in the delicious heat of the falling wind. One finds oneself in cabin number 158 when one ought to be decently tucked up in cabin number 159. The little man in the open shirt who has organised 'sports' is pooh-poohed when the semi-finals of the shove ha'penny Olympics is advertised; the games had ended with the advent of silk pyjamas and Japanese kimonos bought at Port Said. Ras Gharib 'winks and lets us by'. Sinai, glorious in gold and red. An Arab dhow thrashing to windward. Advertisements for whisky and toothpaste indiscriminately sited. And then the Indian Ocean – to quote a poet, 'so soft, so bright, so blinking blue'. Colombo, and Mr. Junous who begged me to take a star sapphire away and pay him nothing if I would offer him 20 per cent more for it at the other end of my journey. And then at last Australia.

Perth: was it a shock? Honestly, just a little. This was 25 years ago, and later I knew Perth better – but yes, to be frank, Perth as a town was pretty awful to the newcomer to look at for the couple of hours I was there in 1913. Port Adelaide: not much more than a berthing place for steamers. At the time one didn't realise that dull stream running by the wharves had a sort of tired beauty in its couple of thousand miles' meander from Queensland. I had no time to go into Adelaide as I received a telegram to say that one of my destroyers had been sent to convey me to Spencer Gulf where the [Australian] fleet was lying. The *Warrego*

Left:
Vice Admiral
Sir George Patey
(AWM)

Right:
HMS *Warrego* (PD)

was the name of the destroyer, and before long we were steaming round to that great gulf, a very fine natural harbour where I found the *Australia* battlecruiser with George Edwin Patey[6] in charge of the fleet as Rear Admiral, a couple of cruisers, and my flotilla[7] – at least, I spotted one other destroyer at anchor, beside the *Warrego*. 'That's all there are,' said Goodchild, my young RAN First Lieutenant, 'except the *Parramatta*, which is refitting in Melbourne. And of course, Captain D's ship, the cruiser *Melbourne*.' 'Captain D's ship? You don't mean to tell me that there is a *Captain* D as well as a Commander D?' I said.

My first thought, rather naturally, was that I had been sent all this way under false pretences. So I had another look at my appointment from the Admiralty, which quite clearly informed all and sundry that I was appointed to the command of HMS *Warrego* and command of the RAN torpedo boat destroyer flotilla. There had been some mistake. In the *Australia* I found a delightful crowd, from the Admiral down. Steve Radcliffe[8] was the skipper, and Hyde, a Commander RAN, second-in-command. I had, however, trouble with *Melbourne* from the word go, or perhaps I should say that *Melbourne* had trouble with me. I regarded her as my parent ship, where my paperwork and paymaster's business should be seen to, but anything else regarding the organisation of the destroyer flotilla was my business and no one else's. Things were not a little difficult at first, but I played possum, partly because I had a keen sense of what was due to a Post Captain and partly because I liked this particular Post Captain. In any case, there was darned little organisation to play with in a flotilla of two boats, whereas I had been used to a twenty-strong flotilla.

Spencer Gulf, magnificent harbour that it is, could hardly be called a beauty spot. Where there wasn't water, there were gum trees and that is about all. Within a day or two the fleet set sail for Hobart in Tasmania. What a harbour! Forty miles wide at the entrance, narrowing down to the deep-water wharves of the city some 30 miles within. A sailor's harbour, make no mistake. This cruise by the fleet was regarded as the annual 'joy' cruise of the year. Hobart for balls and parties and racing, thence to Melbourne in Victoria for a similar programme. Adelaide had already been 'done' before my arrival. Finally, Sydney which, with its

6 Admiral Sir George Edwin Patey, KCMG, KCVO (1859–1935) served as a midshipman aboard HMS *Shah* during the Battle of Pacocha, an action in 1877 with a Peruvian armoured turret ship. *Shah* was then diverted to South Africa to assist in the Anglo-Zulu War. Patey served in a naval brigade which had been formed to fight ashore. In 1897 he was part of the International Squadron blockading Crete. In 1908 he became a naval aide-de-camp to King Edward VII. In 1913 he became the first Rear Admiral Commanding HM Australian Fleet and was promoted to vice admiral in September 1914. In the First World War he commanded the Australian naval squadron as part of the New Zealand Samoa Expeditionary Force that captured German Samoa, and the Australian Naval and Military Expeditionary Force that captured German New Guinea. He also became C-in-C North America and West Indies Station from March 1915. In September 1916 command of the Australian Fleet was transferred to Rear Admiral William Pakenham.

7 In total, the Royal Australian Navy in 1914 consisted of 16 vessels and 3,800 men, of whom 22 per cent had an RN background.

8 Vice Admiral Stephen Radcliffe, CMG (1874–1939) was appointed to command the RAN battlecruiser *Australia* in 1913. In 1918 he commanded the battleship *Superb*. He retired from the RN in 1922.

dockyards, was our normal base. Hobart seemed to me to be about the best place to live in if one had to live permanently anywhere. A lovely climate and grand scenery, Kentish hop fields, and jolly, English-looking people. I have since seen snow in the mountains hanging over Hobart, and gum trees that are real trees. And, not to be disregarded, a very, very solid seafaring people. Did I not spend one of the happiest days of my life on board the old 'timber-getter' *Lunawanna* with just a skipper, a mate and a boy?

My memories of Hobart are therefore pretty fine – if only one could transport it to somewhere get-at-able in the British Isles – with only one bit of fly in the ointment, which I did little, I'm sorry to say, to extract. This D business had fairly stuck in my gizzard. Yet it was not an intentional bit of naughtiness on my part when, one day, the Admiral told me to take the Governor of Tasmania on a trip in *Warrego* to a far-away village. Having embarked His Excellency and set off at full speed, I ordered a course to take us past the *Melbourne* whose whole ship's company at that moment was employed painting the ship's side from rafts alongside. I just did not notice this fact, but the huge wash made by my destroyer purling along at full speed with the Governor on board upset their rafts. I saw a semaphore signal go up. My signalman took it in and handed it to me. The signal read: 'From Captain D. What do you think you are doing?' I quite innocently replied: 'From Commander D. 25 knots.' Goodbye, Hobart. We proceeded to Melbourne.

The *Lunawanna* timber-getter (State Library of South Australia)

Melbourne. Collins Street, balls and parties. Was it wrong of me to slip away from a party with a girl to her home, then from the roof half an hour later watch her parents return in their car, and after a decent interval, led by her hand in the dark, find myself in her pretty room? It must have been, because ten minutes later, to our horror, we heard padded footsteps approaching our door. They passed, and a few seconds later the unmistakable deluge of an efficient sanitary system fell upon our ears, and again the footsteps passed and the faint click of a shutting door indicated safety. The first tram passing in the dawn later luckily woke me. I put my shoes on half way down the stairs and even the hall porter was still asleep.

And then to Sydney. What a city! So different from anything else in Australia, and what a harbour! Perhaps some of the very happiest days of my life have been spent in its so safe and exquisite bosom. Unbelievably beautiful, indescribable.

On the principle that what the eye doesn't see the heart doesn't grieve about, the fly in the ointment as far as I was concerned over who was in charge of my tuppeny ha'penny flotilla was temporarily obscured, the *Melbourne* being 1,000 miles away in Melbourne. But the whole matter was revived from that end, and I was summoned to the flagship to explain myself. Armed with my appointment, I went, lashed up with a frock coat and a sword. At first I was fairly hauled over the coals. But at long last I was allowed to get a word in edgeways. I produced my trump card – my appointment from the Admiralty. It was laid before the

Admiral. There was *no* answer to it. Patey saw the point immediately. He then told me that the self-styled Captain D had written to him to say that he could no longer carry on and, in a few words, if I was not put in my place [the place he wanted me], he would have to ask to be relieved of his command. I responded by saying that I regretted his decision and that it was of no real consequence to me, but as I had this mandate from the Admiralty making me responsible for the good conduct of the RAN Flotilla until it was washed out I proposed to consider myself in full charge.

Patey asked me if I could suggest any way out of this impasse. 'Yes,' I said. 'The simplest way out is to transfer the control of the flotilla office to the flagship, since it appears to me that we should be much more likely to be in closer touch with the flagship than with any one of the cruisers.' Patey thought the idea pretty good, and the day came when the alteration took place. I thought that now, at least, I was what I had come out to Australia to be. The first letter that came to me from the flagship, on some unimportant matter, was signed by jolly Steve Radcliffe with the sub-title 'Captain D.' Over I went to the flagship and buttonholed Steve and pressed the offending document into his hand. 'Well, what's wrong with that?' he asked. 'What's wrong? I'll tell you, skipper. There's only one D in this fleet and that's me. Write me every day of the week and twice on Sundays and sign yourself God Almighty, but cut out the D.' We had a bottle [of beer] on it and Steve saw at once how absurd it was to have a sort of condominium, and that was the last I heard of the matter. I must say for myself that it never entered my head to ask to be returned home failing recognition of my undoubted rights. It never kept me awake at night, nor did I bother much about the principle involved. But it had been irksome to discover, after accepting a particular job, to find someone else installed.

Sydney in those days was a small place of about one million inhabitants. The Coxes didn't know the Boxes, and the Knoxes[9] turned up their noses at both of them. My diminutive flotilla swung round their buoys in lovely Farm Cove with the botanical gardens in the background. There is no more beautiful mooring. Sydney always loved her ships, and in the old days the sailing ships used to secure alongside the circular quay. By the time I arrived these places had been taken by the great mail steamers. It was like having Southampton docks in your back garden. Sydney meets the mail ships, and Sydney sees them off with a thousand coloured paper streamers holding the ships to the wharf until they tear themselves away. In London, I never see my sea captain friends and as for prime ministers, short of going to the House of Commons, they might not exist as far as I am concerned. In Australia, things were different. There seemed to be more of them somehow. I met one [prime minister] on Castlereagh Street one morning outside a sixpenny bar. 'What about stepping inside, Cumberlege,' he said, 'and stopping one? D'you think you could keep one down?'

It was the height of the season when we got to Sydney. Such racing, such balls and parties and picnics, such loveable people. To an easy-going person like myself, it was sometimes difficult to fit it all in. One met and liked everyone. But it was impossible to let oneself go. Talk about being killed by kindness; it was dead easy in Sydney before the war. I jumped at an opportunity to go up-country to a sheep station belonging to one of the Osborne clan.[10] This estate was an example of sheep rearing at its easiest, thanks to an almost permanent supply of water and plenty of feed. The peace of that great estate, the well-ordered house, the company of Henry Hill Osborne and his popular wife Marjorie and a red-headed girl called Auriol are some of my most cherished memories.

I went also to Queensland, a long way from Sydney, to a very attractive cattle station belonging to the Bells of Coochin-Coochin. Three brothers and their two sisters, all young people, and their mother

9 A reference to Arthur Sullivan's first comic opera (before he partnered with W.S. Gilbert): *Cox and Box; or, The Long-Lost Brothers.*

10 Of Kangaroo Valley and Currandooley fame. Henry Hill Osborne (1866–1936).

lived in a great rambling house around a sort of patio. The brothers used to flick cigarettes out of their sisters' mouths with a stock whip. They promised me a stock whip if I could do a 'Sydney flash' (a succession of seven cracks) before I left the station. I have that stock whip still; my father had shown me how to crack a hunting crop years before and a stock whip, being short in the handle, is easier to crack. At the weekend, people just blew in and the jackaroo[11] was kept busy filling sacks with hay to make up beds for them on the verandah. There was a mob of horses in a sort of corral from which one just had to catch a nag and find a saddle and bridle, and then all hands went down to the 'camp' where the fat Herefordshire cattle were 'cut out' prior to being sent to Brisbane, where they were turned into chilled beef. Jimmy Ryan, head stockman, did not go much on new chums, but we got on well together (which was a feather in my cap) partly because he saw that I really could ride a horse and partly because I was able to quote Adam Lindsay Gordon.[12] Bush poetry was Jimmy's hobby. Riding home in the moonlight one night he gave it to us, the real stuff.

Henry Hill Osborne in 1913 ((PD)

Time rolled on in 1914, with very little sea time until June. The Admiral then decided, having collected as much of his fleet as he could, to take it away from the attractions of Sydney for a cruise and 'exercises' with the aim of arriving at Brisbane in time for the Brisbane Cup [horse race]. Our flotilla duty, outside of night attacks and towing targets, consisted of running beef and mail trips for the fleet. I still had only two destroyers to play with, but we spent a most enjoyable month at these games, calling our headquarters the beautiful Palm Islands [off Queensland]. These islands were quite uninhabited but blessed with perfect weather. All my spare time was spent in a pair of bathing bumbachos [baggy shorts] and in my whaler, which I had rigged for single-handed sailing. I used to lie on my stomach for hours gazing down into the wonders of the coral gardens, fathoms deep in the perfect, clear, still waters. Then I would cook my tea in the shade of trees almost overhanging the sea and watch bright butterflies in colour as variegated as the vivid inhabitants of the coral waters.

June went out and July stole in during this delightful mixture of work and play. Everybody was so contented. There were no distractions of beer and beauties for officers or men. Sydney was 1,000 miles away and even mails were few and far between. July was petering out. In day or two we would be leaving the islands for Brisbane and … festivities. We were beginning to look forward to it all. We never got there. That Austrian murder news was a cloud no bigger than a man's hand, but a cloud.

I had gone into Maryborough's[13] deep port for mails, and the flagship was 30 miles away, near Sandy Cape. About 10:30 pm on July 29th in a deluge of rain I got a wireless message ordering me to re-join the flagship immediately and indicating that the whole fleet would proceed forthwith to Sydney. How I got out

11 A young man working on a sheep or cattle station to gain experience.

12 Adam Lindsay Gordon (1833–1870) was a British-Australian poet, horseman, police officer and politician. He was the first Australian to gain recognition overseas.

13 Maryborough is located on the Mary river in Queensland, about 160 miles north of Brisbane.

of that anchorage I shall never know; owing to the tropical rain, I could not see 50 yards. But by lead and great caution I managed somehow. Later I got another order, cancelling the first one and telling me to go at once with *Yarra* (my other boat) to Brisbane and await further orders. When I got to Moreton Bay off Brisbane, I anchored close to the Pile light at the entrance to Brisbane River and got in touch with the city 10 miles up the river by telephone. The local district naval officer kept me informed as far as he could with the march of events in Europe.

CHAPTER 9

At War 1914

The First World War began in Europe. Commander Cumberlege was in the destroyer HMAS Warrego *on the other side of the world in New Guinea, taking part in the first Australian military operation of the conflict.*

Mobilisations. Germany. France. Russia. Surely, we must be in it. No news. A 20,000-ton German liner passed us within a couple of hundred yards, dipping her ensign politely. If only I could have followed her she would have been my property in 48 hours' time. I suppose she went on to intern herself in the Dutch islands.

Early on 4th August I got a message from Melbourne Admiralty ordering the flotilla to proceed with all despatch to Thursday Island in the Torres Straits and attempt to intercept a British oil tanker expected to be passing that way. The route lay right through the inside of the Great Barrier Reef – a mass of uncharted reef-strewn waters with a narrow, surveyed passage of deep water and intricate navigation, stretching 1,000 miles parallel to the coast and through which Messrs Lloyd's [insurance] would not permit a ship to pass without a pilot.

We left immediately at full speed. A moment came when I had to alter course and could not see an islet which I needed to pass. My lynx-eyed signalman sang out: 'What's that, Sir? Right across our bows?' 'That's it! Hard-a-port, ease the helm, amidships. Steady as she goes!' A dark shape, with wavelets lapping, slid by not 50 yards along our side and vanished astern.

It was 1:00 am on 5th August 1914. A little destroyer, 1,000 miles from her base. Beside me stood my young First Lieutenant, my coxswain, a couple of lookouts and the man at the wheel, his face illuminated by the compass light. My writer, standing beside me, hands over a piece of paper. 'Just come through, Sir. I've deciphered it.' I take it to the light shining in the compass bowl and read: 'A state of war exists between Great Britain and Germany and Austria.' I hand it to my First Lieutenant with the remark, 'Seven years.' Goodchild reads it out slowly. 'Oh, impossible, Sir. Seven years! More like six months.' 'Seven years,' I reiterate.

Next day we arrived at TI, as Thursday Island is called. The oil tanker had not arrived. I went ashore to this fly-blown place and met some of the famous Torres Straits pilots. One asked me where we had come from. I told him. 'You're a liar,' he said. I replied: 'Maybe you're a bastard?' He shot back: 'But you must have come through at about 20 knots?' I said: 'Twenty-five. Go and look at my log.' 'God's blood,' he responded. 'Is that a fact? 'For goodness' sake don't tell them that if you ever go back to Sydney or we poor blokes are likely to lose our jobs.'

I anchored the ship way out so that I could keep a lookout for my tanker, kept steam up and rode at a short stay.[1] German wireless transmissions were resounding,

---

1 With the anchor chain somewhat slack – neither vertical nor fully extended.

perhaps from German mail ships scurrying for the [neutral] Dutch East Indies or perhaps from one of the few German gunboats known to be in the Pacific. The tanker turned up that night. She was loaded with can benzene but had some 700 tons of fuel oil in her tanks as well. The skipper was a Welshman. The First Mate was a German. I was sorry for the man; he was serving in a British-flagged ship so that he could get a UK Masters certificate. And, of course, he was a German naval reservist. I gave him in charge of the local authorities in TI and imagine that he passed the next four and a half years in an Australian prison camp. Pretty hard.

That was my first operation of the war. I cannot very well cut out five years of my life in this account, but nor do I intend to give you chapter-and-verse about the war. I will therefore confine this to my own doings and not attempt to draw conclusions or get involved with broader aspects of the conflict. As it turned out, my experiences were not ordinary and on November 11th, 1918 they ended as they had begun, with me at sea more than 1,000 miles from land. Throughout this war not an hour was spent on an office stool, nor a minute of leave in the home of my fathers. Instead, I had the honour and exquisite pleasure of commanding continuously one or other of His Majesty's ships of war at sea. I made no *recorded* mistakes, and made every endeavour to avoid the penalties attached to Article One of the Articles of War.[2] Had I lived in 1790 I would have made a fortune in prize money. As it was, I touched about £300[3] and secured three bits of metal [medals] to hang on my chest whereas one would have done.

The oil tanker skipper was a bit flabbergasted when I informed him that my orders were to take him with me and rendezvous with the fleet 1,500 miles away somewhere in the Coral Sea. 'If we fall in with the bastards, I shall go up in blue flame.' 'That's right,' I said. We hit the rendezvous somewhere south of the German-held islands called the Bismarck Archipelago[4] on about 9th August. The fleet consisted of the battle cruiser flagship *Australia*, the light cruisers *Melbourne*, *Sydney* and *Encounter*, a couple of submarines due to arrive later, and my flotilla, which now had three destroyers.

On arrival I received a general signal to all captains to repair on board *Australia*. It was a lovely day and I manned my whaler and went over. Patey, the Admiral, was on the quarterdeck when I arrived. 'Hullo, Cumberlege. I have a job for you which I'm sure will be to your liking,' he said. 'I'm going to sent you to Rabaul in New Britain, where we believe the German Pacific Fleet is lying. I want you to make a night attack on it. There will probably be half a dozen ships, including the

Rabaul harbour in 1914 (AWM)

2 It is unclear if CLC is being ironic or sarcastic. In 1759 Article 1 stated: 'Divine worship. All commanders, captains, and officers, in or belonging to any of His Majesty's ships or vessels of war, shall cause the public worship of Almighty God, according to the liturgy of the Church of England established by law, to be solemnly, orderly and reverently performed in their respective ships; and shall take care that prayers and preaching, by the chaplains in holy orders of the respective ships, be performed diligently; and that the Lord's Day be observed according to law.' It was still in force during the 1982 Falklands conflict.

3 £300 in 1918 is equivalent to about £18,000 today.

4 The Bismarck Archipelago is a group of tropical volcanic islands off the north-east coast of New Guinea in the western Pacific Ocean. New Britain and New Ireland are the largest islands in the archipelago.

Gneisenau and *Scharnhorst*.[5] Don't waste your torpedoes on the smaller craft.' I felt like saying 'Oh yeah?' Downstairs, round a table with the other captains, a great scheme was elaborated. I soon realised that nobody had the foggiest idea where the German fleet actually was; all that was known for certain was that it had left Taingtau [now Qingdao or Tsingtao] in China on a certain date. Everything pointed to the fleet going to the Bismarck group with its fine harbour which, rumour had it, had been fortified with 10-inch guns and minefields. *Sydney* was to lead the destroyers to a point near the entrance to Rabaul harbour at dark of the moon. I was then to detach myself and make the night attack.[6]

The moment to begin the operation came at about 5:00 pm on a glorious South Seas evening. We were about 70 miles from our objective. *Sydney* drew out, closely followed by me and my other two boats, and we started off at 22–24 knots. As we passed close to the flagship *Australia*, its band was playing 'A Life on the Ocean Wave', 1,000 men crowded her side and gave us a roaring cheer, and a valedictory signal of good luck was flying from her masthead. An inspiring moment.

Night fell rapidly, with a slight following wind which blew black volumes of burnt oil smoke straight into the blue-black heavens. No moon. Some 15 to 20 miles from Rabaul we saw the vivid white light of distant searchlights. We kept going. Quite suddenly, no more lights. 'To be exercising those lights probably means they're not expecting us,' I said to myself. Well, we were up to our necks in it by then. Soon we closed up[7] the gun crews. A perfect, still warm night. The men shed their flannels, Nelsonically, and chaffed [teased] their mates or slept, according to temperament, at their places.

We arrived at the point where we should leave *Sydney*. With a spoke of helm, we passed her close by. There were no entrance lights to the harbour, which was divided in two parts, and we had been a couple of miles short of the agreed departure point, but there were no outlying dangers so it was immaterial. I headed off to the southern shore of the larger harbour while *Yarra* angled off to a smaller harbour, and *Paramatta* laid a course for the steep shore. Not a word was spoken except in whispers. We got to a biscuit's toss of the beach. I actually saw a group of natives sitting around a coconut fire, oblivious to our proximity. 'Someone signalling to starboard, Sir,' my signal boatman whispered: a vivid white light, flick, flick, flick, flick. 'Can you make out what it means?' 'No, Sir.' Our bow gun swung round silently; the torpedo tubes were already trained abeam.

Lights from houses on shore showed up. The signalling ceased. We stole silently and very close inshore. We approached the head of the harbour, curving with the lie of the land to starboard all the time. 'Stand by!' There, right across our bows, was a big black mass. By God it's them, not 100 yards ahead, I thought. 'Hard-a-port!' We swung round and missed hitting a wooden pier by yards. 'Stop engines!' The harbour was plum empty! It was odd lying there in that great harbour. *Paramatta* crept alongside, and we laughed and talked from bridge to bridge, then cleared out, found *Yarra* and joined *Sydney* outside. We had had a thrill all the same. The lights that we had seen earlier had come from a terrific bush fire that was smouldering all down one side of a large mountain called Mother. The flashing signal light had been an acetylene light hung on a bungalow verandah.

We rushed off at speed to another possible harbour[8] round the corner from Rabaul, a few miles away.

5 In reality, as Admiralty documents such as ADM 137/7 in the National Archives demonstrate, neither the British nor the Australians had any idea where the *Gneisenau* and *Scharnhorst* were.

6 The Secretary of State for the Colonies, Lewis, Viscount Harcourt, had previously informed the Governor General of Australia that 'the Germans are fully prepared for surprise attacks on wireless stations by warships and … have made arrangements to hide instruments in order to start stations again when the danger is past.' (ADM 137/7 on 19 August 1914).

7 Ordered the gun crews to their positions.

8 Kabakaul Bay.

As the moon rose night became day. Then we heard a wireless in plain German stating that there were 'three English warships in Talili Bay'. Where on earth had that come from? For the moment, there was nothing to be done. By then the flagship knew that the harbour had been empty. We waited for orders. The sun rose and awakened me on deck. What a transformed scene! On each side was every shade of green. Towering close above the extinct Mother was her lively daughter, sulphur-capped, smouldering at her knee. The flagship wandered by, and I again entered the harbour, this time at speed. Men at action stations. We pulled up at the pier. Handsome natives stood around, naked except for brilliant loin cloths. I spotted figures in tropical white and khaki peering round the corners of sheds. A group eventually pushed out. I hailed; they shrank from view. I went alongside at the end of the pier and landed – perhaps the first man to set foot on German soil in the war. I hailed again. This time the group pushed out, somewhat shyly. I was unarmed, my guns behind me trained on the sheds. I ordered the guns to train amidships. They swung round reluctantly.

Two men in white uniforms appeared. 'Where is your Governor?' I asked. 'Gone away along a bush,' they answered. 'No matter. Who are you?' I said, pointing to one man. 'I'm his secretary.' 'You will do! Tell me, where is the wireless station?' 'There is no wireless station.' 'That's a lie. I have your signals.' 'There is no wireless station here.' 'I can see that for myself. Tell me where it is.' I had the chart of the island. 'Show me where it is.' 'There is no wireless station.' Just at that moment my signalman brought me a message in plain German reporting the presence of our sister ships some 15 miles away at sea. 'Now,' I said, 'where was that signal sent from?' 'I don't know.' 'Very well, I would hate to make a mess of these charming-looking natives with whom we have no quarrel, but if this wireless doesn't cease instantly, I will blow the whole town to smithereens.'[9]

At this point my signalman approached with a signal from the Admiral; the flagship was recalling us. And another one in German: 'English Commander threatens bombardment. This is last signal coming through.' I decided that the only way to find out the location of this station was to shanghai [kidnap] the secretary on board and obey the order to re-join the fleet outside the harbour. I wirelessed my plan to the flagship and got, in reply, another signal: 'Re-join me forthwith. Enemy's cruisers sighted south Tally west. Disembark German.' I had not taken him on board yet, so dismissed the group, saying I would be back. We rushed out of the harbour at full speed.

We found our fleet with engines stopped and no apparent notice being taken of the enemy cruisers supposedly to the south-eastward. A signal came in from *Melbourne*: 'Propose to discharge one Able Seaman to you after supper.' 'When you please,' I replied, 'but meanwhile, where are the German cruisers?' There had been a slight mistake. *Encounter*, far southward, had reported a tramp steamer which she had mistaken for a German man-of-war! By this time Patey had far out-stripped his slow-moving colliers in his laudable determination to locate and bring to action the German Pacific Fleet. So before anything else could be done it was necessary to go back and meet the colliers, hundreds of miles south in a huge Eyrie Reef harbour or lagoon. The destroyers took turns in keeping a lookout on patrol during the operation.

While here, Patey got news that the New Zealanders were about to send a force of soldiers to Samoa, so he rushed off with his cruisers to escort them. I was sent to Port Moresby in Papua to arrange for the arrival of an Australian force as part of the occupation of the Bismarck group. Von Spee and his quite important fleet had vanished, and nobody had the slightest idea where he had gone to until, later, he was located. The Pacific Ocean, big as it is, was a highly unsafe bit of water for ambling troopships, to say nothing of ordinary commercial vessels. This lack of information added a piquancy to what otherwise might have

9 At some point in this situation HMAS *Warrego* destroyed the telephones at Rabaul post office (Source: Raffin).

been a humdrum state of affairs. The needle in a haystack was dead easy compared to what George Edwin Patey was confronting. In those days he had no means of locating anything.[10] Von Spee did, however, have a system, and it is almost certain that at all times he had a fairly accurate notion of the whereabouts of the *Australia* battle cruiser.

I arrived at Port Moresby with my three boats to find a collection of transports loaded with the usual necessities and a few hundred enthusiastic volunteers who, from a dim distance, looked like soldiers. These ships were scattered about the reef that formed the harbour – a blaze of light by night, occupying the most conspicuous position alongside the little town pier. The reason was that Port Moresby had no natural water supply, and by the time I turned up, the water question for the ships had become acute. The *Kanowna* troopship had run out of her stock (but when I went on board, I noticed a large communal lavatory, and walking inside found three taps running to waste). Something had to be done, as Port Moresby could not be depended upon. I shifted all the ships immediately into a well-protected and invisible spot.

Ashore, I got in touch with the livewire Governor, Sir John Hubert Murray, one of the best. On the outbreak of war he had formed a local volunteer force and arranged for guards for the sandbagged wireless station and so on. Through him, I arranged for posts to be set up some 20 miles up and down the coast to act as sea and coast watchers who might be able to give some warning of the approach of hostile craft by day. By night, two of my three boats patrolled outside the harbour, the third one generally being employed evaporating water for the *Kanowna* and her troops. A big strain for a little craft. We also collected the best of the few motor craft belonging to the port to act as vedettes [small patrol vessels]. I put them in charge of a Mr. Powles on the recommendation of the Governor.

Sir John Hubert Murray (PD)

Mr. Powles was a Conway[11] boy who had settled in Papua as a purveyor of labour. New labour laws had outlawed 'blackbirding', and things had gone all wrong with the business. I sent for Powles. He turned up on board at once in a black beard, a sweaty vest, dungaree trousers and no shoes. 'Have a drink?' 'Don't mind if I do, though I can't usually take anything at this time of the day,' he said with a twinkle. 'Now then, what do you know about the reefs hereabout?' 'No more than any salt-water boy. Where there are reefs, you've got to keep your eyes open. There are plenty of passages.' I opened a chart. 'Are there any other passages leading in or out of the barrier fit for us to use?' 'Surely,' he said. 'There's a good one here and another there ...'

What I wanted was to have a 'getaway'. By night, German wireless fairly bellowed. There were at least three German craft in our part of the world within, say, 600 miles – but, for all we knew, within 10. It would never have done to be caught, or bottled up and unable to do anything. It happened several times later. Thereupon, I installed Mr. Powles as Reef Pilot with the temporary acting rank of Sub-Lieutenant – and,

10 Very true. Patey was receiving contradictory information from the Admiralty in London, from eye witness reports from all over the Pacific and from the admiral commanding the China Station who had overall responsibility for RN operations in most of the seas north of Australia. At the time the British government was only interested in two things involving the RAN: finding and sinking the two German cruisers known to be in the Pacific, and transporting a 20,000-strong Australasian Force to the battlefields of Europe.

11 HMS *Conway* was a naval training school founded in 1859 and housed for most of its life aboard a 19th-century wooden ship of the line. The vessel was stationed on the Mersey near Liverpool, was moved to the Menai Strait during the Second World War and then, while being towed to Birkenhead for a refit in 1953, ran aground and was wrecked. The school moved to purpose-built premises on Anglesey and continued to 1974.

with the help of a kindly Chinaman, rigged a barrel at the masthead to create his eyrie. More to amuse the troops than anything, we also formed a 'Torpedo Harbour Defence Scheme'. Meantime, the armada in the harbour was increasing visibly. The *Kanna* collier arrived, carrying a few thousand tons of Westport coal. The *Kanowna* was short of coal (she always needed something), so the law looked the other way while a local policeman shanghaied a village to do the work.

The first month of the war petered out, and on the first day of September the fleet returned from successfully shepherding the troops from New Zealand to Samoa. Still not a sign of von Spee.[12] A troop transport, *Berrima*, with 1,000 Australian troops, joined us, and we all went off for the Bismarck Archipelago. *Kanowna* immediately began to play up and dropped astern. I turned back to see what the matter was and got a signal from her: 'Unable to keep steam. Firemen have refused duty!' or words to that effect. This struck me as odd, and I made a signal in reply pointing out that there were 500 or so soldiers on board and, in as many words, 'What the hell are they there for?' Back came a reply that the officer-in-command had detailed volunteers and shortly she would be able to keep steam. I went back up the line and informed the Admiral, who thereupon sent *Kanowna* back to Australia.

Captain John Glossop (AWM)

September. Precisely one month after our first descent on the German possessions we made a second night reconnaissance on Rabaul harbour and found it still empty. I re-joined *Sydney* and here Captain Glossop detailed an operation which was to take place the following morning. This was to consist of landing two parties at two different locations to find and take over the wireless station. This, we were told reliably, was at a spot some 4 miles inland up a 'good motor road' from the coast. *Sydney* was to land one detachment, and *Warrego* was to land the other a few miles further along the coast. It was expected that the detachments would meet somewhere in the neighbourhood of the wireless station and 'take over'.

Naturally, my first question was: 'Am I to understand that the Germans have agreed to hand over the wireless station?' I was told that nothing had been said about that. Meanwhile, the troops in *Berrima* would have landed at Rabaul and peacefully occupied the seat of government; we knew there were neither troops nor guns in the place. 'Anyhow,' said Glossop, 'I'm sending you 30 men under a couple of officers and a doctor from the Australian Naval Brigade.[13] And you must land them here, where the road commences, at daylight, simultaneously as I land the main force here.' Glossop showed me a picture which showed two roads not more than a few miles apart and a connecting path fairly near the coast, hardly a road. For the rest, bar a few hundred yards of open cocoa nut groves beside the beach, the island was covered with impenetrable jungle.

For some reason, I felt this plan to 'take over' did not have quite the right ring about it, but Glossop's information came from headquarters which had come by it in Sydney from well-connected people who had had commercial dealings with the German islands. So all I could say was: 'But suppose the local Germans

12 Admiral Maximilian Reichsgraf von Spee (1861–1914) was a naval officer of the Kaiserliche Marine. He commanded the German East Asia Squadron. On the outbreak of the First World War in July 1914 he led his squadron across the Pacific to the coast of South America. Here on 1 November, he defeated the British 4th Cruiser Squadron under Rear Admiral Sir Christopher Cradock in the Battle of Coronel. A month later von Spee attacked the British naval base in the Falkland Islands. In the ensuing battle Vice Admiral Doveton Sturdee's squadron destroyed the East Asia Squadron. Spee and his two sons, who were serving in two of his ships, were killed, along with 2,200 other men.

13 Volunteers had joined up especially for this operation.

don't want to hand over the wireless station? Supposing they show fight? Thirty men don't seem much of a crowd to operate in a country as big as Belgium.' Glossop's answer was that his landing party would be co-operating, and that the combined force must surely be able to deal with anything that might occur once the junction had been made. I definitely did not like this plan, and said so. I added that I would send any available men I could spare from my two destroyers (the third was acting as a sort of despatch boat with the flagship). I added: 'And I shall land and take charge of your landing party when and where this junction takes place. I shall be in supreme command.'

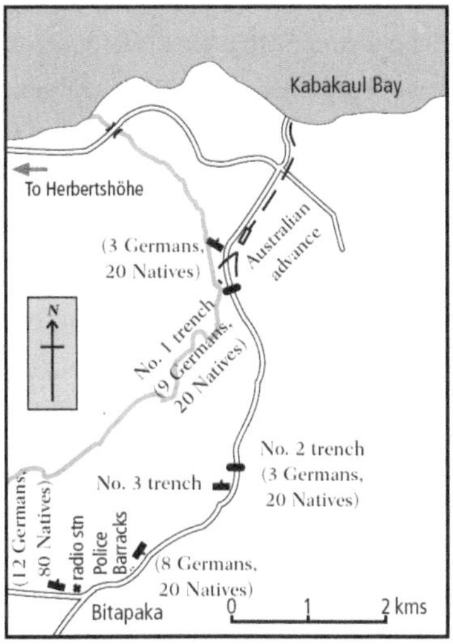

The landing site at Kabakaul, New Guinea (AWM)

'No, Cumberlege, I'm awfully sorry, but I have to give you definite orders from the Admiral that in no circumstances are you to land a soul from the destroyers. We haven't the remotest idea where the German fleet is, and it may be round the next corner. At any moment your boats may be required. All you are required to do is to land the men and await further orders, keeping steam for full speed.' Thirty men dressed in sailors' clothes were then put on board my ship in charge of a youngish officer dressed as a Lieutenant, a Sub-Lieutenant and a young male doctor. I anticipated daylight by an hour and found the place where I had been told there was a pier; and at the crack of dawn my 30 men landed.

In these latitudes daylight rushes up as though a light switch has been turned on. I had anchored within half a cable[14] of a little stone jetty. I spotted a shed or two and a handsome ketch, anchored close inshore. Palm trees fringed the beach. A sea of forest beyond. 'God is in his heaven and occupied with it,' I thought, on this exquisite still morning. An entrancing scene – the absolute calm of it all. We watched, drinking our morning tea, as the men went ashore. I saw the officer talking to some natives. They remained in sight for what seemed like a long time beneath the palms. I disobeyed orders from the word Go by landing half a dozen of my men under a level-headed gunner called Mr. Yeo, with orders to keep in touch with the 30-man force. I reasoned that if the wireless station was 4 miles away, my connecting links would be spread at one every half-mile or so, and it would not take long to reassemble them. After a time, the force disappeared in open order through the palm trees. The officers-in-charge, with whom I had discussed possibilities during the night, very sensibly preferred to go through the forest rather than march amiably up the middle of the road.

14 A cable could vary from about 170 to about 220 yards/metres, so half a cable would have been approx. 85–100 yards/metres.

I landed; yes, I landed.[15] The attraction of that lovely scene was too much for my artistic fancies. My admirable young engineer McNeil came with me and my gunner Mr. Bacon and the 'Admiral', by which sobriquet our Reef Pilot, Mr. Powles, was now known.

Our first call had been at the motor ketch. The Admiral reported that all was well with the engine, but there was no fuel. Then we landed. There might easily be petrol in one of the sheds. The road ran straight from the pier between a few houses and a big copra store or barn. We entered one of the dwellings. Empty. Not a soul anywhere. A little empty cash box was upended and lying on a table. Soapy water in a tin basin, splashings on the floor. 'H'm, evacuated hurriedly. *Why*?' I wondered.

We came to the copra store with a big black door, padlocked. On the door, outlined in white chalk and life size, was my portrait. I say *my* portrait because the side-view face was decorated with a small, upturned moustache and a little imperial[16] under the lower lip. On the head was a peaked cap with wriggly lines representing the oak leaves of a Commander's headgear. Now, all my officers had decided to grow beards at the outbreak of war. I had met them half way, to the extent of cultivating a small moustache and a tuft of hair under my lower lip. The rest of my mug was clean shaven. Above, across the door, was a legend in Roman characters which read, more or less: 'Stop Along Nother Side This Door.' Evidently, 'Don't Go Through This Door.' Rather an invitation, we thought, and set about breaking open the padlock. This was soon done. The store was empty, except, oh joy, for a few tins of petrol. These the Admiral took on board the ketch.

I stepped outside to have another look at my portrait, pondering. 'Stop Along Nother Side This Door'. Suddenly, the meaning flashed across me. 'Don't go any further than here' – might not that be the meaning? Who had put it there? Very odd, and to this day I do not know. We marched a bit further up the road and came to a pretty garden with a smart bungalow and a tennis court. I was dressed in flannel trousers and a vest, and carried a spear. Mr. Bacon had on flannels and a green Homburg hat, and carried a large pistol. I pondered further. Topping a slight rise, the bungalow came into full view. I saw a white man in khaki step hurriedly from the verandah of the house followed by a Great Dane hound. There was no cover. 'Bear away to the left,' I

The road to Bita Paka wireless station (PD)

15 From the book *Australians in Action* by L.C. Reeves: 'The *Warrego* was the first to hear the news [of the fighting on land], and great praise is due to all the men of the destroyer for the promptitude with which they landed to assist the force on land.'

16 Beard named after that of the French Emperor Napoleon III.

Left: German and native troops New Guinea (AWM). Right: Captain Brian Pockley, AAMC (AWM)

said to Mr. Bacon, 'and put that pistol out of sight.' Casually, as if we had seen nothing, we strolled diagonally away from the house to lull any suspicions this gentleman may have had that we were thirsting for blood and hoping that he would be much nonplussed. A few seconds later, we arrived out of the line-of-fire sight from the part of the house into which the khaki-clothed gent had retreated. I said: 'Stand by, Mr. Bacon, to rush in when I give the word.' A white cockatoo was perched on the side verandah. 'Pretty Polly. Pretty Polly' I called out, matey-like, and altered course towards the bird.

At that moment I saw a dozen or so natives fade into the forest about 80 yards beyond the house. 'Now,' I shouted, and we rushed full speed at the house, entered, went quickly from room to room and found it empty. Khaki man must have mizzled along with the natives but I hadn't seen him. Suddenly, I heard the clatter of horses' hooves on the road some 50 yards away. I saw one of my own men galloping along on a tiny pony and shouting to attract my attention. Simultaneously, I heard the ragged rattle of rifle fire. My man excitedly gave me the information that our force was completely held up. It had located the enemy's position which consisted of a trench dug right across the road. For the moment, the force was all right, with most of the men hiding in the dense jungle on the left-hand side of the road. But they were heavily outnumbered and must have reinforcements.

In five minutes I was back on *Warrego* and signalled my other boat, 'Land every available man.' In each ship I had seven rifles, twenty-two .45 pistols and half a dozen cutlasses. Counting officers, I could land 60 men immediately. The men went ashore in the rig they were in. Stokers climbed up from below in boiler suits, carrying a rifle, a bag of ammunition or a bag with a pistol, and a water bottle. They tumbled into the boats and were ferried ashore. First come, first served; when the rifles ran out, they left with slogging hammers.[17] The *Yarra*'s cook was seen striding up the middle of the road with his white cap on his head, his apron rolled up round his waist and a pistol in one hand and a cutlass in the other.

My orders to them were to go inland through the bush and get in touch with our original force and waste as much ammunition as they pleased. 'Never mind if you can't see anyone. Just go plugging away,'

17 With only one person needed to use it, a slogging hammer is said to be more efficient than a conventional hammer, having more direct impact, particularly in tight spots.

I told them. 'There's tons more ammunition.' I wanted to establish a funk. I also wirelessed the flagship, explained the situation and recommended that a heavy force be sent over from the *Berrima* troopship. They were 20 miles away 'peacefully occupying' the seat of government. Then I landed again, but very soon was overtaken by questions from the flagship which had to be answered.

Shortly after, the first casualty was brought in – a German with a shot and shattered hand.[18] I had him stuffed with morphia, and wirelessed for a doctor. Meanwhile, the officer-in-command had been knocked base over apex by a shot that – only just – did not go through his head. A seaman, Williams,[19] was hit and, falling into the road, was attended to by the doctor, a young Australian named Pockley, but while doing so he was mortally wounded with a shot through the stomach.[20] By a great stroke of fortune our lads had collared the German Officer-in-Command and his First Mate: von Kempf and von Mayer. These two had hurried across from the village where they lived some 2 or 3 miles away and, thanks to the fact that we had landed our men so early, practically walked into our hands.

All this took time, but eventually *Berrima* and *Australia* arrived off the anchorage and landed about 70 men. I hurried over to *Australia* and personally gave Admiral Patey all the information about the fighting. I explained that everything was going very well, but he did not seem to think that whatever had happened was strictly in accordance with the original idea of 'taking over' the wireless station. I got ashore again in time to oversee the landing of the reinforcements in charge of a Lieutenant Commander Elwell[21] and a Commander

Left: Lt Cdr C.H. Elwell, RAN (AWM). Right: Where Lt Cdr Elwell and PO Williams were buried initially (PD)

18 Sergeant Major Mauderer.

19 Able Seaman W.G.V. 'Billy' Williams (1885–1914).

20 Captain Brian Pockley (1890–1914) was shot on Bita Paka Road near Kabakaul, 11th September 1914, He died of his wounds in HMAS *Berrima*. He was one of the first two Australians to be killed in action in the First World War. After they encountered German soldiers on the Bita Paka Road, Able Seaman Williams was shot in the stomach. Pockley gave his red cross armband to another serviceman, Stoker Kember, to carry Williams to the rear; Williams died later in HMAS *Berrima*; Pockley was shot shortly after. He had enlisted in the Australian Military and Naval Expeditionary Force five weeks earlier. He was buried in the Rabal (Bita Pika) War Cemetery. His plaque reads: 'Heaven's morning breaks and earth's vain shadows flee'.

21 Charles Elwell (1882–1914), emigrated to Australia from England with his family at the age of eight. From school he joined the Royal Navy, and in 1913 was lent to the Royal Australian Navy. He became gunnery instructor at the Royal Australian Naval College at Geelong in early 1914 and joined the Australian Naval and Military Expeditionary Force at the outbreak of the war. Lt Commander Elwell led No. 6 Company Royal Australian Naval Reserves which disembarked from HMAS *Berrima* at Rabaul, and led a bayonet charge against German forces. Just ahead of his men, he was mortally wounded. An article in the *Sydney Morning Herald* described Elwell as 'intensely popular' with both cadets and officers, charming, quiet and 'full of energy'.

Beresford.[22] I remember saying to Elwell as he landed: 'My word, you *do* look well. Cut along through the trees and you'll find the trouble soon enough. There's no mistaking the way.' Poor Elwell and a few of his men nearly got round the flank of a trench, but there the bush had been cut away and he must have exposed himself, as a bullet got him right through the heart.

That was the end of it. Up went the white flag in the trench; the whole position was ours and its occupants were taken prisoner. That evening, a detachment took over the wireless station which it found not 4 miles inland but 8. We gathered all the prisoners and, keeping the most important ones in *Warrego*, I shipped all the rest under guard to Rabaul, where *Australia* and *Berrima* had returned for safe-keeping. I had Elwell and Williams [the sailor] buried, their graves fenced with railings pulled off a verandah and their initials carved in two overhanging palm trees. Pockley and a wounded sailor [Harry Street] were sent off to hospital, but both, unfortunately, died. I knew they could not live; I had wrapped a towel around one of them to keep his insides from falling out. How a tiny .303 bullet could make such a wound utterly defeats me.

That evening I was sitting in my cabin. Von Kempf was in my easy chair sipping a whisky and soda. Von Mayer was doing the same in my other chair. I was on the bunk – nowhere else to sit. We talked over the day's work quietly. I said that I thought it a lousy trick shooting at my doctor. 'Good Lord,' they said. 'But had he anything to show he was a doctor – any Red Cross armband?' I had to admit that he had not. 'But why not? All our troops, white and black, have green cotton armlets round their arms.' I had noticed this. 'Our orders to the natives were to avoid shooting at anybody with an armlet on,' said von Kempf. 'I give you my word that we gave those orders because it would not be understood by the natives what any particular armlet meant and, of course, to avoid potting anybody on our side in the dense forest.' Pockley had given first aid to the first German hit, amputating the man's shattered hand there and then without any anaesthetic. A stoker was told off to carry the man back to the pier. 'Here,' said Pockley, 'take this. You will have to go into the road,' and pulled off his brassard [armband]. 'I don't want that,' said the stoker. 'I'll get him down [the road] all right.' 'I order you to take it,' said Pockley.[23]

Later that night, taking a man with me, I went up the road to see how the troops had fared. It was a bit eerie in the pitch darkness and utter silence of the virgin forest. Even my man, whom I felt was on edge and to whom I was chatting brightly, suddenly came to the charge. 'What's that light? There's a light!' 'Hold on, old boy. Have another look,' I said. There was an undoubted light, not 2 yards from the muzzle of his rifle. It was the intermittent glow of a friendly firefly. Not difficult to understand. That day, for the first time in his life, my companion had seen dead men. And dead men are damned ugly. He would have fought like a tiger to avoid their fate. Nerves. Eventually, I found the force bivouacked on the scene, but a bit short of water. So I sent up a party with beakers of water; it reported a most violent battle with purely imaginary foes on the way back!

Next day, we re-embarked the troops and slipped over to Rabaul and the fleet. It turned out that *Sydney*'s landing party, after walking all day and seeing nothing, had very properly returned to its ship. So much for the Intelligence Service. Meantime, the occupation of Rabaul, the capital of German New Guinea, had taken place. The only other battle round these parts was quelled by half a dozen rounds from *Encounter*'s 6-inch

22 Commander Joseph Beresford RAN (1861–1952).

23 According to Admiral Patey the fighting lasted 18 hours and was spread over about 6 miles. Being so early in the war and on the other side of the world, it led to an unseemly bureaucratic struggle in London which lasted throughout 1915 over who should be decorated and what should be published about the action. Eventually, in the *London Gazette* dated 11 January 1916, Cumberlege was one of 12 men Mentioned in Dispatches. One man, Lt T.A. Bond RANR, who had been a leading figure in the battle around the wireless station, received a DSO. No posthumous awards were given. The Australians lost 5 men killed, the Germans 20–30.

guns, which plastered a ridge where a fire had broken out amongst some bamboo trees. Burning bamboo sounds quite like machine-gun fire.

We then spent nights patrolling. By day, I nosed and poked about the neighbouring reef harbours. That was grand fun. We found a small steamer on the edge of one barrier reef, her decks awash and partly burnt. She hadn't much in her except for reels of barbed wire. Outside, though, in the clear depths we sighted what looked like a machine gun. We managed to get hold of it by diving, and sure enough it was an old-fashioned Hotchkiss revolving cannon[24] with four or five barrels. Later, we found out that the steamer had been bringing Germans to reinforce Rabaul and had piled up on the reef. Before quitting her they had thrown the gun overboard and set fire to the ship. Mainly, though, I was intent on locating a big German government yacht about which there were all sorts of rumours. I never did find her, but it seems she was never far away – just round the next corner, hidden in a creek. After we had left she was found, taken to Sydney and turned into a gunboat.

One night when out patrolling, I got a quick summons from the flagship. On board, Admiral Patey told me that two German man-of-war ships were reported to be in a harbour in New Ireland island, 40 miles away. He had told off *Melbourne* to investigate and take one of the destroyers. I chose my own craft because I was already under way, and anyhow, I thought, the excursion would be more amusing than patrolling. Away we went. Next morning, *Melbourne* went round the island to block another possible getaway while we picked our way through the barrier reef into a vast lagoon studded with little islets and bristling with reefs and shallows – a most beautiful spot. The entrance to the lagoon looked as if it had been handmade ages ago, with nature left to beautify it with vivid green tropical trees. We skimmed through this strange water 'street' in the indigo blue of profound depths, the faithful Mr. Powles in the barrel at the masthead. Once we were inside we found the waters of the lagoon an unimaginable, still pastel, hue. From the barrel aloft Mr. Powles cried out to us on the bridge: 'Starboard a bit, midships steady. Ha, ha, missed the bastard. Starboard hard over, midships, port. Go on, give it her, *hard over*, or you'll swing your stern into the bastard! Hee, hee – keep her steady now.' Over the side you could see the coral growths waving pale colours and sliding by.

We approached a hidden harbour formed by two fair-sized islands. There was a very narrow passage between the islands. Here I went dead slow; just round this corner should be the enemy ships, and once in there I could not have reversed owing to the narrowness of the waters. My plan was to poke in until I had a fair view and hope to back out at full speed before I was damaged. The harbour was empty! No, not quite. A very attractive steam yacht and a handsome island schooner were there. We nobbled a native in a dug-out canoe. He spoke pidgin English and told us: 'Two feller fight ship sit down this place one Sunday before.' Which meant: 'There were two fighting ships here a week ago.' To this day I have no idea if this information was good. They might have been the Geier and Riasan,[25] or one of them attended by a collier. I wirelessed Melbourne the news. She replied, telling me to get back to Rabaul and leave the yacht, which I felt was bad luck on us [by forfeiting prize money] having done the dirty work of the excursion. I did take the precaution of sending over an officer to the yacht, and he returned to say that the German skipper was desolated because his vessel had broken down irretrievably and could not move. Naturally, I had to send over my engineer, McNeil, to report on the damage. He reported the curious fact that the boat had steam up

24 The Hotchkiss arms company made several machine guns in the late 19th century. The best-known is the 1.65-inch light mountain gun. There was also a 1.85-inch navy gun, and a 3-inch version.

25 Geier was a cruiser commissioned in 1895 for service in German overseas colonies. In 1914 it attempted to link up with von Spee's East Asia Squadron but failed and was interned in Honolulu, Hawaii in October 1914. *Riasan* was a Russian merchant steamship captured by the Germans off Japan in 1914 and interned in Guam, also having failed to link up with von Spee's fleet.

but the slide valve group was missing. The skipper claimed he had sent it to Rabaul to be repaired before the war began, but had not received it back.

I considered this story a very naughty lie. Now that *Melbourne* had cleared out, it was my duty to deal with the case without wasting time by informing higher authority of my intentions. I gave orders for the skipper and crew to quit the boat instantly, and directed McNeil to retain her engineers (who were Chinese) and apply whatever persuasive power he considered suitable with a view to the rapid recovery of the slide valve group. Then I prepared to take the ship in tow. Within in a few minutes McNeil – one of those delightful people who do things without wasting time on back chat – had 'persuaded' the Chinese to cooperate. In another ten minutes the white ensign had been substituted for the German Imperial ensign. Once more we picked our way through the heads of coral, with the white yacht keeping accurate station behind us. It was filled with all sorts of delicacies and had evidently been prepared as a getaway for the local authorities. The delicatessen was highly appreciated by all hands, as we were tired to death of bully beef.

About this time the flagship decided to convoy some of the soldiers to New Guinea, and the Admiral left me to look after the shipping and port of Rabaul during his absence. I requested, urgently, that he allow me to accompany him, but he did not consider it necessary. Had I gone, it is not at all likely that any of us in *Warrego* would have returned. Not more than 5 miles from Madang,[26] off which port *Australia* lay while disembarking the troops, was a hidden anchorage in which, at that moment, the ex-Russian fleet steamer *Riasan*, fitted as an armed merchant cruiser, was lying! It is inconceivable that I would not have located her, as it was my invariable custom to nose into every nook and corner within reasonable distance. *Australia* was, however, utterly oblivious to the proximity of this vessel, but one can imagine the feelings of the gallant officers and men of the *Riasan*, lying there watching every movement of their powerful enemy and expecting every moment to be their last. That night, after *Australia* had left, *Riasan* slipped away under cover of darkness and very sensibly interned herself in Guam.

Left as sea guardian of Rabaul, we amused ourselves by organising a patrol flotilla out of the nondescript collection of prizes we had taken. Through the goodwill of the Torpedo Lieutenant of the flagship, I had borrowed his 14-inch torpedoes and dropping gear, and attached the outfit to one of our prizes. I had also borrowed a 12-pounder field gun from one of the ships, and this was mounted in *Nusa*, the yacht I had taken, together with a maxim gun and a wireless. The other craft were kitted out in similar fashion, manned by the irrepressible men of the shore-based Naval Brigade. These craft relieved my flotilla of a certain amount of patrolling and left us free to search out and expose the crops of rumours and vague reports continually coming in. We still had no notion where the German fleet was.

One day one of our two submarines[27] was missing. Customarily, the submarines used to go out in turns. I do not know what conclusions the inquiry into the loss came to, but it is probable that she over-dived herself and could not recover. Shipwreck can be ruled out, as the weather was absolutely perfect and the sea was as flat as a board. But it is possible she hit a rock while submerged or ran into a coral wall while under water. My flotilla combed the sea for days in the hope of finding her broken down and drifting with the strong currents known in these parts. I had searches made of lee beaches and reefs where some evidence might be expected such as floatable objects. I also went to a group of islands nearby, which we knew the

26 A town on the north coast of New Guinea first settled by the Germans in the 19th century.

27 HMAS *AE-1* was an E-class submarine of the Royal Australian Navy and the first to serve in the RAN. It was lost at sea with all hands (35) near East New Britain on 14 September 1914, after less than seven months in service. The submarine was found in 2017, during a 13th search mission for it near the Duke of York Islands.

submarine must have passed, and anchored our three boats in a natural harbour half a cable from the shore. Then I ordered a search of the fringing reef, which was flat and covered with coconut palms, while I went off to search the reef-strewn waters in my German yacht.

Warren,[28] Captain of the *Paramatta*, was searching the beach here when he happened to turn his view landward and to his astonishment saw a big yellow funnel plainly showing through the ranks of palm trees on the other side of the island. Without a moment's hesitation he made his way back to his ship, wirelessed me the news and immediately manned and armed the [whaler] boats, hiding rifles in the bottom of the boats and hoping to make it seem as if they were merely landing for a bathing party. Getting round a point which formed a tree-fringed bay, he judged that he must be near the hidden ship. Without any more camouflage, he gave the order and the boats raced to the presumed spot. There she was, a German Lloyd[29] steamer, completely hidden by foliage with palm trees lashed to her mastheads. In an instant the ship was in his hands. Hurrying there in *Nusa*, I boarded. The German skipper, a pleasant fellow, seemed almost relieved at being caught. 'Three times have I ventured out in the hopes of getting away and each time I have seen one of your infernal destroyers and have had to return here and replace my decorations,' he said. That his screen of foliage and trees was admirably designed may be judged by the fact that no sign of her was evident from our anchorage close by. In an hour or so she was steaming out in company with the flotilla to be added to the collection in Rabaul harbour. I wished that she had been the submarine.

Commander William Warren (AWM)

Admiral Patey now decided that all German territory having been occupied, a government of sorts should be set up. It was clear to him that the German Pacific Fleet was not in these waters. He decided to shift his base from the western to the central Pacific, and he and two cruisers set off for the Fiji Islands, leaving me to convey the collection of store ships, colliers and so on over 1,800 miles of Pacific Ocean or so in that part of the world. What a voyage! I have so often heard people say: 'Oh, to go to the South Pacific, how marvellous!' There we were, doing what millionaires sometimes do and paying £30–40,000 for their amusement, while we were actually being paid, perhaps a little meagrely. The weather was mostly good, if hot. Our speed was that of the slowest ships – 7½ knots. And at the end, we were twice 1,800 miles from our nearest home port.

The Pacific is a size or two larger than the North Sea.[30] After a lot of sheep-dog work with this decrepit fleet of hangers-on, eventually we got within a day's steaming of Fiji. I left them there and barged on at speed. We were wanted by the flagship. That night, we caught it fair and square. Did it blow?! The wind was followed by impenetrable cyclonic rain, worse than fog. The first I knew that we were near our port was when I found myself in the backwash of the Pacific rollers beating on a barrier reef, which made me put my helm hard over. The reef could not have been more than a couple of hundred yards away, and *Warrego* was

28 Commander William Warren of the destroyer flotilla (1877–1918) had joined the RAN in 1908 from P&O. He became commander of a RAN destroyer flotilla of his own on 1 April, 1917. He died in a drowning accident in Brindisi, Italy, on 13 April 1918.

29 Norddeutscher Lloyd (NDL) was formed in 1857, offering passenger and cargo transport between Bremen and New York. In 1914, 32 of its vessels were interned in US ports. Those NDL ships surviving the war were confiscated as reparation, leaving the company to start over from scratch. Today it is part of Hapag-Lloyd.

30 60 million square miles, as opposed to the North Sea's 200,000 square miles.

travelling at 18 knots. Still, we did discover an entrance to Suva harbour, where *Australia* was lying. I found a lovely nook up at the head of the harbour, entirely landlocked and out of sight, where I moored my three boats. Marvellous pellucid fresh water ran into the sea between overhanging tropical vegetation.

One destroyer had to be outside the harbour patrolling, as we still had no notion where the German fleet was. At last, one day, we got some definite news – a German cruiser belonging to this fleet had appeared off French islands a couple of thousand miles east of Fiji and sunk a ship at anchor. Admiral Patey realised that von Spee was heading east, either to intern his fleet in Spanish-American ports or to make a magnificent try to get home to Germany. He decided at once to follow. His slow-moving colliers would follow. I begged him to take my flotilla with him. He said the idea was ridiculous. How could we possibly steam all that way? I replied: 'I'll get there if I have to sail the damn things,' but it was no good, and I have no doubt that he was correct. So we were sent back on the long journey to Sydney.[31] At this point we had been at sea for over four months, and our one casualty was a bent propeller in *Yarra*, which had hit an uncharted rock. The damage was repaired quickly with the help of divers.

En route, we stopped off at New Caledonia for a night and gave the crews a run ashore. A friendly French officer told me that he had seen a bluejacket full of absinthe fast asleep on a bench in the park. Knowing that I had given orders for all hands to be back on board by 6:00 pm, he had approached the man with the idea of giving him a shake and telling him it was almost 6:00 pm. At that moment, a huge cheap American clock clasped to the sailor's bosom sounded off. The alarm had been set for 6:00 pm. I happened to be walking on my small quarter deck at about that time when a young sailor from the submarine staggered onto my ship on his way to his own. As he was full of wine, his language was awful. Our leading stoker, Oxo, remonstrated gently with him. He replied with another volley of abuse. The stoker's right fist caught him under the chin, lifting him clean off the deck. He stayed there, flat out, for another 20 minutes. That's what I call '*esprit de vaisseau*' [vessel]!

And so at length we got back to our home port, sound in wind and limb. A few friends killed,[32] a submarine lost and a country as big as Europe added to our possessions[33] – to say nothing of a feeling of thanks to Almighty God for a rewarding time and the unbelievable sensation of loyalty. Yes, I admit it – I think the affection given freely to their boss by all hands *and* the cook in *Warrego* speaks for itself.

31 2,000 miles.

32 Six Australians and one German died during the capture of German New Guinea in 1914.

33 Australian historians assess this episode more meaningfully. It was the country's first overseas military expedition, the first joint operation by the Australian Army and Navy, and the first amphibious landing by Australian wartime forces. It involved the first recorded acts of bravery by Australian servicemen and the first Australian deaths of the First World War. Effectively, it marked the end of German colonisation in the Pacific region and led to *de facto* Australian control of New Guinea for 60 years until Papua New Guinea's independence in 1975.

CHAPTER 10

Up the Sepik River

At the end of 1914 Cumberlege led an extraordinary mission in HMAS Warrego *with two other destroyers to search for hidden German naval vessels in the remote wilds of New Guinea.*

We went into dock on arrival at Sydney – that was the first thing. My word, what a sight for sore eyes the little ships were. They had stood up to the racket marvellously. We had never let steam down for nearly six months, hardly ever remained at anchor for more than 48 hours, and spent the whole time in enemy waters and in the Tropics within a few degrees of the line. We did touch the flagship whenever possible for fresh meat and rooted vegetables, and if ever a stray cow hove in sight it finished up on our dinner tables. No cinemas, no beer, no leave of any sort and none of the softening influences of feminine society. Yet no one went sick, sorry, sore or sad. The statement about beer is not strictly accurate. On one of our nosey-parker expeditions we found a German naval store full of casks of bottled pilsener. Such a find was impossible to keep secret. The flagship got wind of our Aladdin's cave, and had the brass neck to commandeer what was left and *sell* it to us.

We had not been 48 hours in Sydney when the Intelligence Service came to me with some very curious information. It appeared that it had a German prisoner who was half Danish, and who had told it that he knew of a German plan of interest to us. He would disclose it if he was given his liberty and some cash to live on if his information proved to be correct. I immediately had an interview with the man, together with the Intelligence heads, one of whom was Bertie Keely. As intelligent as he was charming, he was a member of the family of the same name which included a couple of British admirals. We agreed to the German's proposal. His story was as follows:

The Germans had decided, he claimed, on the outbreak of war and the probable occupation of their possessions in the Pacific, to send one of their man-of-war ships inland up one of the great rivers in Papua. At the end of the war, maybe in about six months' time, they would have argued that we had by no means occupied their territory.[1] A reasonable plan, similar to that of the Rufiji river episode in Africa; the main difference was that in Papua naval ships could have been far more easily secreted, and at much greater distance in unsurveyed and most difficult country inhabited by large numbers of hostile natives. Our informer was able to give us the name of the river selected – the Kaiserin Augusta, or in the local language Ngu

---

1 In 1914 the most powerful German ship in the Indian Ocean was the light cruiser *Königsberg*. After an engine failure following its sinking of the British cruiser *Pegasus*, *Königsberg* and its supply ship hid in the delta of the Rufiji river. HMS *Chatham* discovered *Königsberg* in the delta towards end October 1914. *Königsberg* was then blockaded. By March 1915 its food supplies were low, and many crew had died from malaria and other tropical diseases. Eventually the British navy began to shell *Königsberg*, assisted by shore-based spotters. *Königsberg* was reduced to a wreck and scuttled. After that the British were by far the strongest naval power in the Indian Ocean.

Sepik, meaning the Great River. He did not know the identity of the warship selected, but believed it to be one of the Russian Volunteer Fleet which the Germans had captured – fitted with 4-inch guns and arranged to carry about 1,000 men.

Such information could not possibly be disregarded. After consultations with the Navy Board in Melbourne, the job was put in my hands. All refitting work was stopped and within a week of arriving in Sydney, the flotilla was off once more on the long, long trek to Papua, some 1,500 to 1,800 miles away. I had my three torpedo destroyer boats, a couple of small craft to act as minesweepers or mine lookouts, *Nusa*, which I took along to act as a scout in the event that we encountered unsurveyed waters unsuitable for destroyers, and as many soldiers as could be spared from the Rabaul detachment once I had got there; they were to be dumped on board from a couple of ex-German island steamers. In Rabaul my plans were laid before the new military government headed by Colonel Petherbridge, a rare good fellow. My plan was to locate the ship using the destroyers, and then to use the soldiers to guard bases and act as circumstances developed.

While these plans were being arranged in Rabaul, I slipped over to New Guinea and anchoring at Madang, a very beautiful port on the north coast, landed there to get hold of the local commandant, a sportsman by the name of Major Martin.[2] It had not been considered necessary to evacuate the German planters living in the area, so that in my walk through the small collection of bungalows with their gardens of flaming tropical flowers I passed them by. For some reason, this caused a great deal of amusement, especially to a large crowd having a beer party on a verandah a few yards from the road. They were, in fact, quite evidently poking fun at this absurd object in a sweaty vest and a pair of trousers who was carrying a native spear. One very stout dame, the wag of the party, caused roars of guffaws with her pleasantries, but unluckily I could not understand a word she was saying or I would have joined the merriment.

At length I found Martin and over a whisky and soda broached the reason for my appearance in his domain. He saw at once the need for absolute secrecy in the initial conduct of our plan and said: 'The first thing to do is to round up every squarehead[3] within a radius of, say, 25 miles and lock 'em up.' 'My idea exactly,' I replied, with tender thoughts of the beer party down the road. Martin immediately put his organisation into motion by dint of telephone and emissaries. I wended my way back to the port. The beer party, escorted by native police and Australian Non-Comms [NCOs] crossed my path *en route* to the local Calaboose [prison]. I will remember all my life the malevolence in the somewhat bloodshot eyes of the fat dame as she stepped across the road and entered the palm leaf portico of the local gaol.

The 'troopships' arrived. One had lost itself temporarily, there being no aids to navigation, but I discovered her during the night sensibly awaiting daylight some miles up the [north] coast, and put her on her way. Next day, I steamed up the coast to a place where I knew there was a Catholic Mission. Here I found a charming elderly gentleman, the head of the Mission, to whom, after some conversation, I felt I could unburden myself to some extent. He was perfectly straightforward. He said that he was certain that no such armament as I had heard of existed in the vicinity, and went so far as to offer to come upriver with me as a guarantee. 'I have had

2 Brigadier General Edward Martin, CB, CMG, DSO (1875–1950) joined the Australian Naval and Military Expeditionary Force (AN&MEF) in 1914 and sailed for New Guinea. Here he led the capture of Toma. After the German garrison surrendered, he was sent to Madang with infantry and naval reservists. He remained District Administrator until February 1915, when he returned to Australia. In May 1915 Martin joined the 17th Battalion of the Australian Imperial Force. He fought with the battalion in France 1916–18 participating in the capture of the Pozière, being Mentioned in Dispatches five times and winning a DSO. In March 1918 he assumed command of the Australian Imperial Force (AIF) 7th Brigade and then the 5th Brigade. In August 1918 the 5th Brigade took Mont St Quentin, one of the AIF's finest fighting feats. For his part in the 1918 fighting Martin was made a Companion of the Order of the Bath (CB) on 3 June 1919.

3 A contemptuous 19th-century British term used to refer to a German or Dutch person or a Scandinavian, especially a Swede.

no opportunity for months, thanks to you English bagging all the steamers, to visit my farthest outpost some 40 or 50 miles upriver.' This information was rather a shock to my hopeful plans, but I was so convinced of his honesty that I took him at his word, shipping him and his mate, and set off for the river.

We found the entrance without difficulty. Carefully sounding [depth-checking] our way, eventually we arrived at his 'outpost' – a mission station and a German police post. The police had vanished but the local priest was at home, glad to see somebody. At the back of my mind, while I believed the old gentleman, I thought he might be wrong. He told me that the *Riasan* had been in *his* harbour when *Australia* had turned up[4] only 5 miles away – and how the poor skipper of *Riasan* had passed such an anxious day before clearing out after dark and escaping. He did not think *Riasan* had carried out what he said was her original intention of secreting herself away up the river. My chance of immortal glory somewhat faded. Still, I thought it my duty to make absolutely certain, and decided to proceed as far as possible up the river to this end. I returned the divines and collected my other destroyers and *Nusa* and, with my enthusiastic accomplice Major Martin, set off on the most interesting voyage I ever had in my life.

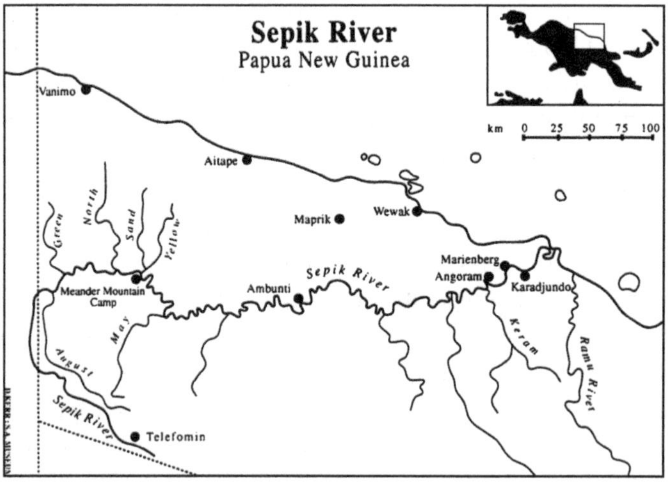

The terrific Sepik River[5] runs directly into the ocean on the north coast of New Guinea. Its source is somewhere up in the mountainous backbone of the island whose peaks are still waiting for the feet of men. There is something of wonderful interest to me in nosing into places where no one [no Westerner, that is] has been before. It is a real thrill. There had been one or two expeditions in these parts – but very, very little of the region was known to anybody but the primitive natives who lived and loved and fought with axes of stone, and bone-pointed arrows. We found the actual entrance to the river flanked with solid, tree-covered ground; within was a vast sago [palm] swamp through which the river meandered. From time to time the swamp gave way to solid ground covered with tropical forest, impenetrable to the eye, with a curtain of flower-spangled creepers. At other times, level savannahs stretched as far as the eye could reach, like some vast park with its clumps of trees like dark islands in a sea of grass.

4 See Chapter 9.

5 The Sepik is the longest river on the island of New Guinea, and the second largest in Oceania by discharge volume. The land around it is mostly swampland, tropical rainforest and mountains. In 1884 Germany asserted control. For most of its length, the Sepik twists and turns north to the Bismarck Sea, flowing directly into the ocean. It is navigable for much of its 700-mile length. Along its course it flows through the territories of dozens of Sepik languages. In the early 20th century, several expeditions collected flora and fauna, studied its tribes and produced the first maps. The town of Angoram dates from 1913.

The Sepik river from HMAS *Warrego* (AWM)

A Sepik river village above Angoram (AWM)

With little *Nusa* ahead sounding the depths, we wound our way obeying the 'law of the ebb tide' – that is, searching for the deepest water by keeping close to the banks whose angles were concave and steep. There was a uniform tide running of 3½–4 knots, which eddied and increased in speed at bends and narrow reaches. At Angoram – the farthest-away post of German authority with its police 'station' – we went alongside the bank and secured to trees in 5 fathoms[6] of water. Here we decided to establish a temporary post of our own people. We found a very sick man [acute malaria] who told us that the police officer and his 'boys' [local men] had left a long time previously. Meantime Martin, while preparing the accommodation for a few men he intended to leave there, sent out his 'boys' [all German-trained] with orders to scout out the neighbourhood in case the sick German's story lacked anything.

The heat was terrific ashore, the river cool, if filled with crocodiles. Nevertheless, we bathed. While we were engaged in this pastime an Australian 'digger' [soldier] arrived and informed us that the native sergeant in charge of the police 'boys' had been fired on a couple of miles away in the bush. Martin, as soon as he heard this, at once organised his small force with a view to investigating the matter. McNeil (my Chief Engineer) and I joined him and, with a dozen splendid young natives armed with rifles and bayonets, we plunged off through the bush. Eventually, we made contact with the sergeant. His name was Kundoo and he was a most delightful little chap. Martin told me that Kundoo was the only man to stick by him when the whole lot of ex-German police 'boys' had cleared out of the station and gone into the bush after Germans had put it about that it was the invariable custom of the English to eat their policemen! For his loyalty, Kundoo had been raised from the ranks before the assembled 'boys' on their return to duty, and the gold chevrons of a full sergeant had been pinned around his muscular, bare arm.

Now, hidden in the high bush, Kundoo reported that he had seen the German police officer with a large number of 'boys', that they had mutually recognised each other and that the Germans had at once opened fire. Kundoo had effaced himself and hurried a man back to report the matter. With our dozen police 'boys' and Kundoo, we started off in pursuit. It was a most interesting hunt. Personally, I could see nothing. But in that virgin forest it was evident that Kundoo and his lads were systematically following some tracks. We came to a river, and our pack of two-legged hounds turned left for about 100 yards. Evidently, this was a false trail, for suddenly they all swung back together and made off up the river instead. Even in the forest, the heat was terrific. Wearing only a vest and pair of pants, I was soon in a muck sweat and finding it hard to keep up with the easy speed of the aboriginals. When the pace got even hotter, I realised that the enemy could not be far away. Every man jack of the 'boys' suddenly threw themselves on their bellies on the ground. I chose a vast hardwood tree

6 Five fathoms is the equivalent of 30 feet.

and took excellent cover amongst its buttresses. After a few minutes, Kundoo raised a wary head and, scenting the air, moved forward followed by his 'boys' in the manner of the serpent. We followed, silently and slow.

We found ourselves climbing a gentle rise in the forest when nearly all the 'boys' simultaneously jumped to their feet and rushed up the hill. Following them, we found ourselves face to face with an absolutely typical Prussian Sergeant Major, standing before a relatively newly-made bush shelter and utterly deserted by his 'boys'. He was very big, and terribly hot and was cursing his former supporters heartedly: 'For 14 years I have trained these swine hounds, and this is the first time I've ever really needed them. This is what happens.' I relieved him of his automatic [weapon]. 'Ach, you must not take it. I paid £3 for it only a month ago,' he said.

Kundoo and his 'boys' were sent into the forest to get in touch with the runaways.[7] Kundoo spoke pidgin English,[8] that curious language used by the members of the many different tribes on the river whose languages are dissimilar. From the emerald depths of the still forest, we heard him calling: 'Come back, you boys, come b-a-c-k. German fellow master he no plurry good, he die finish. Good fellow Englishman sit down this perlace. Come back, you boys, altogether. Come back!!' Very soon, furtive and frightened, they drifted in twos and threes into the clearing round the leaf house. Most of them carried their rifles, some were unarmed. 'Where your gun? Go fetch quick,' was answered by a pointing of the chin into the forest. Soon, all were re-assembled – some 50–60 splendid young fellows in neat red lavalavas[9] and armed with Mauser rifles, belts and bayonets. We didn't bother to disarm them or even take away the bolts of the rifles. 'Pfall in,' snapped Kundoo. 'All together, you boys. Pfall in! By right, dress. Numbah.' *Ein, zwei, drei* and so on rippled up the line – the only German these handsome lads knew. Kundoo, with a stamp of his bare feet, turned to Major Martin and repeated: 'Boys all present and correct,' with a salute that would have done credit to a Royal Marine. And the poor German police officer slowly scratched his shaven poll [head] and murmured '*Mein Gott, mein Gott!*'

Our late enemy declared to us that there was no other force or any sort higher up the river. I felt it prudent to make absolutely certain. We were only 50 miles up the river and it was believed to run for something like 1,000 kilometres, to say nothing of large tributary rivers. It was too late to proceed further that night as by now the Sepik, with its twirls and bends and snags, was unnavigable by night. Adding to the dangers were the large numbers of vast forest trees continuously drifting downstream, any one of which would have stoved a hole in our thin plates or bumped off a propeller blade if any contact was made. Next day, after a quiet night, we proceeded, taking Major Martin and a few of his 'boys' and, of course, Kundoo. With Martin's concurrence, before we left I decorated Kundoo in front of the assembled natives

HMAS *Nusa* moored at Meander Mt. camp (PD)

7 Cumberlege took part in this hunt across 'undulating country covered with grass chin-high, then into cane and forest' according to S.S. Mackenzie in *The Australians at Rabaul.*

8 Tok Pisin or New Guinea Pidgin English or simply Pidgin is a creole language spoken throughout Papua New Guinea. Today it is an official language of the country and the most widely used. Some one million people are thought to use Tok Pisin as their primary language and it is slowly crowding out other languages.

9 A lavalava is an article of daily clothing traditionally worn by Polynesians and other Oceanic peoples. It consists of a single rectangular cloth, like a sarong.

Claude Cumberlege, shirtless on left, surveying the Sepik river from the 300-foot Timburke lookout post, now Ambunti (AWM)

with the crossed anchors and the three gold chevrons of a golden first-class petty officer's badge of rank, which I attached to his bare chest.[10]

Above Angoram, we got into really wild New Guinea. What a wonderful experience! How fine was every outlook! Getting a fairly regular seven fathoms by closely following the ebb tide law, I surmised that it was very possible that this good depth might be accounted for by continuous and heavy rains somewhere up inland. I noticed that the great trees drifting downstream were denuded of foliage, which indicated that they must have lain for some time in the water. I concluded that it would be some time before the river decreased in volume to such an extent to render it unnavigable for our boats, which only needed a fathom and a half of water in which to float.

New Guinea, although one of the largest islands in the world, is quite devoid of wild and savage beasts other than crocodiles, alligators and snakes. Only 'man is vile'. Immediately westward there are all sorts of carnivorous beasts, and in Borneo there are elephants. But in New Guinea the fauna is similar to that in Australia, to which it was doubtless attached long ago. If the lion lay not down with the lamb in this entrancing vale, the osprey and the eagle seemed to regard the billings and cooings of gentler species with no greedy eye. Paradise birds in colours unthought of by van Gogh flirted or feasted on the same branches as the drill toucans with their megaphonic beaks.

Connection by wireless with the outside world was almost entirely severed (thank God) owing to the violent atmospherics, but once at evening we received a fragment which could only have been intended for us. The mutilated message ran: '... and not to proceed into uncharted or dangerous waters pending further instructions.' Although it was cryptic and a bit late, I had to take some notice of it. So I anchored the flotilla and gave instructions to make as wide a search as possible in the creeks and by-waters we had encountered. Then, taking Major Martin, my engineer McNeil, my gunner Mr. Bacon, one or two others and a small posse of soldiers, I trans-shipped to the *Nusa* and continued our voyage into the unknown.

To recount at length the incidents that occurred, or to describe the ever-changing vistas of flood and forest of mountain and plain in that unforgettable journey, would fill a volume.[11] Non-stop incidents

10 Sadly, Cumberlege leaves the method to the reader's imagination.

11 CLC wrote a full report on his return to Australia which is in the archives of the Australian War Museum – 'Report of 'Warrego' Sepik River Expedition December 1914' (AWM 33, Item 64/3). *The Official History of Australia in the War of 1914–18, Volume X: The Australians at Rabaul* by S.S. Mackenzie describes Cumberlege's report as 'vividly phrased and full of picturesque incident'.

Thomas Rodonia, photographer (University of Newcastle, Australia)

Sepik river tribesman at the time of the *Warrego* visit (Macleay River Historical Society)

occurred. Rodoni,[12] our self-appointed photographer, lost himself in the bush at one place where we had stopped to cut down trees to fire the boilers, and was not missed until we had gone on a long way. He got no sympathy from us, and was told by his mates that he had no call to be afraid as no respectable native would think of bothering to put such a meagre wretch on the spit. It was on that firewood stop that we saw the great forest butterflies, including the unbelievable Ulysses moth.[13]

One of the best turns came as we swung round a sharp bend into a hidden stretch of river. On the bank, within half a cable, were a couple of hundred stark naked warriors armed with great bows and 10-foot spears. Apparently utterly unaware of our approach, they were engaged in a war-dance or some sort of fiesta. I have seen pretty good nude dancers at places like the Folies Bergère in Paris, but the *figurantes* [showgirls] have always been of the gentler sex. The beauty chorus before our astonished eyes were of sterner stuff, and every man jack of them had his phallus rigged out in most formidable fashion, like the flying jib-boom of a clipper ship. In an instant they vanished in the bush and no applause or roars of laughter on our part would bring them back again to take a 'curtain'. For the first time in my life, I decided to venture behind the scenes.

Anchoring well away from the bank, I awaited developments, telling the men to remain quiet and do nothing that might cause alarm ashore. I wanted to establish friendly relations. Sitting on the rail, clad only in a native lava, as indeed we all were, and burnt by the sun to a hue comparable to that of any native, I kept my eye on the river bank and smoked my cigarette. Half an hour elapsed. Not a sign of life ashore. Then, out of the high bulrushes fringing the river bank emerged the prow of a big dug-out canoe. I saw a magnificent native standing up with one foot in the boat and the other on its gunwale, and balancing himself with a very long paddle.

I turned my back on him, as if uninterested. He made a stroke with his paddle. I picked up a roll of brilliant red cotton, unrolling a yard or so. Another stroke of the paddle. Unhurriedly, I tore off a strip, rolled it into a tight ball and flung it near the canoe. He fished it out with his paddle, inspected it, made an exclamation and drifted towards the shore. Two hundred men rose up out of the forest and came to the water's edge. Spears and bows and arrows were left in the natural arms-rack of the bushes and they came armed solely with a weapon that they did not need to carry in their hands. As they had sent a single ambassador, I thought the compliment should be returned. So, hauling up the dinghy which was astern, one of my crew jumped into it and ferried me towards the shore. On my way, I scanned the mob and chose one I took for the chieftain, a tall and grizzled man. As the prow of my boat grounded on the bank, I stepped

12 Thomas James Rodoni was born in 1882 at Hotham East, Victoria, to Swiss and Irish parents. In August 1914, while living in Sydney aged 31, he joined the Australian Naval & Military Expeditionary Force and sailed to German New Guinea in HMS *Berrima*. He remained in New Guinea for five months and came to know Cumberlege well. After leaving New Guinea and returning to Australia in 1915, Rodoni worked in a munitions factory. He died in 1956 as a result of a car accident in Waratah, Newcastle, NSW.

13 The Ulysses butterfly (also known as the blue emperor), is a large swallowtail butterfly of Australia, Indonesia, Papua New Guinea and the Solomon Islands. Its size varies but the wing span can be about 10.5 cm (4.1 in).

out with empty hands and a smile and walked straight up to my chieftain. Grasping his hand in my right, I laid the other hand on his bare shoulder with the words: 'Hullo, old cock. How are you feeling today?' Immediately, the silence was broken with smiles and exclamations, all hands came crowding round and insisted on trying this novel form of evidently friendly greeting.

Relations had been established. 'Talks' continued. I had a close-up view of these fine fellows' anatomy and found that the alarming erection that had caused our amusement from the distance was a sort of tube [a penis sheath, phallocrypt] made of finely woven strips of cane which was fitted over their whatsisnames and tied up with a bit of native twine made fast to another piece of twine tied round the waist, whether as a decoration or a lure to the ladies or merely protection I know not. We visited their village, but it was a long time before the women and children bucked up the courage to come out of their hiding places in the forest. The red cotton was distributed and small metal objects presented as gifts, and returned in kind with native weapons and carved 'devil-devils'. Peace reigned in the forest. From then on, whether or not messengers were dispatched to villages higher up the river, or possibly thanks to that obscure system of bush telegraphy employed by native peoples, we never had an unkind word or nasty look from these real children of nature wherever we went.

We left them and proceeded on our voyage. We passed by or stopped at places of extra interest, entered great castles of houses where the young men lived apart – with the houses always built well off the ground, some at great heights as prudence dictated. It is difficult to get a shot with a spear or arrow at occupants of houses erected 50 feet off the ground on hundreds of tree trunks.

The steel axe did not exist, but there were stone ones, beautiful ones of a lovely greenstone, which were used mainly for carpentry and ship-building. We found a shipyard and saw the whole process of construction. A huge forest tree, recently felled, was being trimmed. Next to it was a 70-foot bole [trunk] being slowly hollowed out with burning stones. Beside that, a more advanced and finished article had a figurehead of a carved crocodile. The houses, too, were often of great size. Complete trees formed 'rooftrees', carved at their ends with grotesque figures of men and women, crocodiles or toucans. The sleeping places were formed of long tubes of matting into which the people crawled one after the other. The last to bed put out the light by closing a matting flap. These arrangements were made, of course, to keep out the ubiquitous mosquito. Carved, three-legged stools and wooden pillows, also cut in the shape of lizards or crocodiles, were the only furniture.

Tobacco had been smoked here long before it came to England from America. All sorts of vegetables were carefully cultivated. Sugar cane, taro, tapioca, yams, fish, terrapin, wallaby and birds formed the daily fare. Cannibalism certainly existed, but I have my doubts if human flesh was a popular form of diet. I feel that it may have occurred after the frenzy of the fight and was more in the nature of a religious rite, as we might act a charade. I could not speak their languages, and all I can say is that I believe that the inhabitants of villages but a few miles apart cannot understand each other. We were also far from any knowledge of that strange lingo called pidgin English in China and *bêche-de-mer* (literally, sea slug) in the South Pacific.

Limitless plains gave way to hummocky hills; the river increased its speed. Foothills of mountains developed from the hills. Beyond lay the great Papuan ranges, as virginal as the forest that surrounded us. We turned round a bend and far ahead saw what looked like a motor boat. McNeil threw the contents of the paraffin lamp on the boiler fire, forcing up the steam. Anything might have been round the next bend. Nothing was there. We had made quite certain; nothing, at least, of any sort could have got up the Sepik any further. The great idea had not materialised. The *Riasan* had not been discovered; maybe her heart had failed her when she had seen *Australia* from the priest's harbour a couple of months before and she had quit for neutral territory. We did, though, find a German here who was looking after a depot belonging to a German scientist[14] and a few police 'boys'. Dr. Thurnwald was somewhere in the neighbourhood but very stupidly pretended that he was not aware of our arrival.

Having completed my job, all that was left to do was to return to my ships. Somebody said it was Christmas Day, so we gave Kundoo a gun and two cartridges. He returned 100 per cent hits with a fruit pigeon and a huge goura pigeon as large as a turkey.[15] There were six or seven of us in the state cabin in *Nusa*, and the next day there were still drumsticks and carcass meat left over from our feast. Major Martin elected to stay upriver for a bit, so I left an Able Seaman with him for company and a bottle of whisky, and arranged to send up one of the small steamers to meet him. He was hoping to get hold of Dr. Thurnwald but never did. Later, this 'doctor man' made a terrific song-and-dance about the way he had been treated, and put in a claim with the Australian government for thousands of pounds' damage. A war had been on, however, and in the ordinary course of events he would have been shot for all sorts of things if he had been caught.[16]

We got back down the river safely and, having accounted for all possible enemy activities, I was able to return to Sydney for our interrupted refit.[17] Our voyage south was not without incident. We hit a terrific cyclone in a part of the world where it was impossible to avoid it. I did not expect to see the storm through, but somehow there was no more damage than the loss of our whalers and a lot of deck fittings. Arriving in Sydney in the middle of January 1915 we went for a refit, and this kept us there for some weeks.[18] Meantime, all the RN officers who, like myself, had been lent for service in the RAN, applied to be sent home, as it was evident by now that there was no further use for our services in Australia. But the Navy Board replied to the effect that no applications of this sort could be entertained. All we could do, therefore, was to make long cruises up to Brisbane and Townsville which, though full of interest, lacked warlike excitements. How we would have welcomed some raider to be reported! The *Emden*[19] had been dealt with by John Glossop and *Sydney* on the other side of Australia. The only part of the world that might have produced some action at this time was the Dutch East Indies, where several fine German ships were interned, and many might, without much difficulty, have been organised as commerce destroyers.

14 Dr Richard Thurnwald (1869–1954) was an Austrian anthropologist and sociologist, known for his comparative studies of social institutions. In 1912–15 he was the first European to enter the highlands of central New Guinea along with Walter Behrmann who was also a member of the Kaiserin-Augusta-Fluss Expedition of 1912–13.

15 The goura or crowned pigeon includes four large species of pigeon that are endemic to the island of New Guinea and a few surrounding islands. It was introduced by the English naturalist James Francis Stephens in 1819. The lifespan can be over 20 years.

16 CLC seized three motor launches and one engine from Thurnwald's camp at Meander Mountain as well as rifles, stores and ammunition. The anthropologist claimed that CLC had 'vandalised' his camp, but CLC argued that this had been done by Thurnwald's 'boys' later.

17 According to S.S. Mackenzie in *The Australians at Rabaul*, the Sepik River Expedition led by Cumberlege penetrated 450 miles up the river.

18 During this refit Cumberlege submitted a tracing map of the Sepik river to the RN Hydrographer. 'The work has been rendered in a very satisfactory manner and reflects great credit on all concerned in its production. It is based on a German plan but contains many important additional details including soundings.' It was suggested by the hydrographer that 'their Lordships' appreciation' could be conveyed to Cumberlege.

19 SMS *Emden* was a light cruiser completed in 1909 armed with ten 10.5 cm (4.1-in) guns and two torpedo tubes. Early in the war *Emden* captured a Russian steamer, joined the German East Asia Squadron and was given an independent raiding role in the Indian Ocean. It then spent nearly two months operating in the region, capturing nearly two dozen ships. Eventually, *Emden* raided the Cocos Islands and landed sailors there to destroy British facilities. Shortly after, it was attacked by the Australian cruiser *Sydney* on 9 November 1914. The more powerful Australian ship forced *Emden*'s captain to run his ship aground to avoid sinking. From a crew of 376, 133 were killed in the battle.

I decided that something must be done. Vague reports had come in that a certain amount of activity among the interned vessels had been noticed by consular and other agents - a ship here seen to be scraping her bottom; a ship there seen taking on coal from one of the others and so on. I worked on the feelings of the RN officers and enlisted the invaluable aid of the Governor-general, then Munro Ferguson,[20] a magnificent character, and got permission to go to the Torres Straits, where at least I would be in a position to watch the approaches to the Australian east coast and feel that we were doing something for our money. Away we went.

Munro Ferguson, Governor-General of Australia 1914–20 (PD)

At Thursday Island I met someone who knew the Dutch Archipelago [Indonesia] well, having had business interests there. He volunteered to make a tour of the islands and report to me his observations on enemy activity. We made a private code which he could use at Dutch wireless stations, the messages being arranged to appear that he was simply sending information about such things as coconut plantations, commodity prices and so on, and all couched in perfectly plain business language. The difficulty was to get him to the archipelago. Luckily, an old French gunboat wandered into TI, homeward bound from Tahiti, and the skipper agreed to give my man a passage and land him at the nearest island. My last words to this admirable pirate were: 'Whatever you do, find me a raider!' Away he went, and within a few days I had my raider, all cut and dried. His exact wording escapes me now, but it was to the effect, when de-coded, 'suspicious movements had been observed' etc. Quite sufficient for me.

I left TI with my huge fleet, heading west, and wired *Melbourne* to say that I was proceeding to investigate reports received. Then I cut off all wireless contact, on the grounds that if it was used my position might be located by enemy wireless. We nosed here and we nosed there in that great expanse of the Arafura Sea.[21] I cannot image a more desolate ocean. After ten days, I decided to pop into Timor and try to obtain some fresh grub and a cool drink.

My 'fleet' consisted of the three destroyers *Warrego*, *Paramatta* and *Yarra*, the ex-German imperial yacht *Una* fitted with two or three 4.7-inch guns, and the oil tanker *Esturia* fitted with a 12-pounder. I had recommended to the skipper of *Esturia* that he mount this gun aft so that if he was chased he could have a bang with it over the stern. 'Chased, what d'ye mean?' he said. 'If there's any chasing to be done I shall do it myself.' 'Oh, all right,' I answered. 'Have it your own way and nail it to the forecastle head.' *Esturia*'s Mate had the Chinese crew trained to a hair in no time, but after seeing the rough-and-ready job made of holding the cannon down, I begged the skipper not to fire off the thing except as a last resort.

Our armada now approached the beautiful harbour at Dili in Timor, where I had every intention of dallying for a few days to 'refresh' my ships' companies, as I felt that in this out-of-the-way place the local officials might be sufficiently 'got at' to look the other way and not insist on us returning to sea in the usual time limit of 24 hours. We anchored and hauled our sterns, and secured them to a row of great silk cotton trees.

20 Munro Ferguson, 1st Viscount Novar, KT, GCMG, PC (1860–1934) served as the sixth Governor-General of Australia, from 1914 to 1920. Initially he had pursued a military career before being elected to the House of Commons for the Liberal Party in 1884. He lost his seat in 1885 but was re-elected in 1886. In Australia he was influential, forming a close bond with Prime Minister Billy Hughes, and was also committed to his role as nominal C-in-C during the First World War. He became Viscount Novar in 1920, and from 1922 to 1924 served as Secretary of State for Scotland under Bonar Law and Stanley Baldwin.

21 800 miles long and 350 miles wide.

I sent for Jackson,[22] my next senior officer, a very short man, and told him that I would require him to accompany me as Chief of Staff on a visit to the Governor of the islands; I felt an impression ought to be made. Jackie said: 'Of course, but all chiefs of staff invariably wear aiguillettes. I must have aiguillettes.' So we un-wove a couple of sword knots and pinned as fine a pair of golden aiguillettes on his white tunic as ever anyone saw. The only material difference was that they had a couple of gilt balls or knots in place of the usual pegs. 'Fine,' said Jackie, admiring himself in my mirror. 'Now, I wonder if you have a dud half-crown or something like that? All chiefs of staff are invariably decorated … !' I had not, but even better I produced half a dozen old French five-franc pieces which had been lying in a box for years. An artificer soon had a neat hole drilled through each one, a selection was made of the gaudiest neckties available and little Jackie had a row of decorations that would not have disgraced Mark Kerr.[23]

Dressed in our best, we sallied to the Governor's Palace. Arriving before the frowning porticoes, we clambered up the marble staircase. Suddenly, the great doors were flung open and a nice-looking man stepped forward with outstretched hands. 'Welcome,' he said, 'and welcome in the name of Portugal, England's oldest ally.'[24] We had very nearly put our foot in it. The Governor was an ex-Portuguese naval officer, so no time was lost rounding up fresh food, and everything possible was done to make things easy and pleasant for us in the few days we spent in Dili. Being in 'almost Allied' territory and not even in neutral waters, as I had stupidly supposed, there was no sort of enemy activity, but we got a certain amount of useful information. On leaving, I laid my course for the Dutch Archipelago.

Arriving in these waters, we were kept busy holding up traffic of all sorts. Part of the information I had received dealt with the activities of German agents who were coming and going freely not only in the archipelago but to the Manilas [the Philippines] and even China. These activities were immediately knocked on the head, partly because we boarded every ship that hove in sight and partly because it was reported from end to end of the archipelago that a vast fleet of English destroyers was scattered in these waters. We achieved this sleight of hand by deploying a destroyer in one part of the islands and doing the same thing the next morning with the same destroyer 100 miles away under a different name. At the same time, we got on the right side of the authorities by interfering as little as possible with the Dutch mailboats and island steamers. If we delayed a mailboat, we would send a couple of officers aboard and request the skipper to continue his voyage while we searched. A destroyer would follow up and retrieve the search party a couple of hours later. Little time was wasted, and the steamers were able to keep to their schedules.

Of course, we had our moments. I got wind, for example, of a far-away islet, well out of the track of steamers, where wild stag or deer abounded. On landing in a most picturesque harbour full of reefs, I met a native who produced a piece of paper which I understood was his certificate, or 'commission', as headman.

---

22 Commander John Metcalfe Jackson, RN (1884–1918) spent most of his naval career on the Australian Station. In 1914 he was posted to *Warrego* as second-in-command and took part in the German wireless station operation in New Guinea. Later he commanded *Una*, 1914–16, and the depot ship *Penguin*. He contracted malaria sometime in 1916 and returned to the UK in 1917. That year, seemingly recovered, he was given command of an RN minesweeping trawler, HMS *Daisy*. However, malaria returned, and Jackson died in March 1918 aged 35.

23 Admiral Mark Kerr, CB, CVO (1864–1944) was C-in-C Royal Hellenic Navy in the early part of the First World War, and C-in-C British Adriatic Squadron in 1916–17. He was then involved in the creation of the Royal Air Force in 1917–18.

24 Portugal remained neutral for 18 months from the start of the conflict in 1914. But there were many hostile engagements with Germany during this period in Angola and German South West Africa (now Namibia). Tensions also arose because of German U-boat warfare which hit Portuguese trade with the UK. Ultimately, these tensions resulted in confiscation of German ships interned in Portuguese ports, to which Germany reacted by declaring war on Portugal on 9 March 1916. Approximately 12,000 Portuguese troops died during the course of the First World War.

This personage made a speech which might have been double Dutch for all it meant to me. I felt sure it was an invitation to stay as long as it suited me and thanked him profoundly. He set about arranging a shoot for daylight next day. We saw plenty of deer but at the first light of dawn they all faded away from the open where they had been grazing in the dark. However, we bagged a large number of pigeons and purchased, with good English gold, as many chickens as we could get – a welcome change to the endless sweaty bully beef.

After this interlude I decided to pop into Makassar, on Sulawesi, to see if the Governor there would sell us a few head of cattle. Shifting into the *Una* gunboat, we proceeded to Makassar, leaving the other boats 15 miles away. The Governor turned out to be a very pleasant fellow. He asked where we came from. I said Sydney. 'Yes, but I mean where have you come from *now*?' 'Oh,' I said, innocently but smelling a rat, 'We called at Thursday Island in the Torres Straits and popped in to Timor and had a look round one or two places. Didn't stay a moment longer than we were invited to … !' He smiled. 'I see,' he said. 'Well, what can I do for you. Do you want coal?' 'No,' I answered, 'but if you could let me have a few head of cattle I would be much obliged.' He gave me 20 head of fat cattle on payment, and we shipped the lot on board *Una*.

Later, I went for a drive after a really wonderful Reiss Tafel[25] in Makassar, which lasted from 1:00 to 4:00 pm followed by a siesta and an enjoyable fresh water bath. During my drive (with the Governor's Secretary) I wondered how his boss had known about our stay off the deer island. He told me that a native *prau*[26] had arrived from that very island, and the artistic-minded skipper had drawn pictures of our boats with a piece of charcoal on bits of bark! Soon after, I began to run short of oil fuel. I took a chance and planned to send the bloodthirsty skipper of *Esturia* into Balikpapan, where I knew there was fuel oil for the buying. Then I had a look at the ship's atlas and found, to my delight, a patch of red not very far away, in the northern part of British North Borneo. So off we paddled to the big harbour of Sandakan. Here I unearthed a wireless station and transmitted a message to the Admiral commanding at Singapore, apprising him of my arrival in Borneo.

At Sandakan, I met a Japanese cruiser with an elderly man in command, Yotsomoto. He received me in a real old-fashioned Japanese custom, hissing and rubbing his knees. On being asked what he proposed to do to keep the good work (against Germany) going, he replied: 'Anything you'd like to suggest!' So I said: 'Perhaps you'll raise steam as soon as possible and do a bit of holding up traffic, because I want a bit of rest!' He was delighted and off he went. I made great friends with him and, having come by a beautiful 'wawa' monkey, a friendly sort of ape smaller than an outang, I gave it to him. To see these two walking his quarter deck, hand in hand, was a sight for blind eyes. We had something in common – a fondness of music. He taught me some charming Daimyo [nobleman] songs and wanted to learn some English ones. I chose Harry Pélissier's[27] 'Moon, Moon, Serenely Shining'; I used to sing it and he would chip in, always half an inch too high.

We did have one major difficulty, when *Paramatta* got stuck on a reef in the Sulu Archipelago [Philippines] which was American territory, where we had no right to be. We got her off without any damage, but the difficulty then was to find a suitable reef comfortably outside the 3-mile limit. I had to lie fluently to answer all sorts of leading questions from the British Admiralty and 'diplomatic sources', but got away with it, which, no doubt, was what the Admiralty wanted.

25 *Rijsttafel* is an elaborate Indonesian meal adapted by the Dutch and consisting of up to 40 side dishes accompanied by rice.

26 Or *prahu*, is a fast, sharp-ended rowing or sailing boat that is widely used in the region and was once popular with pirates. The prau is long and narrow, rigged with one or two fore-and-aft sails. Modern praus are generally open and relatively small. In earlier times the boats were decked, and could measure as much as 60 feet (18 metres) long.

27 Harry Pélissier was an Edwardian music hall star. A fast-living, flamboyant personality who composed over 60 songs and whose show, *The Follies*, packed the Apollo Theatre before the First World War, he died of cirrhosis of the liver in 1913.

Admiral Sir William Grant (IWM)

Not long after I got a wireless message ordering me to go to Singapore. I arrived and called on Admiral Grant,[28] the C-in-C. He was delighted with the grand fleet I had brought him, and I was pleased to go so far westward. Grant had a couple of ordinary tugs to check the whole vast traffic passing through the [Malacca] Straits; they were capable of dealing with perhaps 10 per cent of it. Any additional fast-moving craft were a godsend to him. Then we suddenly got wind of a ship that was operating as a trader and flaunting the German flag up in the Gulf of Siam. That was rather too blatant. At that date she might have been the only ship on the high seas flying that flag. Off we went.

It was horrible weather; the clouds almost touched our mastheads. Day after day in that thick, humid atmosphere. No land, nothing in sight. At this point, to my astonishment, I went down with rheumatic fever, possibly developed from the hard bout of malaria I had had after the Sepik River expedition, when anopheles[29] mosquitoes had grazed on me. I ordered a boiling hot bath, but the pain was awful. We had a young medical student on board and I made him give me a strong dose of cocaine. In about 20 minutes I felt as if I was floating on rose leaves about a foot above my bunk. I remember no more, but 12 hours later, when I woke up, I was completely cured! Meanwhile *Paramatta* had nobbled the ship, German ensign and all, and I had her skipper sent over to me. Poor wretch, he had little thought there were three destroyers waiting for him in the Siam Gulf when he had swanked out of a river flying an extra-large flag. This matter having been settled, I moved on to Saigon, the French base in Cochin China [now the southernmost parts of Vietnam and Cambodia], carrying a personal message from Admiral Grant to his French counterpart.

28 Admiral Sir William L. Grant, KCB (1864–1929) C-in-C, China Station 1915–17; C-in-C, North America and West Indies Station 1918–19.

29 Anopheles is a genus of mosquito. Within it about 460 species are recognised, of which some 100 can transmit human malaria. However, only 30–40 commonly transmit the parasites which cause malaria in humans in endemic areas.

CHAPTER 11

Cruiser Commands

Aged 38, Cumberlege was promoted to captain in June 1915. Soon after, he left his destroyer flotilla, took command of the cruiser HMAS Encounter *and gave up hope of returning to the UK. At the end of 1916 he assumed command of a new-build Australian cruiser, HMAS* Brisbane.

HMAS *Encounter* (PD)

Just before leaving Singapore for Saigon, I received a telegram from Melbourne Navy Office offering me, as Post Captain,[1] command of *Encounter*. At that moment she was approaching the East Indies from the Pacific.

For all I knew, the ship was liable to remain on the East Indian station, or perhaps the Pacific, indefinitely. My object, however, was to get back to England as quickly as possible. I consulted Admiral Grant. He said that even if I was to get home there was very little chance of an immediate command, and I might easily be sent to the Cape Station or anywhere other than the Home Fleet, in command, say, of an armed merchant vessel. At least, he pointed out, that as *Encounter* was a man-of-war, and for her 6,000-ton size a very hard-hitting one, I ought, as I had only recently been promoted Post Captain, to consider myself damned lucky. I took his advice. *Encounter* was deflected to Saigon so that I could join her immediately.

I hated leaving my small flotilla. There seemed to be a mist in the Saigon River when I left *Warrego* with my dog and my parrot – not hard to understand, having passed the last 15 years in command of destroyers. But no sooner had I got on board *Encounter* than I received orders to intercept an American mail steamer from China to the Manilas. This done, I sailed to Western Australia, to protect the lines of transports and shipping which used Fremantle as a starting and stopping place. How one lone cruiser was expected to carry out this duty efficiently over such a vast expanse of sea is not for me to say. Fortunately, there were no German raiders around.

Not long after, I went off on an extraordinary hunt for a submarine 2,000 miles away in the Cambridge Gulf.[2] Intelligence had picked up a story that a native boy had reported to his master that somewhere in those huge, uncharted desolate waters he had seen a 'big fella dinghy with house along top which sat down in passage. He go along top of water, bynby he go along under water and come up a long way off.'

1 Post captain was a military rank above commander and below flag rank (admiral). When an officer was posted as a captain, he was entitled to wear a captain's epaulette on the right shoulder of his uniform. When he had attained three years in that rank he was entitled to wear an epaulette on both shoulders.

2 An inlet on the north coast of the Kimberley region of Western Australia – a gulf within a gulf, at the southern extremity of the Joseph Bonaparte Gulf in the Timor Sea. It experiences two large tidal flows, between 23 and 30 feet, daily.

The Benedictine Drysdale River Mission, Western Australia, 1900 (PD)

An accurate description of a submarine, and a description utterly impossible for the Aborigines at that time to have invented. I left immediately, taking my faithful collier *Kanna* with me (I had annexed her to replace the oil tanker *Esturia*). Needing something small to nose about this most dangerous, unlit and unsurveyed coast, in Broome I hired a sailing ketch and a pearling schooner with an engine.

We got to Cambridge Gulf, and I located the probable anchorage supposedly used by the 'dinghy with a house along top'. The gulf was said to have a regular depth of 100 fathoms to bottom according to soundings taken by Dampier[3] more than 200 years earlier. I'm sure the old pirate made no mistake. But after such a lapse of time, our soundings found a regular 10 fathoms! There was no sign of any submarine in this weird but beautiful part of the world. Perfect weather. No sign of life except for the tracks of a great number of Aborigines (who we never glimpsed) and their warning fires. When I landed near the entrance to a great river, I was more than astonished to come face to face with a robed and hooded monk, adorned with a huge black beard. We passed through the bush to his abode, where I met two other monks. They were glad to see me, having not seen a white face for over two years. Their home consisted of a couple of corrugated iron shacks and a wonderful garden stretching more than 3 acres, which grew every sort of vegetable, all enclosed by an unclimbable barbed wire fence. The nearest white man lived about 1,000 miles away! But large numbers of Aborigines came and went, and the fence was for protection. It was more than these monks' lives were worth to venture further than a few hundred yards from this settlement. The head man of this group told me that he had got a spear through his shoulder one day when overtaken by some natives just as he arrived at his entrance gate.

I sat and talked with these gents in their shack, conversing mostly in Spanish which, being Portuguese, they understood. Idly, I turned the pages of a four- or five-year-old *Illustrated London News* from a heap of periodicals that some pearler had left. The oldest monk told me that they had long ago given up any attempt to convert the Aborigines, but now and again sick men would come in to get the benefit of their medical knowledge. On one of the pages I found some photographs of the launching of a new submarine

3 The first European to explore the area was William Dampier, who visited the region aboard *Cygnet* in 1688.

in an English yard. I enquired: 'When these natives come to get doctored, do you ever show them these pictures?' 'Oh yes,' replied my monk. 'It's curious to see how interested they are in pictures of any sort. I always encourage them to ask questions.' I handed him the big picture in the magazine and said: 'I wonder if by any chance you remember explaining this particular picture?' 'Why, yes,' he answered. 'The only type of boat the Aborigines use is a collection of tree trunks lashed together to form a raft.' I followed up: 'Do any of these natives use pidgin English?' 'Very, very few. Now and again, one finds a man who uses it who may have been taken up by a mission and returned to his tribe.'

'Suppose,' I said, 'you wished to describe a submarine – this picture – to a native. How would you do it?' 'I would say,' he replied, "this big fella dinghy with house along top—" 'Stop,' I cried. 'I've found my submarine!!' 'What submarine?' And I told him what had brought me to this wilderness. Did we laugh! Still, I felt grateful to the simple man, who had listened to the yarns of his compatriots spun round a camp fire and passed them on, for having brought me to this enthralling country, as wild as New South Wales when the First Fleet had anchored in Botany Bay.[4] As an indication of the virginity of this country, my men found two brass cannon from the *Rose of Seville* offshore, which must have lain there for 300 years. Burnished and mounted, today they adorn the grass lawn in front of the Naval Commandant's office on Garden Island, Sydney.

I spent a generally thrilling fortnight investigating and making a rough survey of this district, including mapping the entrance to a 700-mile river, the Drysdale.[5] Then, with *Encounter* due a refit, we visited Darwin, poked our nose into the Gulf of Carpentaria, and returned to Sydney via the Torres Straits, having circumnavigated the continent. At Sydney I found that the first man-of-war to be built south of the Equator was very nearly completed at the dockyard on Cockatoo Island; this ship had been earmarked to go to England and join one of the light cruiser squadrons of the Home Fleet. I went to Melbourne and made my bow at the Navy Board. 'Now, Cumberlege, what can we do for you?' they said. 'Give me the new cruiser,' I responded. 'Hold on,' said the second naval member, an RN captain.[6] 'I thought she would do for me.' 'Oh dear, Sir,' I answered. 'For God's sake, don't think of leaving the Navy Board. What would we do without you?' I urged on the Board the fact that I had only accepted *Encounter* to please it after I had been prevented from going home. Surely, as the oldest inhabitant,[7] I was justly entitled? And, anyhow, I wanted this ship very badly indeed. I got her. She was called *Brisbane*.

HMAS *Brisbane* (PD)

The next few weeks were beset by incidents. Sabotage, in a very serious form, had set in. Expensive fittings, like electric ring mains, as soon as fitted had a chisel passed through them resulting in complete replacement at terrific expense. I took command, and was given about 80 men to act as a nucleus crew

4 A fleet of 11 ships that had taken the first European settlers to Australia. In 1787 this fleet, with over 1,400 people (convicts, marines, sailors, civil officers and free settlers) on board, left Portsmouth. After 250 days it arrived in Botany Bay, New South Wales, where the resultant penal colony would become the first European settlement in Australia.

5 The Drysdale river is in the Kimberley region, the northern part of Western Australia. It rises in the Caroline Ranges, flows in a northerly direction and discharges into Broome Bay near Kalumburu. It was named after a director of the Victorian Squatting Company, Thomas Drysdale, by the company's surveyor in 1886. The traditional owners of the area are the Ngarinjin, Miwa and Wilawila peoples.

6 Vice Admiral Sir Arthur Gordon Smith, CMG (1873–1953). In 1913 he had been lent to the RAN to serve as captain of the cruiser *Encounter*.

7 At the time, in October 1916, CLC was a post captain aged 39, and had been in the RAN for two and a half years.

for clearing-up duties while hundreds of workmen were employed doing overtime onboard. I divided my men into four watches[8] and put a couple in every compartment, armed with home-made truncheons and .45 Webley pistols with orders to bash or shoot should any sort of sabotage take place. I met the public prosecutor and warned him that if I or any of my men were charged with murder, to deal gently with the case. He promised me that there would not even be a prosecution.

Soon after joining the ship, I overheard a conversation among some friendly men working on my after-cabin. One said: 'There's a bloke working on the forecastle who has been painting the capstan for the last four days, going slow on the job – the bloke who wears a Panama hat.' I went on to the forecastle. A man in a Panama hat was assiduously painting the capstan. I returned to my temporary cabin and called for the master-at-arms and my chief gunner's mate and two chief petty officers (both very strong men). I said: 'I want you to go on to the forecastle where you will see a man painting the capstan and wearing a Panama hat. You are to request him, politely, to give me the pleasure of his company at once.' In a few minutes my men returned with the rat. I asked him to take off his hat. He obeyed. 'Now, I want to ask you a few questions. Firstly, I was informed that you are a member of the IWW.[9] Is that so?' He stood up for himself much as I had expected, looked vicious and showed temper. He demanded to know by what right he should be dragged before me and be questioned.

'I will explain,' I replied gently, and produced from a drawer an official document which I had recently mastered, since it described me as a 'competent authority'. It gave me the most bloodthirsty powers such as acting as hangman. 'Now, there you are, sonny,' I said. 'That's that.' I had him searched thoroughly just in case he acted foolishly, and then continued the conversation. He soon got quite matey. Yes, he said, he was an IWW member, but that did not mean he had done anything naughty – and we had good chuckle all round at the latest bit of dirty work that had happened. Eventually, I decided that he had given himself away quite sufficiently for my purpose even though he had not owned up to any act of villainy. I closed the interview by asking one my strong men to hand the rat to the chief warder on Garden Island gaol and lock him up. He was surprised and hurt.

I landed at once and called on Sydney's Chief of Police, a fine fellow called McCullock. On hearing my story he had a good laugh and said: 'But my good fellow, it's all utterly illegal.' My answer was that the blighter had been locked up and that was that. McCullock said he would send a couple of men to the gaol: 'Perhaps they will be able to work out something more definite to go on.' Away I went with two detectives to Garden Island where the chief warder put an 'office' at my disposal. It was a gloomy sort of cell, and we three sat down on kitchen chairs at a small table. With much rattling of keys and shooting of bolts, my friend was led in by two stern-faced warders.

If I had been suave, the detectives, taking turns, were sugar-suave. In a few minutes, everyone was on

8 Sea life involves four-hour periods of work called watches. The first watch is from 20.00 until midnight; the middle watch is from midnight to 04.00; the morning watch is from 04.00 until 08.00; the forenoon watch is from 08.00 until noon and the afternoon watch is from noon to 16.00. Then there are two dog watches, each of two hours, resulting in a switch of the hours for the crew members on watch. In the two-watch system, which applied at the time, each four-hour watch was followed by four hours of rest; it must have played havoc with the crews' body clocks, hence their ability to function effectively. Since then three-watch and four-watch systems have been introduced, allowing much longer rest times. NB The word 'watch' also means the two sets of crew involved: the starboard watch and the port watch.

9 International Workers of the World (known as wobblies). The IWW opposed the First World War from 1914 onwards, and was at the front of a worldwide anti-conscription fight. In Australia it never had more than 500 members. A narrow majority of Australians voted against conscription in a bitter, hard-fought referendum in October 1916, and then again in December 1917. Australia was the only belligerent in the First World War without conscription.

the best terms and our friend seemed to be enjoying himself. Then, crack! The tone changed. 'So,' barked one of the detectives, 'you are doubtless aware that in wartime the law is a bit different and a court martial has a nasty way of doing things that perhaps a magistrate might think twice about.' A lot more in this tenor followed, suggesting that a cold morning against a brick wall loomed but ... Turning to me, the detective said, with a quiver of the eyelid: 'Well, I think that's all we need to know. I have his name and know where he lives. So if you agree I will take him with us and allow the higher authorities to decide what to do.' I never saw or heard of the man again; he may easily have become a Member of Parliament for all I know.

After this I got hold of that great and good man, Munro Ferguson, Governor-General of Australia. He was extremely interested both in the ship and in our difficulties. By now (December 1916), *Brisbane* was complete in every detail except for the electric gun circuits and fittings and a few other details. Yet in spite of our vigilance, we were worried that something serious might happen to her. My plan, which I adumbrated to Ferguson, was to clear out of the shipyard unexpectedly and do the work that remained in, say, Singapore or the first dockyard we reached. He agreed, and so did G.G. King-Salter, the dockyard manager. Then I went to Melbourne, and the Navy Board agreed. I came back to Sydney and made our plans secretly.

The last shift of some 100 or so workmen was in the habit of leaving the ship at 11:00 pm. We fixed a date, and during the evening casually removed all gangways leading to the ship, except one. I went ashore for dinner and arrived back on board at five minutes to eleven, to find King-Salter and his chief assistant anxiously pacing the quarterdeck. The bell for the shore rang. A mob of men trooped on to the quarterdeck towards the only gangway. At the bottom stood certain dockyard officials. Their job was to tell each man as he left the ship that his job was finished. As the last man departed, we sighed a sigh of great relief and went and had a drink. Next morning, dense fog enveloped Sydney harbour and the dockyard, and the tugs to tow us out lost their way and never turned up. I decided to kick *Brisbane* off the wall and turn into the stream for Sydney Heads. At that moment the early morning fog lifted and we got under way in blazing sunshine. Dropping off King-Salter and his wife and daughter by Garden Island, I said: 'Take her out, Navigator, telegraphs half speed, revolutions 15 knots.' Homeward bound at last.

On the way out of the lovely harbour, the ship kept swinging to starboard against helm. 'I'll take her, Navigator,' I said, and ordered hard-a-starboard. Still, she swung to starboard. The helm was not functioning. All this took but a few seconds. 'Full speed astern,' I ordered quietly, and then went to the forecastle where the men were still at their stations. I ordered: 'Stand by to let go both anchors.' By now the engines were turning at full speed astern but we were very close to the Bottle and Glass rocks.[10] 'Let go starboard anchor, let go port anchor. Don't snub her. Let it run.' I was afraid of snapping the chains. The twin chains tightened like bars on our flanks and we came to a standstill. 'Stop engines.' Then, to the leadsman: 'What water have you up and down?' 'Four fathoms, Sir.' We were still afloat; my cigarette was still alight.

My Engineer Commander and good friend McKean got busy. I tried the helm – nothing whatever the matter. The only thing to do was to weigh anchor and proceed on our voyage. The most thorough investigation showed absolutely nothing wrong. Sabotage, naturally, was suspected. Ever after I could never trust the gear and always had a second string at the conning tower. (One morning, 18 months later, I was having breakfast when McKean brought me a sort of brass plunger which had a series of small holes drilled in a collar through which water had to pass. 'I've got it at last,' he grinned, and with a pin picked out a lump of solid grease from one of the holes. It turned out that this piece of mechanism had been sent from England

10 The oddly-shaped Bottle and Glass Rocks were so named in 1799 because the sandstone columns resembled glassware. Once much taller, the columns were supposedly shattered when used for target practice by passing ships.

and laid aside until wanted, most carefully greased with some heavy gelatinous preservation grease – which had solidified in the little holes and prevented the full flow of water necessary for its proper working.)

Singapore Dockyard could not do our work, so we went across the Indian Ocean, through the Suez Canal and on to Malta. We arrived on a Sunday evening, 24 hours before we were expected; there was a delay letting us into the harbour. When we did get in, an unpleasant-looking blighter of a Post Captain was on the wall trying to find fault, but failed. A few days later, four of my men (out of 550) went down with measles. To my amazement, the ship was put into quarantine at once. Was I furious! The Post Captain was getting his own back. I went ashore and got hold of the Maltese government doctor. He told me that something like 10 per cent of the whole population had measles. '*Quarantine!*' I said. 'Good Lord, you may as well start to quarantine for colds in the head.' I went to the general officer commanding the military in Malta. Was there, I asked, a camp somewhere on the island where I could house my gallant men? He had one at his disposal 6 miles out in the country, by the sea: 'You can go in tomorrow.' He put half a dozen lorries at our disposal. Then I politely adumbrated my scheme to the Post Captain. He hadn't the guts to veto the plan. Leaving a small care and maintenance party on board, which we relieved at intervals, we marched, with our band playing, to our delightful summer resort and passed a very happy six weeks there. Lord Methuen,[11] the Governor, and his charming family, made it a regular port of call.

At Port Said I had wired my wife Laetitia, whom I had not seen since 1913 (it was now the end of 1916) to say that I knew I must remain at Malta for probably three months and, if she considered it safe to travel by sea, she should come to Malta. If there were difficulties, I was sure I could get leave and meet her in Sicily or some Italian city. I got no reply to that, nor to a confirmatory letter I wrote on arrival in Malta. I had kept up a regular correspondence with her in all my wanderings, so rather wondered why. But it is amazing how time flies, days suddenly become weeks and weeks months. I knew Laetitia was working[12] and she might quite easily have been in France, and letters do fail to get home. Much later, I learnt from a young lady in the Malta office that my letters had been suppressed; the authorities wanted to curtail, probably with good reason, the coming and going of non-combatants, especially women.

Malta was a rum place in those days. The harbour was full of French and Italian ships which might have been better employed elsewhere. I met a lot of old friends and made some new ones. But at last the day came when *Brisbane* was ready for sea. Off to Queensferry.[13] A signal came. 'Admiral wishes to see Captain.' I went to the office and encountered a sardonic old blighter[14] whom I had not met before – a hard-faced man. He handed me a letter, my sailing orders. 'Better read them,' he said. I opened the letter. '... you are to proceed with all despatch to Colombo, Ceylon, and place yourself under the orders ...' He saw my face fall and

11 Field Marshal Paul Methuen, 3rd Baron Methuen, GCB, GCMG, GCVO, DL (1845–1932) was a British Army officer who led British forces in the Boer War and was badly defeated at the Battle of Magersfontein. He was later captured by the Boers at Tweebosch. After the war he became General Officer Commanding-in-Chief in South Africa in 1908, Governor and C-in-C of Natal in 1910 and then Governor and C-in-C of Malta in 1915–19.

12 It is unclear what Laetitia was doing in 1916. The couple's son Michael (born 1905) was away at school. Daughter Diana (born 1910) lived with her. Laetitia certainly had a job for much the war, and the records show that in June 1918, aged 32, she joined the Women's Royal Air Force in an administrative capacity and was based in Hurst Park, West Moseley, Middlesex.

13 The naval base close to Edinburgh.

14 Rear Admiral George Ballard, CB (1862–1948) was Senior Officer in Charge at Malta and Admiral Superintendent of Malta Dockyard from September 1916. He was not popular with his peers. In May 1917 he was criticised by the Board of Admiralty for the torpedoing of SS *Ivernia*, having allowed it to proceed through the Cerigotto Channel by day, contrary to instructions. On 17 September he was informed that orders had been given in a 'haphazard' manner regarding an operation in which the vessel *Zeus* was lost. He remained in Malta to 16 November.

The German raider SMS *Wolf* (PD)

heard my muttered 'Well, I'm buggered.' His demeanour changed. He was smiling. Few, it's claimed, had seen such a phenomenon. 'Sorry,' he said. 'That's from the Admiralty. It appears that a German raider called *Wolf*[15] is operating out there, and the Melbourne people are anxious about their transports. Your ship is the only 6-inch gun ship available here. When can you get away?' 'Tonight,' I said, and went.

Arriving at Colombo, I cross-examined the local C-in-C about *Wolf*'s whereabouts. He did not know. It was suspected that she was lying doggo at sea somewhere south of Ceylon [now Sri Lanka]. I took on board a Sopwith Pup[16] and her pilot, Clemson,[17] and ranged those wide seas. Fine weather, luckily. I had a zone to search. At dawn, I would hoist out the seaplane and Clemson would buzz off on a huge triangle. He would come back in an hour or so. I would then steam along our course until an hour before dark. Then off the plane would go and scout out again until near-dark, so that *Brisbane* could safely steam a certain distance during the night without missing our quarry. Next day – repeat the tactics. No wireless, no observer, just Clemson. If he sighted the craft he was to return immediately, make certain signals with a Verey pistol and fly off in the direction of his find. I would take my course from him, and drop a whaler with plenty of tins of petrol and grub, and a compass, mast and sail to which he could return while I was dealing with the enemy. Not a sign of *Wolf*, and suddenly they got news that she was 5,000 miles away. We were recalled, and joined a convoy of three large ships protecting West Australia.

This extremely boring service – doing nothing, really – at length came to an end. We were due to go to Sydney for a refit when a rumour arose that something was happening some 2,000 miles away, in the Solomon Islands east of New Guinea. I made for Tulagi, the seat of government, and its magnificent harbour. Rumour was rife, and I saw at once there would be difficulties if I started tearing off to investigate every report coming in from anywhere in the Pacific Ocean. *Kanna* by then had wandered up behind *Brisbane*; as soon as we had cleared her I sent her back to Australia for more coal while we did everything we could to conserve our resources, even trying to burn young wood from the local forests in our furnaces (a complete failure).

We looked around for some other remedy. It turned up in the form of the jolliest and broadest man that I ever saw. His name was Norman Wheatly. He arrived on board in customary island costume, an

15 SMS *Wolf* was an armed merchant raider. It was equipped with six 15 cm (5.9-in) guns, other guns, four torpedo tubes and over 450 mines. It laid minefields in the Indian Ocean and off Australia's southern coast, which claimed several ships. Its advantages included deception (fake funnel and masts which could be erected or lowered to change its appearance), false sides which kept its weapons hidden until the last possible moment, and a range of over 32,000 nmi (59,000 km) thanks to a coal bunker capacity of 8,000 tons. On 30 November 1916 *Wolf* left its home port of Kiel with a crew of 348 men and returned to Kiel in February 1918, having destroyed 35 trading vessels and two warships totalling 110,000 tons and carrying 467 prisoners of war aboard; without support of any kind, *Wolf* had made the longest voyage of any warship during the First World War. For the rest of the war, *Wolf* was employed in the Baltic Sea.

16 The Sopwith Pup was a British single-seater biplane fighter aircraft built by the Sopwith Aviation Company. It entered service with the Royal Naval Air Service and the Royal Flying Corps in the autumn of 1916. With docile flying characteristics and good manoeuvrability, the aircraft proved very successful, but eventually, outclassed by newer German fighters, it was replaced at the end of 1917. This particular Pup was evidently one of the rare models with floats instead of wheels.

17 Probably Flight Commander Alfred W. Clemson, DSC of the Royal Navy's Aerial Reconnaissance Unit.

immaculate white vest and equally spotless duck trousers. He had a walrus moustache and wanted to join up, but told me that he was too large to be accepted by the Australians. 'Haven't got an inch of fat on me,' he said, and seized my hand and laid it on his armour-plated stomach rippling with muscle. It was not clear why he wished to join up. Then I spotted a seaworthy islands schooner. 'Whose ship is that?' I asked. 'Mine,' he said. 'The *Ruviana*. Built her myself. Got a good engine.' An idea came to me. There must be others like *Ruviana* in the islands. Fitted with wireless, perhaps they could be sent out to do the rumour-exploding while I lay at anchor conserving my precious fuel? I had come by half a dozen sets of portable wireless gear while in Sydney. I put a few bluejackets and a warrant officer or lieutenant in each of them, retained their owners as (unpaid) pilots, and gave each of them a home-made Commission which looked official.

Next day, led by a proud Mr. Norman Wheatly, this 'fleet' put to sea. We blew out every rumour in this vast group of islands. Having done so, we shifted eastward, calling at Ocean Island because I had heard I might find a stock of coal there. We did, but it was three parts guano. Even so, we took a few tons on board of which all but a handful went up the funnel. Life would have been tiresome were it not for the endless, enlivening sense of responsibility. And there were compensations; one day I had the feast of my life with the Commissioner – coconut crab and millionaire's salad.[18]

On this particular voyage, I once ordered my collier, the faithful *Kanna*, to meet me on a certain date thousands of miles east, in one of the Gilbert Islands. To do this, she had to steam 1,850 miles to Sydney to fill up with coal, then make another 2,000-mile voyage. I had absolute faith in the skipper of the *Kanna*. The Senior Naval Officer in Sydney once told me that he had tried to discover from the skipper where *Kanna* was going after she had loaded with coal. The skipper had replied: 'You may be SNO here, but you aren't the SNO who gave me my orders. Captain Cumberlege would hang me as sure as they hung Doctor Crippen if I let him down!' By the time *Kanna* reached the Tarawa Lagoon in the Gilbert Group, we were short of everything, so we made arrangements to live on the land in case she was late. By the evening of the agreed rendezvous Engineer McKean and I were pacing the quarter deck and talking shop when something – just a tiny speck in the sky in the south-west – appeared. It was the *Kanna*, 30–40 miles away, but still with a few hours in hand.

---

18 The coconut crab looks like a lobster, climbs coconut trees and lives off coconuts. Millionaire's salad is so-called because it needs the destruction of a complete palm tree to get at the succulent young innermost shoots of palm leaves.

CHAPTER 12

The HMAS Australia 'Mutiny'

In 1917–19 Cumberlege ran into a succession of disciplinary issues in HMAS Brisbane, *and from April 1919 in HMAS* Australia, *the flagship of the Royal Australian Navy. Those problems had a lasting impact on his naval career.*

There is a sentence in the half-sheet of parchment called a 'Commission', elaborated at vast length in a volume called *The King's Regulations*, that has something to say about seeing that everybody under one's command behaved themselves. Frankly, I funked *The King's Regulations*, but it was my Paymaster's job to know it by heart. Fortunately, he never did. But by the time one becomes a Post Captain, one has probably absorbed by example and tradition a condensed version of these Regulations.

In 1917 in the Pacific I had an occasion to abide by my Commission on the question of behaviour. This led to a certain ship's boy to behave himself to the tune of a dozen over the arse with a well-and-truly laid cane administered by the awful arm of the Master-at-Arms. Never, never again will that boy, or his boy or his boy's boy, commit the particular atrocity for which he was punished. On another occasion, a grown man who had been very clever in avoiding the arm of the law, at length tried it on once too often. This particular crime included rudeness to his superior officer, who instantly knocked him down, which is not in the Regulations. On my orders, this gent [not the officer] was sent to languish in the gloomy portals of Sydney 'detention' barracks for 90 days – to the infinite relief of his 500-odd shipmates, be it said. At this point, a Labour member of the Federal Parliament used malicious remarks in that assembly in referring to me. Hansard published his stupidities. The local Admiralty in Melbourne repeated the libel, enclosing a copy of Hansard, and asking me what remarks I had to make on the subject. My answer – that these remarks did not concern me in the least – evidently met the case.

Be all that as it may, in *Brisbane* our lives were passing in extraordinary peace with half the world aflame. From the Gilberts, we went to Fiji and from Fiji back to Australia in January 1918, passing Sydney Heads in as fine a blow as ever I did feel. We docked, we refitted, we loved – what is more necessary to good ships and their crews? At last, in October, came the order to sail for Europe. One thought obsessed me: I was going home, to my mother, to my England. On November 11th 1918 – as on August 4th 1914 – I was 1,000 miles out at sea. By wireless, we got the news: the war was over. I forget what I did. I certainly did not have to think or plan what to do. The Commander [Hare] brought me the cipher. I said the only thing I could: 'Ring the bell for Divine Service.'

An order arrived: 'Proceed to Mudros.'[1] We went, and stayed a few days. Mike Seymour, [2] by now in Constantinople with his fleet, suddenly realised that a fine cruiser, with one of his old destroyer lads and lifelong admirer in charge, was within hail. 'Come here,' said Mike, in official language. I went happily, and barged into the entrance of the Dardanelles, crashing through a minefield I had had no knowledge of until someone in a motor launch flagged me out of it. At Chanak[3] I embarked 200 Royal Marines, a pleasing sight, as Royal Marines do not exist in the RAN. We arrived at the Golden Horn at 11:00 pm after a glorious day's work. Dawn next day came, a late-November dawn. I went on the bridge in my pyjamas and overcoat. What marvels I saw! The sky was opal over Asia. To the west, I saw Seraglio Point, the Tulip Mosque, St Sophia and 10,000 chimneys sending up a blue wisp from kitchen fires. It was the most beautiful sight I had ever seen.

'Sound the officers' call,' I told my bugler. Instantly, pyjamaed lieutenants, engineers, warrant officers and sub-lieutenants came racing up, pulling on British Warms[4] and grumbling. I said nothing. There was silence. And then the old, old sun, a glory of red and gold, rose over Asia and I said, 'Sound the disperse.' And then, and not till then, did they realise why I had sounded the officers' call.

Shortly after I received an invitation from Mike Seymour to breakfast. I went, taking with me two pats of Australian butter (we had loaded 4 tons into *Brisbane*'s refrigerators before leaving Australia). When Mike emerged, he said: 'Good Lord – what's that, Steward? Where did you get that? Butter, man, fresh butter!' He went on: 'Claudie, I want you to run the Marines over to Sebastopol and land them there.' Breakfast finished, away I went, landing the Marines to cheers from my men. Who knows what happened to them? We were potted at by Bolsheviks on the way into the harbour. There were half-sunk Russian ships, a destroyer on the Marine Parade (her Bolshie crew had rushed her at full speed onto the beach). On shore, ordinary people stood about, waiting to be murdered.

The job done, back to Constantinople. 'Claudie, I must get a ship to Smyrna[5] instantly and before any other foreigners get there,' said Mike before explaining why. 'You'll have to get through a swept channel by daylight. About 20,000 mines were thought to have been laid. 'I can do it, Sir, if I go at once.' 'Well, don't take any risks.'

I went. Another glorious trip. We did it at 27 knots and passed, at a distance of 50 yards, the newest French battleship nosing up at 4 knots. At Phocis, at the entrance to the Smyrna Gulf, I was joined by one of the finest sailors I have ever met. His name was Captain George Todd and he commanded a couple of the latest minesweepers. Before the war, he had held the rank of Mate in some obscure steamer in the China trade. He had joined up and been pitchforked into the minesweeping business in the North Sea. In the Dardanelles he had a kite balloon to help him with the balloonist signalling back the location of mines ahead. He got to work immediately and swept a 30-mile clear channel to Smyrna. The first man I met there

---

1 Now Moudros, a town on the island of Lemnos, North Aegean, Greece. In the First World War its harbour was used as an Allied base, commanded by Admiral Rosslyn Wemyss. On 30 October 1918 it was the site of the signing of the Armistice of Mudros, which saw the end of hostilities between the Ottoman Empire and the Allies.

2 Vice Admiral Sir Michael Culme-Seymour, KCB (1867–1925) At the end of the war he was appointed Rear Admiral Commanding 4th Battle Squadron and soon after Rear Admiral Commanding the Black Sea and Caspian Squadron.

3 Chanak, or Çanakkale, is a city and seaport on the southern shore of the Dardanelles at their narrowest point.

4 A British Warm is a type of woollen overcoat based on the greatcoats worn by British Army officers in the First World War. It first appeared around 1914 as a military greatcoat for British officers. It is typically a heavy double-breasted coat made from a 100 per cent wool cloth, taupe-coloured, with peak lapels, leather buttons and epaulettes.

5 Greece occupied Smyrna (now Izmir) in May 1919 and put in place a military administration. The occupation of Smyrna came to an end when the Turkish army of Kemal Atatürk entered the city on 9 September 1922, at the end of the Greco-Turkish War (1919–1922). In the immediate aftermath a fire broke out in the Greek and Armenian quarters; the death toll is estimated anywhere between 10,000 and 100,000.

was Alan Dixon, an RN Commander – just the man to handle the unexpected, and the involved cases of jealousy that were cropping up among the jumble of nationalities. Not that it mattered a hoot what we on the spot reported or suggested; the British government had settled on its policy[6] regardless. I am thankful to say I was far away when the result of that policy developed into the sack of Smyrna.

Whilst in Smyrna I met a number of interesting personages. Nureddin Pasha,[7] the Turkish military governor of the Vilayet[8] of Smyrna, used to row to *Brisbane* to 'give me the dope' on what was going on onshore. Nur, of Albanian descent, was the victor of Kut.[9] He claimed that in that battle he had been at the end of his tether: 'Things on our side were going from bad to worse.' Then an imam of the district had come to see him and told him that he had seen a vision of the golden scabbard sword of Hassan, nephew of the prophet Mohammed, being taken from his tomb, followed by 'the utter defeat of our enemies'. So he had had that holy place opened, and had seen the scimitar which had lain untouched for 2,000 years. The imam had handed it to him – and the result was victory! He also told me of the awful march of dying British prisoners – no medical stores, no possibility of relief, no transport. The sword now hung in Nur's house in Bursa. The civilian Governor was called Edhem Pasha. It was said that he had £1 million worth of carpets on the walls of his palace. If he saw one somewhere that he liked, he would ask the owner to name a price. Regardless of what he was told, he would send someone that evening to walk off with the treasure. Maybe so, but he paid handsomely.

One day a big and bearded Frenchman came to me in the uniform of a Capitaine de Frégate [Senior Commander]; he owned a few old-fashioned minesweeping trawlers. He told me he had received orders to sweep a certain patch of water well out of the fairway in the Gulf of Smyrna. I pointed out to him the great danger of the project. I knew that these mines lay about 11 to 12 feet under water and that his boats drew at least 13 feet. I explained that my own boats, which drew about 10 feet of water, would do the job as soon as they had finished another job. He said that his orders were for the work to be carried out instantly. I pointed out that I was the senior Allied naval officer present and it was for me to decide when and where mines should be swept. I said that I had no objection to him informing his C-in-C of my attitude. 'Impossible, impossible. I obey my Commander-in-Chief.' I tried another tack, working on his feelings. To no purpose. He went. Half an hour later he and 30 of his men went sky high – lavishly praised at a terrific funeral, and a fat lot of good to his wretched wife and seven young children, all of whom I had seen when he had produced a photograph of them from his inner breast pocket.

There were a hundred and one incidents like this, many fixed by the Italians. We dealt with most of them, and it might have become boring, but suddenly we were ordered to England to take part in an act of welcome for an Australian ship in Portsmouth, where we arrived to the cheers of assembled ships and

---

6 After the First World War the Allies split on the future of the Ottoman Empire: the French favoured some territorial integrity for a new Turkish state that would include Smyrna; the British ended up supporting Greek claims to Smyrna; the Italians claimed that Smyrna was their possession. Meanwhile, the Greek claim over Smyrna, which had a large Greek population, was supported by the USA and Woodrow Wilsons's Fourteen Points, which emphasised the right to autonomous development for minorities in Anatolia. In April 1919 the Italians landed and took over Antalya, and began showing signs of moving troops towards Smyrna. Eventually the Italians accepted Greek occupation.

7 Nureddin Pasha (1873–1932), was a high-ranking military officer who served in the Ottoman Empire during the First World War and in the Turkish army during the Greco-Turkish War (1919–1922). He was the only high-ranking Ottoman officer during the Greco-Turkish War (1919–1922) who sported a beard. He played a leading role in the massacre of Greeks, Armenians and Kurds in Anatolia.

8 A first-level administrative division of the Ottoman Empire in the south-west of Asia Minor (Turkey).

9 The Battle of Kut (December 1915–April 1916) was the Ottoman Army siege of an 8,000-strong British Army garrison in the town of Kut, 100 miles south of Baghdad. Following the British surrender the survivors were force-marched to imprisonment at Aleppo. Ten months later a newly-recruited British Indian Army re-conquered Kut.

a dense fog. For the first time in five years I set foot upon native heath and saw my wife, children and mother. Shortly after our arrival, I heard from Australia that a new captain[10] for *Brisbane* had been appointed and was coming to take her back to Australia.[11] Meanwhile, there had been some hitch in the arrangements for a new Admiral to command the battle cruiser *Australia*. The job was then offered to a Senior Post Captain, who was given the rank of Commodore. This brought me into contact with one of the most loveable and extraordinary characters I met in my life, a man called Dumaresq,[12] the new Commodore of the RAN. When he asked me to take on the job of his Flag Captain, he told me quite frankly that he had been hoping to get someone else but had been turned down. I accepted at once, partly because I was not looking forward to the probability of waiting a couple of years in England for a ship, partly because I was very willing to get away from post-war England, and partly because John Dumaresq intrigued me. My cronies told me I would not last six months, if that, in the job, given Dumaresq's record with seconds-in-command. All I can say is that I never had cause to regret the step I had taken; I lived cheek-by-jowl with him for two-and-a-half years, and when he found that life was not worth living under these conditions [at sea] our parting was not on my side.

Rear Admiral John Dumaresq (PD)

I took over *Australia* from Jimmy James[13] and found that pretty well all the RN officers were quite new to the ship and that a second-in-command Commander had not yet been appointed.[14] The crew was mainly Australian with some RN Petty Officers predominating in the non-commissioned ranks. It did not take long to realise that the rank-and-file had developed a grievance, which was well worked up by a small minority. The basis was the fact that they were being treated like conscripts – quite forgetting

HMAS *Australia* (PD)

10 Admiral Sir George Francis Hyde, KCB, CVO, CBE (1877–1937) transferred to the RAN in 1912. In 1913, as a commander, he sailed in the battlecruiser HMAS *Australia* to Australia. In 1915 he was appointed to command HMS *Adventure* in the Coast of Ireland Command; during the Irish Easter rebellion in 1916 he was commended for performing his duties 'with great tact and ability'. Promoted captain in April 1917, he became director of the war staff at the Naval Office in Melbourne, later taking HMAS *Brisbane* back to Australia. He became the second naval member of the Australian Naval Board 1923–24. In 1926 he took command of the Australian Squadron. In 1928, he was the first RAN officer to become an aide-de-camp to King George V, then after a year in the UK he returned to Australia as the first naval member of the Australian Naval Board in 1931 – the first seagoing officer to hold the position. He was promoted admiral in 1936. His health deteriorated in 1937, and in June that year he killed a pedestrian whilst driving his car. Although an inquiry exonerated him the incident caused him enormous distress, arguably contributing to his death from pneumonia in Melbourne eight days later.

11 HMAS *Brisbane* left Portsmouth after a refit in April 1919. In the interwar years it was decommissioned twice before being broken up in 1936.

12 Rear Admiral John Saumarez Dumaresq, CB, CVO (1873–1922) is remembered as the inventor of a device named after him which helped users calculate the rate at which the range to an enemy ship changed over time. He was the first Australian-born officer to command the Australian fleet. His period of command was marked by disagreement with the Australian government over expenditure on the RAN. In April 1922 he was posted back to the Royal Navy, but on the return journey he contracted pneumonia, and on 22 July 1922 he died in the US Military Hospital in Manila.

13 Vice Admiral Thomas James, CB (1878–1965) assisted the Second Sea Lord at the Admiralty from August 1914 to end 1917. He was freed from desk work to command of HMAS *Australia* on 1 September 1918. Later he became flag captain to the Rear Admiral Commanding Second Battle Cruiser Squadron.

14 It turned out to be Commander Francis Brabant.

or disregarding the fact that in peacetime they had contracted to serve for a certain number of years (five, I think) *and* for the duration of any war that might occur in that period. I have no idea how they stood legally, the war now being over, but it was quite apparent that the malcontents had decided to regard themselves as passengers, as far as they dared, on the impending passage home to Australia.

My cheery-faced but gloomy-minded Master-at-Arms [George Smith] said to me: 'How we shall ever get out there, I don't know. There's a party on board this ship what calls themselves F.I.Fs., Sir.' 'What do you mean?' I inquired. 'Sir, if you will pardon the language, F.I.F. means Fuck It, I've Finished.' I had to laugh. Commodore Dumaresq's counsel on the subject was to do nothing drastic, given that as soon as we arrived at our destination the whole crowd would be put ashore time-expired and we could start again with a new crew. His idea coincided with mine. A few days before sailing, the Prince of Wales came on board to say goodbye; the occasion passed off very well and even the F.I.Fs. did their best to get the ship more or less decent after the months of refitting, lying alongside a dockyard and its dirt.

Dumaresq was a hell of a man for 'policies'. They all centred round one particular policy – to show the world what a highly efficient service the RAN was, is, or would be. A very praiseworthy policy too. Elaboration of this policy entailed no end of work by Dumaresq (the hardest-working man I ever came across) and his staff, of which I was the 'Chief'. That this abundance of work never irked me was due to the fact that every other officer in the ship seemed to be on the staff, or co-opted on to it. That left me very little to do. Nevertheless, I did enjoy the ship. *Australia* was a fine old craft and a very handsome one. If policies dominated conversation even at table, the atmosphere was conspicuously good, and particularly so in the wardroom – mostly young and forward-looking gentlemen anticipating new countries or returning to their homes. Until we arrived in Port Said, the voyage developed comfortably enough.

In Port Said, however, there was an unfortunate incident, hinging on the date of pay day. I forget the precise details, but some capital was made by the F.I.Fs. of the fact that I had ordered the crew to be paid at Port Said. This was so that the men would have a chance to buy those little odds and ends so beloved of sailors to take to their girls back home. This seems to have been taken as a sign of 'weakness' by the malcontents instead of an act of ordinary thoughtfulness for their welfare.

Aden was our next stop. Here, according to policy, the very smart officers of the native Indian cavalry regiment were entertained on board by the Commodore. Our date of departure was postponed so that a quite important Arab Sultan could also be welcomed. Next Colombo. Thence Australia.

According to our schedule, Melbourne was to be our next port, where we should have discharged our time-expired men. But it occurred to Dumaresq, in his pursuit of policy, that it might not be a bad idea to look in at Fremantle, to give the inhabitants of Western Australia a chance to see the flagship they had helped to fund. He asked me if I would care to take the ship into this port. I replied that I certainly would, even though there would only be 2 or 3 inches of water under *Australia*, which did not exactly suit a manoeuvring battle cruiser. To Fremantle we went, and secured up to a couple of buoys without difficulty. Here Dumaresq decided to do things well. To this end he obtained from the Melbourne Navy Office a small extra entertainment allowance for the ship, which amounted to some £50 or £70.[15] For their part, the hospitable inhabitants of Perth and Fremantle arranged a truly Australian welcome. Officers and men were fêted to the utmost. We marched round Perth and invited the populace to visit the ship on a certain day and take tea on board. We had no way of gauging the probable number of our guests. That is where the snag came in.

15 Equivalent to £2,750–£3,850 today.

The galley-capacity of the ship was limited so that catering for this tea party was put in the hands of a local firm. We thought that perhaps 2–3,000 people might turn up, and tea on the quarter deck was arranged for these numbers. The local steam ferryboat was hired to transfer such a crowd on board, in return for a small fixed fare. The day arrived – a beautiful day. If 10,000 people got on board that day, another 10,000 only got as far as the steamboat jetty. There was no chance of our tea for 3,000 being extended. At five o'clock the ferry steamers' crews struck for higher wages! Dumaresq had to hoist out the lifeboats to land the crowd. It was only a matter of 100 yards or so, but it was getting on for 9:00 pm when the last boat left the ship.

The Commodore was staying with the Governor of Western Australia. We were scheduled to leave Fremantle when he came aboard at eleven o'clock next day. Perth was some three-quarters of an hour's journey by train from Fremantle, so it was necessary to give leave until the arrival of the first train in the morning at about 9:00 am. Normally leave might have been given to 7:00 or 7:30 am, which did not allow time for liberty men with a slight hangover to imbibe another hurried pint; 9:00 am is a dangerous hour. At 11:00 am the ship was ready for sea. The men were all at their stations with the Commodore momentarily expected and the steam barge ready to bring him. There were no stragglers among the liberty men. But the Commodore was late. We waited a quarter of an hour and then I ordered steam at short notice and fell out all hands. Arriving on the quarterdeck, I noticed a fairly large body of men on the far side. I assumed it was the watch falling in. Then the barge came alongside and Dumaresq, running up the ladder, was full of apologies. His car had broken down on the road and he had had to wait for another one.

On sighting the barge coming off, the Commander of *Australia* had sounded the bugle call for stations for proceeding out of the harbour. Steam had been ordered and 'Ready to proceed' repeated. 'Shall I proceed, Sir?' I asked. 'Yes, whenever you're ready,' Dumaresq answered. I turned to the Commander and asked him about the party on the other side of the quarterdeck, a good few of them still out of the rig-of-the-day and in their Number One rigs such as are worn on leave. Instinctively, I sensed trouble. The Commander reported that a delegation had requested to see me to ask if the stay in Fremantle could be extended. Immediately, I stepped across the deck with the Commander and told the men that I understood what they were there for and that I would not listen to any collective request but if any one person had anything to say he could say it to me.

After a good deal of hesitation, a young fellow replied that he had been asked by his mates to say that the people of Perth had been very kind to them and that the ship's company as a whole felt that it had not had sufficient opportunity to return their hospitality. Would it be possible to postpone sailing so that this might be remedied? I replied, quite quietly, 'No; my orders are to proceed to sea now,' and added that even if I or the Commodore wished to remain here our orders were quite definite and originated from a higher power, to wit the Navy Office. 'Dismiss this party,' I said to Commander Brabant, who thereupon gave the order which was obeyed but not without a bit of noise and remarks such as 'What about the bloody Gyppos?' I realised that this was a reference to the ship's delay at Aden. Imagine an Arab Sultan being referred to as a 'bloody Gyppo'!

I went straight up to the bridge. It was a lovely day. Everybody was at their stations. 'Let's go aft,' I said to the young Lieutenant on watch, who immediately transferred my order to the telephone operator on the bridge. I knew it would take two or three minutes to cut the seizings and take off the turns of heavy wire hawsers holding us to the stern buoy. Suddenly, while I was waiting for the anticipated reply 'All clear aft, Sir', the telephone from the engine room buzzed. I heard the operator answer: 'Oh, what's that? Oh cripes! Here, Sir!' The Officer of the Watch took the mouthpiece. 'What's that?' He turned to me. 'From the Engineer Commander, Sir. Please don't move the engines. The stokers have left the stokehold.'

Luckily, the last big 5-inch hawser was still in place. Puffing and blowing, the Engineer Commander, Llewellyn Howell, arrived on the bridge some 70 feet up and reported that a posse of masked men had entered the boiler rooms and terrorised the stokers on watch into leaving the stokeholds. Only the petty officers were in place. I told the Navigator to look out on the bridge and went down the ladders. Meeting the gunner, a real wise fellow, *en route*, he said: 'I've cleared the pistol racks and locked 'em up in the magazines.' 'Good man,' I answered, went into the Commodore's cabin where he was changing into uniform and reported the matter to him.

'Come on,' said he. 'If there's going to be a riot, let's bog [*sic*] into them.' I replied: 'Sir, your orders are for the ship to go to sea. I shall take her to sea, but thought you ought to know what's going on.' I left him, followed by my good-looking 6-foot Australian coxswain. I strolled aft on the after deck where the majority of 1,000 men were congregated, most of them screaming like a lot of lunatics. I pushed my way in and managed to get myself heard. 'So,' I said, 'this is what I get from a lot of dirty tuppenny-ha'penny bastards who have never seen a shot fired after bringing you 10,000 miles in safety.' I really got down to bedrock. 'I don't need you, and thank God that I'll soon be rid of you miserable half-baked Sydney rats. But the ship goes to sea, here and now.' There was a moment's silence. Then I heard: 'Come on lads. He's Jonnick.[16] What about it, mates?' A scream of beer-laden hatred followed: 'Shut up, you bastard. We'll pull it off. Up the F.I.Fs!'

My very tall, very hard Chief Boatswain had followed me into this horrid collection. I turned to him. 'Pipe Petty Officers fall in on the quarter deck,' I said, and left. I must say that a way was made for me. By now, I had recovered my normal method of quiet speech. All I had said on the after deck was pure acting, although I admit I had enjoyed talking to them in their own colloquialisms. It then took about 20 minutes to replace the poor fools who had left the engine room department, and I returned to the bridge. The Commodore had been splendid, dying for a scrap but never interfering. After perhaps half an hour the Engineer Commander arrived on the bridge and reported ready to proceed.

We edged out of Fremantle harbour with 3 inches of water under our bottom and nearly 1,000 lunatics screaming with beer on the afterdeck. A pretty sight for casual onlookers. Down below, midshipmen and young paymasters were handling the shovels in the boiler rooms. 'What are you going to do now, Sir?' asked the Commander. 'Do?' I said. 'Nothing. Let the bastards sleep it off and let me know when it is seven bells [3:30 pm].' At seven bells I ordered 'Pipe Sweepers.' They appeared and shamefacedly swept the decks. The Commander then reported to me that several of those fallen-in on the quarter deck wanted to have their names taken as having had no part in the mutiny. They were mostly old-fashioned able seamen who had joined the RAN after discharge from the RN. Next, all the leading seamen fell in with a complaint that they had not been summoned when I gave the order for petty officers to fall in on the quarter deck. They were dismissed with a kind word, and an apology for forgetting them in the heat of the moment.

I ordered 'Sound off Quarters'. Everybody turned up; I had never seen the quarter deck so full. As a rule, all sorts would wriggle out of attending these parades. Time went on, the great quarterdeck awning spread over all. It was a beautiful Southern Indian Ocean evening. Commander Brabant and I walked up and down the serried ranks. 'All present and correct,' the Commander reported. I went on walking up and down in the twilight. Usually, the men would begin to shuffle and suck their teeth if kept waiting. Not so this day. Absolute stillness, not a move. What I had expected. After five minutes I seemed to realise that the ship's company was still there. I stopped. 'Midshipman,' I said, 'go up to the bridge and tell the Officer of the Watch

16 Fair. Australian slang 'Jannock'.

to stop engines.' A midshipman ran up the ladder on his errand. We heard the telegraphs clang and felt the movement of the engines cease. The great ship heaved gently. What absolute silence! I turned to my young clerk. 'Get me the Articles of War.' He was gone like a sky rocket and instantly reappeared with the folio. 'Commander, kindly call the ship's company to attention.' He did.

I mounted a raised iron uptake to give me height, and read out the heading, which went something to the effect that this 'is an act for the better guidance' etc etc. I began very profoundly, in measured terms. 'Article Ten: Any Captain, Commanding Officer or Officer in Command of His Majesty's ships who shall not make some endeavour to bring the enemy to action shall suffer … death.' Then I turned over a couple of pages and proceeded, rather casually: 'Article Nineteen. *Any person who shall commit mutiny shall suffer death.*' I clapped the book shut, handed it to the clerk and climbed off my pedestal. I don't ever remember such stillness. I paused perhaps a minute, maybe two. Then I turned to my great, gaunt, hard-bitten Chief Boatswain's Mate, and ordered: 'Pipe the first watch of stokers. Fall in on the after deck.' The long shrill of his pipe broke the silence. Movement in the ranks followed. A moment later, he reported the watch present. 'Follow me,' I said, and walked aft. 'Tell off your Steaming Watch and relieve the officers at their posts, and let me know when you are ready to proceed.' Then I went back to the assembled multitude and, nudging my Commander, walked up and down the ranks for perhaps 20 minutes.

At length, the Engineer Commander arrived and reported that he was ready to proceed. I ordered half speed ahead. We heard the gongs clang, and soon the regular beat of the propellers. 'Sound the Disperse, Commander,' I ordered. The mutiny was over. Mutiny? Ye Gods and little fishes. To call it even a strike would be an exaggeration. The origin of it had been vanity. The war was over. The mood was 'Everybody has told us what damned fine fellows we are. Let's have a bit of fun and show the stay-at-homes it's a fact.' One thing is absolutely certain. Personal violence towards either the officers as a whole or to individual officers was neither attempted nor, probably, envisaged. Nor was any attempt made to interfere with the casting-off of the hawsers. For a day or so the officers felt the disgrace that must attach to the very word 'mutiny'. For myself, I felt composed. I also had the fact up my sleeve that I had actually taken my ship to sea. What troubled me most was that now I had to turn myself into a first-class detective to lay my hands on the organisers of the *bagarre* [brawl].

Dal Rudd, DSM, as shown on the cover of the book *Mutineers*

We set about the matter methodically. We knew which men had been in the stokeholds and who had left them. We had the leave books, which showed who had been on leave that morning. Through their petty officers, we were able to eliminate all deck hands who had remained at their stations. We were thus able to boil things down to five men in liberty men's clothes, with black handkerchiefs tied round their faces, as the ones who had rushed into the stokeholds and terrorised those working there. The rest was fairly easy, especially as one of the stoker petty officers recalled that one of the masked brigade had worn a distinct medal ribbon. It was a Distinguished Service Medal. He was a Zeebrugge[17] hero! This man now had a swelled head combined with a natural instinct for trouble.

17 The Zeebrugge Raid on 23 April 1918 was an attempt by the Royal Navy to block the Belgian port of Bruges-Zeebrugge by sinking obsolete ships as blockships in the canal entrance, to prevent German vessels from leaving port. Eight Victoria Crosses were awarded. But in 1931 the official war historian wrote that the ships had been sunk in the wrong position and the canal had been obstructed for only a few days.

He was Irish in origin.[18] His brother, out of family loyalty, was one of his assistants. A third was a half-caste Māori, rather a jolly boy;[19] I knew him quite well by sight. The other two hangers-on[20] were nondescripts and uninteresting. These five gents were locked up with a view to court martial. The remaining 50 or 60 implicated in being absent and leaving their place of duty were dealt with summarily.[21]

The HMAS *Australia* mutineers (*Mutineers* book)

We steamed to Melbourne. There one evening, an elderly couple were shown into my cabin. They were the parents of 'Pitta' Thompson, the half-caste. They had not come to try to beg off their son; I have had some fairly difficult moments dealing with parents, sweethearts and wives of my men. The Captain of a ship acts as a local Justice of the Peace or Magistrate as part of his ordinary duty – to say nothing of acting as King's Proctor,[22] stockbroker, solicitor, registrar and (last, but not least) as a sort of de-surpliced 'Divine'. But if many of these complications were entirely humorous, others sordid and some pathetic, this one was poignant in its pathos. The father and mother felt their boy had brought disgrace on their family. I did my best to comfort them, and felt it was useless. The father knew the story, and knew his boy must be punished. He, clearly feeling the weight of a father's responsibility, had come to ask his son's captain's pardon for himself, not for his boy.

The court martial took place on 20 June 1919 in *Encounter* in Sydney harbour. I was the prosecutor. I charged the men with 'joining in a mutiny' rather than with definite mutiny. The former was a much less serious offence than the latter. The accused had chosen a bum little red rag politician[23] as 'prisoners' friend'. This man had wit enough to plead guilty for the lot. He having done so, the Court was cleared.[24] While waiting for the Court to open, I sent a chit to the 'prisoners' friend' reminding him that there would be an opportunity to call witnesses to previous good conduct, if any, of the accused as soon as the Court re-opened, and saying that if he so wished, he might call me on behalf of young Thompson. He did, with the result that the prisoners got two years' hard labour except for Thompson, who got one year.[25]

---

18 Dalmorton Rudd. His brother was Lenny Rudd. A full account of their involvement can be read in *Mutineers* by Robert Hadler, published in Australia in 2021 by Wilkinson Publishing. Dal Rudd was awarded a DSM for his part in the Zeebrugge Raid.

19 This was Wilfred 'Pitta' Thompson. He was often mistaken as being of Māori origin. In fact his great-grandfather had emigrated to Australia from the Cape Verde islands, off the west coast of Africa. He was 5 feet 1inch tall with striking black hair and brown eyes.

20 Bill McIntosh and Ken Paterson. McIntosh was a biscuit-maker from Melbourne: Paterson was a childhood friend of the Rudds, and they had grown up in neighbouring suburbs of Sydney. Paterson had always wanted to go to sea and had a good service record.

21 Summary Hearings and the role of the commanding officer are at the heart of British military discipline and remain the mechanism by which most offences are addressed. Personnel dealt with at a Summary Hearing have the right to appeal to a Summary Appeal Court.

22 A king's proctor was an officer of the judiciary in England who could intervene in actions for divorce, chiefly to prevent collusive proceedings.

23 Dick Orchard, a National Party Member of Parliament and former Sydney jewellery salesman. A larger-than-life character, he had won a reputation in the First World War as the Soldier's Friend by visiting battlefields in France in 1916 and campaigning against harsh living conditions.

24 The President of the Court was Commodore John Glossop, then Captain-in-Charge of Naval Establishments, Sydney. In 1914 Glossop had directly commanded Cumberlege during the RAN wireless station action in New Guinea.

25 This is not quite accurate. Dal Rudd got 18 months, Lenny Rudd got two years, Bill McIntosh got two years with hard labour, and Paterson and Thompson each got one year.

The Australian MP Dick Orchard (PD)

With some relief, I unbuckled my sword as I walked away. Suddenly, I felt someone pluck my sleeve. I looked down into the face of the politician. ''Ere, d'you mind if I tell you [that] you've got me fair beat? I came aboard this ship, for the first time in my life, expecting a sort of super inquisition and vindictiveness, and what do I find? No sooner has the prosecutor finished prosecuting than damn my eyes if he don't turn round and put in a good word for the blighters. If that ain't justice, search me!' I was told later that he held forth in this fashion in the wardroom, over cold gin and water, and finished up by tearing off his red tie and jumping on it. '*Ben trovato, si non e vero*.'[26] The law, at any rate, had been upheld. Our yard arm had been cleared.

I shall always regard the whole episode as no more than a sort of schoolboy escapade. I was quite unconcerned when, a year later, a Labour government released the prisoners. Shortly after this [release] occurred, I happened to be walking along Elizabeth Street in Sydney when a decently-dressed man, looking across the road at me, raised his hat. Not being able to place him, I returned the salute and stepped across the road. He held out his hand, which I took, and said: 'You don't remember me, Sir. My name's Rudd.' It was the ex-hero of Zeebrugge! We stepped inside and 'stopped a couple' [of beers].

In writing these memories I questioned myself if I ought even to mention such a word as 'mutiny'. But I think I have done the right thing. There is no doubt that this episode had an ineradicable influence on my future naval career. It will be observed that I have not attempted to excuse or belaud participants in the matter. It is, indeed, more than probable that if nothing of this sort had ever taken place that I might have become the possessor of a cocked hat.[27] Be that as it may. I was able to wash my hands of the whole affair.

26 Even if it is not true, it is well conceived.

27 The bicorne hat worn on ceremonial occasions by admirals in the Royal Navy until at least the First World War.

CHAPTER 13

With John Dumaresq 1919 1921

Cumberlege remained in the RAN after the war, and spent much of the next three years working closely with John Dumaresq, who became head of the Australian Fleet in March 1919.

My Commodore, who about now was promoted to Rear Admiral, developed his eternal policies with unrelaxed fervour. *Australia* was relegated to the scrap heap in 1921, this and that ship were put out of commission, and the 'fleet' by now could have been run by an honest signal boatswain and a signal pad. Yet the Gunnery Lieutenant, Navigator, Chaplain and Bandmaster were closeted for hours with the high authority. In Sydney, Labour members of the municipality swilled his wines and ate his grub, carefully prepared by my admirable steward, who had replaced the Admiral's, who had returned to England. How I wished that steward's austere presence had been beside me in place of the time-serving grafters that the policy demanded be entertained.

Dumaresq was a sick man. The papers mounted in piles on his desk. His secretary sighed with relief when he had to go to Melbourne; I would spend two days signing off months of stuff. *Australia* had to be vacated; we moved to *Melbourne*, a light cruiser. The chief engineer and the Commander saw their opportunity to quit. I ought to have done, and become another failure, but I liked the little man. After all, it was no concern of mine if he cared to stay up to the small hours flogging out policies which led nowhere. It *did* concern me, though, and I realised that the Admiral was unwell – it did not require the evidence of a pocket handkerchief I had lent him once on some official occasion which he used to wipe away blood from his lungs. I had it every day from the hacking cough in his sleeping cabin. Burning with internal fires, he must have known that he only had a short time. Knowing it, he tried to beat the Man with the Scythe to get what he considered his duty done in time.

Claude Cumberlege in 1920
(Family collection)

Once, we were at Sydney. There was literally nothing to do that could not have been done by his enthusiastic staff. I used all my tact and discretion to get him to take a rest – a few hours' motor journey into the Blue Mountains. I talked to him about their beauties, I tried to insinuate them into the policy. 'You must see them,' I said. 'Go up and take a stretch off the land.' Not he. It might have delayed the inevitable. Nor would he ever have a word with a doctor. Was it fear? No! A more fearless man I never knew.

There were moments when he became boisterous. On one occasion, he stroked a veterans' six-oared galley in a race, a mad thing to do in his condition. It was a case of having a policy to demonstrate a fitness he did not have. More often, he just looked ill. If he went ashore for some official call, he would land and go to his flat where his invalid wife lived. He would be back at his desk by 10:00 pm to pore over those damned official papers. He did, however, have one definite relaxation. He loved music and seldom missed a Thursday at the Conservatorium.[1] After these visits, it was a pleasure to sit with him. Music was about the only topic he ever allowed at table to interfere with his endless references to his pet 'policies'. He had no library worthy of the name; Mahan's *Influence of Sea Power over History* was the only book I saw him read. My ribald quotations from W.S. Gilbert struck no answering chord. I don't believe he had ever read the Book of Isaiah. The painting art came only to him as a policy. 'Yes, yes,' he would say, tapping the table cloth. 'Flag Lieutenant, you must make a list of Australian artists we ought to have to lunch. My policy, as you know ...' Oh, help!

As a host, he was lavish in his hospitality. This generosity, beyond his entertainment allowance, was not confined to 'tosspots' nor to his personal friends, but covered every sort of society. All part of the policy. At his private parties he became, often enough, quite breezy. Maybe this, too, was part of policy; sailors are proverbially breezy. With young people, breeziness was the order of the day, and he was cyclonic. I saw him galloping round his cabin on all fours, snarling and growling and pretending to bite the pretty ankles of young things for 20 minutes on end. A very droll and unexpected sight, if a trifle embarrassing after the first few minutes.

Sydney provided every sort of sport in our leisure hours, and there was always the harbour, the most popular playground for all the *citoyens* – a wonderful sight on a summer's Saturday. What parties and dances there were in private houses and at Mrs. MacLurcan's Wentworth Hotel.[2] We had parties on *Australia* on an almost weekly basis, and were very fortunate in our Bandmaster, Mr. Ventry, who had had the greater part of his band with him in the ship for seven years and organised a dance band, playing soft music between each

Above: Wentworth Hotel, Sydney, at the time of the Prince of Wales's visit (PD)

Right: Capt. Cumberlege (right of Prince of Wales; John Dumaresq on left) on HMAS *Australia* 1920 (AWM)

1 The Sydney Conservatorium of Music dates from 1913 and is a heritage-listed music school in Macquarie Street. Located adjacent to the Royal Botanic Gardens on the eastern fringe of the Sydney central business district, today it is a faculty of the University of Sydney.

2 Hannah Maclurcan (1860–1936) published her first book, *Mrs Maclurcan's Cookery Book: A Collection of Practical Recipes, Specially Suitable for Australia*, at Townsville in 1898. In England, she published *The 20th Century Cookery Book: A Thousand Practical Recipes for Everyday Use* in 1901. That year Hannah and her husband assumed the lease of the Wentworth Hotel on Church Hill, Sydney, in time to capitalise on the visit of the Duke and Duchess of York in 1901. In 1920, after the acquisition of adjoining property, 'a palatial ballroom' decorated 'in the style of the Georgian period' and able to accommodate 1,000 dancers and diners, was built; the ballroom was a favourite haunt of the Prince of Wales when he was in Sydney in 1920. 'Madame' retired as hotel manager in 1932

Claude with daughter Diana in Australia 1919–20 (Family collection)

number. In 1920 His Royal Highness the Prince of Wales came out in the battleship *Renown*.[3] We saw a lot of him at official functions, and what a welcome he got! He was always late for functions owing to enthusiastic crowds holding up his car. There's something in the seaside air that makes Sydney folk less reserved than those in other parts of the continent. Not that 'reserve' is particularly noticeable anywhere. One Christmas we took a flat in Manly. A real party was going on below us. On the third night, the proprietors asked me to try to stop the riot below. I went in in my pyjamas and was at once given a glass of 'pop' [beer] and the empty bottle was hurled out of the window onto the sidewalk below. Next day someone came up to express their regrets that we should have been disturbed and invited us to an evening séance, which we gladly accepted.[4]

Melbourne was not always at Sydney. Economy was the order of the day, but we did manage to make one long cruise in the Pacific, visiting the smaller settlements whenever we could find a suitable anchorage. When I write 'we', I mean the flagship, HMAS *Melbourne;* there wasn't enough fuel to go round to take everybody. The main idea of the Admiral was to bring home to these distant inhabitants that an Australian Navy did exist. Wherever we stayed – the islands of the Western Pacific, Vani Koro in the Solomon Islands, the New Hebrides, Norfolk Island, Pitcairn Island, Lord Howe Island – we had the warmest of welcomes, and met all sorts of interesting folk.

There were humorous moments. When we landed in our best clothes at one remote wharf a group of labourers hardly gave us a passing glance. This was too thick for the policy; the Admiral turned back and,

3 In 1920 the Prince of Wales visited Australia on behalf of his father, King George V. The visit was to thank the Australian people officially for the sacrifices and contributions made during the First World War. The prince visited many cities and towns across Australia, and his popularity was such that he became known as the 'digger prince' – a great compliment from a nation that held its returned servicemen and women in high regard. The prince, however, quickly tired of Australia and never returned.

4 CLC makes no direct mention in this memoir of the months-long 1919–20 period when his wife Laetitia and daughter Diana (then aged nine) lived with him in Sydney.

Claude Cumberlege visiting a gaol in NSW in 1919, where German prisoners of war were held (Macleay River Historical Society)

in his quick, earnest manner of speaking, said to those men: 'Good morning, good morning. I thought you might like to know that I'm the Admiral in command of the Royal Australian Navy. It's my policy to get in touch ...' and quite a lot more. This was Greek to his listeners. Somebody said: 'Come from the war boat?' Another added: 'Fine day, ain't it,' and one, I think, muttered 'Cripes.' That was it.

Once, the Admiral, a non-smoker, told me that I smoked too much. This rather surprised me. He went on to say that he thought he should have to call the attention of the Lords of the Admiralty to his conviction, I responded: 'By all means, and you might add that I've smoked incessantly since the age of 18 and I hope to do so until the limit set by the Psalmist. And it might interest them to know that I was once in hospital with a dislocated knee gained at football.' On another occasion on a wonderful island – gold would not tempt me to give the place away – I found ranks of six-foot-fourers (I am 6 feet in my socks) at my sides; one pressed my forearm against his naked ribs. We came face to face with a golden goddess; our jolly giants presented us to her. She was 'Mai'. A wisp of black straw smote the eye, but that was all. Her perfectly circular thighs ran up to sand-papered hips. Sweet-scented flowers, threaded like jasmine fell between two rosy geranium-tinted breasts, round as apples but no bigger than an orange pippin. No horrid betel nut had stained her pentelikon teeth,[5] shining with good health between full Burgundian lips.

On our visit to Pitcairn Island, it was a glorious, bright sunny day with a fresh breeze into a 70-yard-wide gap which led to a small lagoon surrounded by rocks under low cliffs. There was a small stone landing jetty. I called for my sailing galley, a 30-foot gig, painted black with a white underbelly and two red standing lugsails. She had a six-man crew including Hutchings, my coxswain. We hoisted the sails. The barrier reef was well indicated by the regular but gentle swell breaking in white foam on each side of the entrance passage.

5 'Pentelikon' refers to a famous Greek mountain consisting mainly of white marble.

Just as we were approaching this gap at high speed, I caught sight of my coxswain's face. He was sitting in the bottom of the boat with the mainsheet in his hand, facing me and looking aft. I realised something unusual must be occurring behind me. I looked round.

Oh my God and little fishes! I saw, 20 yards astern, a veritable cathedral of water following us. It was the one Pacific roller of the day. If I had had time, I should have turned up into it. Such a manoeuvre was out of the question. Just as we entered the gap, the toppling crest curled over and the whole mass of water broke. In an instant, our stern was flung into the air. I found myself looking down a steep descent of crashing, tearing foam. The sails were loosely flapping. The whaler was flying at up to 30 mph straight at the rocks and cliffs not 100 yards ahead. All I could do was to keep the boat straight. Surf-riding, nothing more or less. Ahead, those jagged rocks. Twenty yards to go. Something had to be done. I jammed the tiller hard down. Better to be rolled over, I thought, than to hit those terrific cliffs. The lovely boat spun on the rudder. The foaming sea literally slid under us and crashed in a 50-foot deluge of spray. It was the only roller of the 24 hours. Nothing followed. I stepped out onto the stone pier crowded with islanders, my cigarette still burning. A hundred spectators, divested of their clothes and ready to plunge to our rescue, gasped. Once more, I had 'bluffed the eternal sea'.[6]

Next day, I happened to be walking on the island and met a local. We passed the time of day. 'Did you see the way that bloke brought his boat in yesterday? They tell me he was the skipper of the ship. Came in under sail, a thing we never do in the whale boats. You never know when a big wave will break. We always turn and face it before entering the gap. He came slap in on a big breaker and laid his boat alongside the wall. He wouldn't have cracked an egg. Thirty years I've been in the whale boats and I've never seen such a thing done before.' Very encouraging, but it was all pure luck.

In Nouméa, New Caledonia, I spotted an old-fashioned yawl flying the blue ensign. She belonged to a Lt. Muhlhauser RNR,[7] who was sailing around the world. He describes in his book[8] how one of my smart young officers (Lt. Collins) had boarded him soon after our arrival and told him that if he needed my help all he had to do was to say so. At the time, he was in a filthy state, in the middle of pulling his auxiliary engine to pieces, and rather nonplussed at having to receive an officer in his condition. However, putting on his best clothes and coming on board next morning, he was shown into my cabin. A few minutes later, I entered from my bathroom in my birthday suit.[9] About three weeks later in Sydney we met again, and I saw a lot of him and his boat *Amaryllis*. Some years later, I received a line from him at my club in London to say that he would

George Muhlhauser RNR (PD)

Captain Muhlhauser's yacht *Amaryllis* (PD)

6 From Kipling's 'The Ballad of the *Bolivar*.'

7 Temporary Lieutenant RNR George Henry Pasche Muhlhauser served in the Royal Naval Reserve in Q ships (armed trawlers) in the First World War. He left to sail round the world after the war, and died suddenly in 1923. In the introduction to his book, he is described by a friend as 'rugged, honest, straight-to-the-point … one of the finest seamen who ever sailed under the blue ensign.' His meeting with Cumberlege in Noumea is described in similar detail to that in this book. An hour was spent that morning swapping sea stories; Cumberlege, he wrote, had a 'great reputation'.

8 *The Cruise of the Amaryllis*, John Lane, 1924.

9 The night before, the officers of HMAS *Melbourne* had been entertained onshore by the French colonial officers. They did not return to the ship until 4:00 am.

Captain Cumberlege at his desk (Family collection)

Captain Cumberlege relaxing in his office (Family collection)

like to see me to tell me about the second half of his world trip, but for the moment he had had to go into a nursing home for 'a slight operation'. I answered at once to say that I was coming to visit him immediately, but I was too late. He had already set out on the endless voyage to the unknown. More than a decade later, *Amaryllis* was still going strong in the keeping of the Royal Navy at Dartmouth, thanks to a gift from his sister.

Back in Sydney, it was full of fun as usual. One cannot tire of Sydney and yet, somehow, I felt it was time to cut my stick. I felt a little out of place. I was now a fairly senior Post Captain – too senior to be a Flag Captain, and long past the customary two years in command of the flagship. Yet I hesitated to instigate proceedings. I liked the Admiral but, at the same time, had realised practically from the start that I was of little use to him; he had no need of a Flag Captain. Fortunately, the word came from him in the first instance. That was a great relief. He had asked me to come. Now he asked me to go. What was at the back of his mind, I never thought to find out. He worked out the lay [situation] that I was well over my time as Flag Captain and that a younger man from the RAN ought to have the opportunity. The policy crept in from there.

All that was necessary to say on the subject might have been said in one word for all that it concerned me. My yard arm was square. It did not need the presence of the imperturbable, but temporarily embarrassed, secretary who had been called in as a witness – not that I objected to his presence. Like the sailor who 'limited his remarks seeing as how there were ladies present', I retired, instantly to reappear with a written request that I might be ordered a passage to England in the first available steamer. A fortnight later, I had sailed for home.[10]

Within a few months my Admiral was dead.[11] In his case *de mortuis nil nisi bonum* ['of the dead say nothing but good'] is an easy motto; he knew no evil. John Dumaresq – I doubt anyone other than his parents ever thought of him by his first name – saw his way clear in life. Most naval officers,

10 At the start of the First World War the RAN had 18 ships and 3,800 personnel of whom 850 came from the RN. By end of 1918 it had 37 ships and 5,000 personnel. In 1922 Cumberlege was one of the last RN officers to return to the UK.

11 John Dumaresq was posted back to the Royal Navy in April 1922. On the return journey from Australia he contracted pneumonia, and he died in the US Military Hospital in Manila, the Philippines, on 22 July.

very rightly, have 'one eye on the main chance' – by which I mean that while they may have the service at heart, the heart is generally sufficiently capacious to include the ordinary humanities. Dumaresq, however, suppressed all outside sentiments. The Navy obsessed his every faculty and filled his life. Recreation, sport, parenthood, every ordinary virtue, to say nothing of mild vices, were nowhere. His policy was directed for the good of the service. His clear and active brain was like the beam of a searchlight in Stygian gloom.

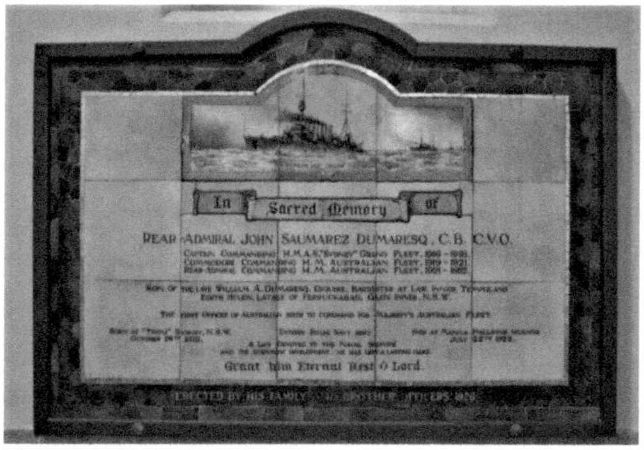

The Dumaresq memorial plaque in Manila, the Philippines (PD)

Physically, Dumaresq was Nelsonic, yet I cannot see him penning a letter such as Nelson did at Trafalgar, and I cannot see him losing his heart to a modern Emma. His intense concentration on policy would not have allowed such a dalliance. As one who lived with him in fair weather and foul, cheek-by-jowl, at every meal, for hours each day, through years not months, I concluded that no clearer or more perfectly-concentrated mind was ever stowed away in one cranium. His curse was ill-health; he merely kidded himself that he was well, and he died of disease of the lungs. Was he a genius? I don't know. The opportunity to show it never developed. Maybe he was just my 'B.F.' [Best Friend]. I really do not know. Possibly the latter. I cannot imagine myself being fond of a genius.

One of the pleasantest pastimes I know is to take a long sea voyage as a passenger in a mail steamer, particularly if one is a professional sailor. A busman's holiday. No responsibilities. No Captain's defaulters, no papers to sign, no guns to go off, no torpedoes to lose, no next ahead, no next astern, no finding fault, no hot air. And on this trip, we had a flat calm from Australia to England. It was early December 1921. We anchored in Cawsand Bay, Plymouth, on a still December night with a full moon. We went on up the Channel and landed at Tilbury. I commenced leave on six months' full pay, which was a very handsome parting present by a generous country which I had had the honour to serve for nearly seven years – Australia. *Conjunctis viribus* – 'with united power'.

I lunched that day at the Hyde Park Hotel grill room. At my club, the main topic of conversation was about the [RN] retirements. Large numbers of my near-contemporaries had already been chucked out.[12] Everybody, I think, saw the necessity of this move at the time, although a good many wondered why 'old so and so' had been kept on and they had not. I had no notion what the procedure was in carrying out this policy but, on the well-established principle that no one is indispensable in this world, it might have been as hit-and-miss as a draw by an office boy out of a hat. Eventually, I received a charming letter from the Secretary of the Admiralty offering me either a couple of hundred pounds[13] a year extra pension to quit at once, or to stay on half pay and be automatically retired at the end of a couple of years in accordance with the regulations. It is not true that I rushed to the post office and accepted the first proposition by telegram in case they altered it. I certainly would not have left at that point if I had thought there might be a chance of further employment. I was, however, fully aware that, being a young,[14] if senior, Post Captain, I would, under

12 For the Royal Navy the end of the war meant a serious cutback in funding; whereas in the 1918/19 Naval Estimates it was allocated about £165 million, in the 1919/20 Estimates this had dropped to a little over £50 million.

13 Worth about £12,000 today.

14 Cumberlege was 44 or 45 when the offer to retire was made to him.

the conditions in the Royal Navy at the time, be a very serious block over many years to younger officers. But that knowledge, too, had nothing to do with my choice; they also chucked out youngsters and reduced the fleet to the point where it could be, and was, pooh-poohed by sturdy-minded gangsters.[15] Now [in 1938] I wonder if they will ask those not-quite-so-young fellows to come back, since the country has seen its mistake. Yet it takes nine or ten years to make a fully-trained officer. As for myself in 1922, I simply did the best that I could in the circumstances, and have never regretted the step.

15 Hitler and Mussolini.

Part Two
Living on his Wits
1922–1963

CHAPTER 14

On *L'Insoumise* 1922–1924

During the next dozen years, after a short false start in England, Cumberlege led a peripatetic life on two boats, haunting the coasts of northern France, south-west France and the Mediterranean.

When sailors leave the sea, some walk inland with an oar over a shoulder until someone round Cheltenham asks 'What is that?' He settles for a life of bridge. Others go all nautical, call their house 'Moorings' and let off brass cannons on the Glorious First[1] because they once served in the same fleet as a famous admiral. Others, poor devils, degenerate to Parliament; this type is also to be found in *Who's Who*. For my part, I unearthed a stable cottage in Henley, ten paces from the waterside, built in the reign of William and Mary with a loft beam that came from Chatham dockyard dated 1797. I took the place for three years,

It was raining very hard when I went into residence on December 10th 1921. On 22nd December the sun was shining and the world was white. My train wheezed to a silent standstill at Sallanches in the Haute-Savoie. I got off, and the silence was broken by the iron tones of a great bell. Lesser tinklings rushed in to help, and the air was filled with the banging of bells. The auberge of the Three Pigeons looked good. Andrée, the pretty proprietor, looked charming but desolate. Her house was full. She offered me a bed in the kitchen for a day or two. I persuaded her to let me have the 'middle pigeon' – her room – not for ten days but for four months.

It was only when the village roads showed through their winter ice that I remembered my stable on the banks of the Thames and went home. By then it was May. And what a May – perfect, glorious weather! I acquired a sailing punt with boxed-in lee boards and a great red sail. One day I crashed it into Hambledon Lock, spun the craft and came to rest alongside the wall without cracking an egg. The lock keeper, in the healthy evening of his days, sternly told me I could not do that. ' 'Gainst the rules.' I learnt that he had been a Royal Marine who had sailed in the old battleship *Canopus*. 'Beer?' I said, and off we went and had a couple of pints. Not long after, somebody gave me the hull of a coastal motor boat of the Maple Leaf type. It occurred to me that if I put a small engine in I could amble about the smooth water of the river at 3 or 4 knots. I looked around the river banks for a place to haul her up, and found a hayfield near a bathing establishment. It was not difficult to make friends. The proprietor of the baths was an ex-Able Seaman; I was made welcome and I hauled the boat up there. She was very large, about 35 feet in length, weighing about 2 tons and built of sewn mahogany. Eventually, I got her out of the water. Then I found a carpenter – an enormous jewel of a man with a high-pitched voice. He took up a lot of time telling me his tales. But by June, the work was done.

1 The Glorious First of June (1 June 1794), also known as the Fourth Battle of Ushant, was the first and largest fleet action of the naval conflict between Great Britain and the First French Republic during the French Revolutionary Wars.

CLC back in England in 1922 with Diana and a cat (Family collection)

Friends from all sorts of places came to my stables. One brought 30 more friends with him. June and early July passed, along with the regatta, and then I went seafaring. First, on the Broads in a wherry. Then *en automobile.* My friends decided they wished to buy a yacht. Early on, I spotted a shallow-draught craft with tip-top accommodation, 80 feet long with twin engines, in Cowes. We went to pretty well to every port in the United Kingdom before returning to the Isle of Wight. Off we then went in the craft to the Channel Islands and Deauville and up the Seine to Paris – a delightful trip. Here I left, and set off to visit French ports in my own search for a ship. I longed for a Fécamp ketch, but they were much too big. The smaller craft, such as French luggers, didn't appeal. I found nothing to suit me, and got as far north as Calais. I was thinking of going to Holland when I met a friend who was sailing his boat to Ostend. I went with him. I found my ship at Ostend.

Going over a bridge at the head of the harbour, I saw a couple of big ketches lying alongside the wall and evidently out of commission. From their watchman I learnt that the Belgian government, having gone into steam for its pilot service, was selling them at auction. A small notice at the police station notified the interested public that *Loodsboots* [pilot boats] No. 17 and No. 7 would be auctioned on 24th November. It was now the end of September. I sailed for England and went over to Ostend on 23rd November. Next day the auction was held in a big room of an old pub. Some 30–40 men, seemingly connected with fishing, were there, and a sprinkling of Dutch businessmen. The ship masters were there, too, thinking they could turn the ketches into fishing vessels. The business types had scented copper. I had selected No. 17, but there was practically no difference between the two. No. 17 was first up. Small amounts were offered but I hung fire, thinking No. 7 would be even cheaper. No. 17 went to a Dutchman with flap ears and a billycock. The bids for No. 7 began slowly. I bid and was immediately capped. Up and up went the price. There was an atmosphere, I felt, of 'the Englishman knows something'. I didn't, and dropped out. An Ostend fisherman got the boat for double the price of the first one.

I was left without a ship. *Que faire?* I singled out the new owner of No. 17. 'I should like to make you an offer, but I must have an answer here and now as I'm unable to remain in Ostend.' I offered him 3,000 more francs than he had paid for her. He hardly hesitated. It was quite good business for him. We shook hands. Number 17 was mine. I hurried on board in the November dusk. 'Good God,' I thought. 'I haven't got a yacht. I'm the owner of a *ship*.' I paced 20 *feet* of quarterdeck beam. Next morning, I passed over my cheque for £170 3s 9d.[2] I went ashore and had a bottle of wine and longed for the day.

What a ship! All oak and teak and copper. I found her plans in the spacious after-cabin. She had lovely lines and had never been built to carry cargo. I just wandered about her. There was filthy water in the well; risking typhoid, I tasted it. Fresh, not salt, water. Good. I found two huge solid bronze pumps on deck, pumped her dry and did not touch those pumps again for six months. I decided to start work on the after-

2 Worth about £9,900 today.

Below deck in the main saloon in *L'Insoumise* in 1924 (Family collection)

cabin so I could live in it and save hotel expenses. There were two big boxed-in berths with sliding doors, an oak table, settees with lockers. It looked as though she had come back one day from shedding pilots, been paid off and locked up. I roped in Bicky – anyone who knew Ostend in the 1920s knew Bicky: retired Commander John Bickford RN. We set about demolishing the cavernous bunds [water tanks] with axe and crowbar, piling the debris on the forecastle. It was grand fun. It did not take long. I hired a carpenter, and inside sheathing with hanging cupboards was soon in place. I bought a full-sized double bed, a complete set of copper navigation lights and a standard compass very cheaply out of a large sailing ship which was being broken up at Ghent. As early as possible, I started to live in the after-cabin, usually dining on shore. It was wonderfully comfortable in this roomy cabin with its huge four-poster.

Just forward of the after-cabin there were two big bays, one on each side of the ship. Here I found a large number of sails. Forward of this was the vast saloon; it was fitted with no less than 16 box bunks with sliding doors in two tiers of four each side. In the middle was a huge sort of box at table height containing water tanks, chain lockers, paint and so on. I demolished the whole lot. Bunks, lockers, bulkhead, bays, all went by the board. In the end I had a great barn of a compartment about 30 feet in length and 21 feet wide with over 6 feet 3 inches under the beams, all ventilated by a massive teak skylight with windows all round. A broad staircase led to the upper deck through a teak companion hatch; there were also a water closet and two single-berth cabins. The engine room was aft of the ladder. I arranged the saloon very simply with a 6-foot settee on each side flanked by large floor-to-deck wardrobes. I covered the oaken inner skin with three-ply mahogany. The bulkheads at each end were finished in mahogany. The ship's ballast had been sold separately, but I was pleased to discover that 15 tons of beautiful pig iron ballast had been overlooked in the centre compartment of the hold. Meanwhile Pieter installed himself as watchman. He was a dear old chap – a fisherman all his life. His passion was brass-work. Day and night, he scoured and burnished, bringing to light the heavy fittings of hatchways. He spoke little, but his words meant a lot. Another Pieter joined up. Pieter number two was a boatswain of sailing ships by trade. A rigger, his work was perfect. Three-inch wire was like silk in his hands. Then there were two young carpenters.

Winter set in and work on deck was not much fun. I took the train for the Three Pigeons. A wonderful change. No ships, no water. No noise other than the deep-toned bell. Andrée was no longer desolated. The great white mountain hung over the auberge. With turned-up planks on my feet, I ranged the mountains with French friends, sometimes for days on end. Over in Chamonix, I met and made friends with Alfred Couttet, a splendid Savoyard guide, and Edgar Bernheim, a Lyons silk merchant, and a second guide, Andre Farini. We pored over maps and planned the most alarming tours. Couttet and Farini, both about 30 and born smugglers, had deserted from their regiment, the Chasseurs Alpins, after the Armistice. It was January 15th 1923. We set out to make the circuit of Mont Blanc. By 2:00 pm we were within 45 minutes of the Col du Bonhomme and its two-storeyed refuge. The sun was shining in a cloudless sky. Over the Col from the south rushed a great ragged black cloud. In a few moments we were enveloped in a tornado of wind and snow. We reached the Col and took shelter behind some rocks. It was impossible to see more than a yard or so. We searched methodically for the hut, but no one found it. With very little daylight left, we dug a hole about 7 feet deep backed by a rock wall, and stowed ourselves in our hole for the night. We lit a fire from old wood we had found, and thawed our big bottles of red wine. Time passed quickly and in the greatest cheerfulness. Inspecting our provisions, we chose a menu and at 8:00 pm began a feast. The omelette was superb. We always carried uncooked eggs on these expeditions.

We didn't sleep – we yarned and yarned. I cheered them with stories of Pacific Island beaches and sunlit blue lagoons. At six o'clock next morning we ate lard and had a large tot of brandy. Half an hour later, the snow stopped; we climbed out of the hole. A beautiful sunrise greeted us. And there, not 150 yards away, was a large two-storeyed building; one of our tracks showed we had passed it at no more than ten paces! 'Leave the mountains alone in bad weather' ran a steel-cut warning carved into the jagged barriers around the refuge.

We were all glad to see a wisp of smoke from a cottage in the first village we reached. After some discussion, we were welcomed in and given beds and a truly wonderful meal. On we went, and stayed the next night at a small inn in Courmayeur.

On the road to Aosta in Italy we got on a rickety autobus. On arrival in the town, we sensed that something was wrong. Antagonistic placards everywhere. Communists! Fascists! Death to this! Up with that! We went to a café; 'No Politics Here' was chalked on a board. Farini, the young devil, started crooning 'La Bandera Rossa' ('The Red Flag'). In an instant, the café was in violent uproar. Nobody suspected us. For five minutes there was utter pandemonium. Suddenly, it all died down.

We trekked on. Through the Italian Alps. Italy into Switzerland, Switzerland back into France. From the little village of Argentière at the foot of a glacier we buzzed along the iced road with our jackets hauled out like topmast stunsails to the dead fair gale over a dozen or so kilometres to brilliant, cosy Chamonix. As pretty a promenade as is to be found; six days going in all, which would have been five had it not been for our night in a snow hole.

March 1923 came, and the snow slipped off the sunny side of the copper Byzantine cupola of the church in Sallanches, and the roofs dripped, which reminded me there was lots of water elsewhere. In my absence, all had been very well with the ship. I bought 30 tons of iron ballast out of the hulk of an old trawler and had it transferred to my hold. The saloon bulkheads were finished, the settees and wardrobes built in. I set about the forward end, making a comfortable single-berth cabin on the port side with a passage past it to the galley. This left about three-quarters of the width of the ship to make a large cabin with a big double bed on the starboard side and a door into the saloon. The forecastle – a huge place fitted for a four-man crew – the forepeak, a space for canvas and the [anchor] chain lockers followed. All very simple and straightforward. I was spending about £20[3] a month on this work, doing it out of income. I

3 Worth about £1,300 today.

thought it better fun and much less expensive than golf. There was little to interest me in Henley; I made a present of my cottage to my friend the Able Seaman owner of the baths. Society, or at least County Society, was not my line, although I called on the county for all sorts of innocent pleasures. What woods! What bluebells like blue low-lying mists! And the River.

In Ostend, work progressed slowly. I could not afford more hands and, anyhow, it was enjoyable. I had many visitors. Once, a fine yacht came into port, barque-rigged, exquisite. A man hailed me and asked me the name of the 'sturdy-looking ship' I was fitting out. 'To tell you the truth,' I answered, 'she hasn't got one.' Another time an old gentleman, who looked devilish critical to me, told me that he had commanded the ship for 12 years. 'Get her down to 10 foot 6 aft and 7 foot forward,' he said. 'It took me three years to trim her, but when I got her right she was the fastest ship that ever sailed out of Flushing. She'd go round off the wind on her heel in as short a space as she would across it, as handy as a tug boat. Mynheer, you have a wonderful ship. Take her out into the Western Ocean, blow it never so hard – have no fear. Haul down your mizen [mizzen], lash your staysail amidships, take one reef in your mainsail, lash your helm down, go down to your cabin and drink beer.' His speech filled me with joy.

I had found quantities of sail stowed in the sail locker and two bays – jibs of all sizes, two staysails, a brand-new storm staysail, a couple of mainsails, two mizens and a square and triangular topsail. Some had never been used. I also found two complete sets of blocks, all for running rigging with roller bearings. I put in wheel-steering and was lucky to find a new double-threaded set of gear made for a steam trawler. One of my helpers, Harry de Wiest, made me a lovely teak wheel. The anchors were very heavy and the chain was of alarming size – a short link with seven shackles of 15 fathoms each. I demolished the oak windlass and designed, and had made, a powerful modern one. Next, I bought a 30 hp Kelvin engine out of a yacht and installed it in an accessible space back of the stairway. It was small, but I thought that almost anything would shove my 170 tons deadweight along at about 3 knots in a calm. It did. I had hankered after something bigger but could not afford it.

The state of the decks was appalling. They were covered with splashes of tar and a couple of years' dust and dirt from the shore which had worked itself into a mass hard as concrete. One day, a gaunt individual with British war medal ribbons came on board and asked for a job. He worked like a tiger for the week he stayed with me, lunching at noon and always returning at 1:30 pm with a useful object. One day I remarked that I needed to buy some new scrapers for the deck. 'Don't do that,' he said. 'I'll bring some back after lunch.' He did. Another day he brought a huge copper ship's kettle. A third item was a mahogany cigar cabinet which was turned into an admirable medicine cupboard. Later, he bought an Alsatian puppy for which I built a kennel, intending to bring him up as a real ship's dog. A few days later, however, the old soldier was missing and a couple of policemen arrived in his stead: could I give them any information about the whereabouts of a man by the name of Smith wearing British war medals? I could and did, and all I said was to his credit. They told me he was, in fact, a German. I never saw him again. At about noon soon after, I went ashore. When I came back, the dog had gone.

Time passed. Twenty years' paint was scraped off the huge teak beams in the saloon. The deck was painted pale yellow. The deck between the beams was painted sky blue, and the beams themselves dark blue. I did my cabin in creamy white with three outlines of gods and goddesses up to all sorts of pretty play. The three spare single cabins were enamelled in white. My furniture was installed, including my fine old brass-bound chest and a couple of old leather-covered armchairs. On my walls I hung my pictures, including some marine paintings of about 1850 by an unknown Dutch artist. The interior began to resemble a Kentish cottage.

CLC with a young Diana in St Moritz in 1923 (Family collection)

L'Insoumise in the early 1920s (Family collection)

Claude's oldest son, Michael, in *L'Insoumise* in the early 1920s (Family collection)

By the Autumn I could live in great comfort. A blazing fire in the saloon and all my books, to say nothing of Ginger, a red Persian cat as big as a young lion but short of tail. Evenings were often passed at the Société Littéraire. There was an hour of *escrime* [fencing] under a very able Belgian instructor who fairly made me sweat. Maybe a call at Mr. Hanson's hospitable hostelry. Visits to Bruges, Brussels, Ghent. One could never be bored. Winter came; the basin froze over. One evening Ginger fell into the broken ice. I ended up in it, up to my neck, as well; Olive, the girl who did absolutely everything for me, had to get a sailor from a steamer to get me out. Cats are rum things where water is concerned. I took Ginger ashore for a bit of a canter the following Spring and he refused to return to the ship. I left him. Back on board, he saw me from 80 yards' distance, calmly sprang into the water, and swam like an otter to my gangway – he knew he could swim if he had to.

That Winter (1923–24) I went again to the Three Pigeons, and later to Chamonix to call at the little wooden chalet which had given us shelter the year before. Andre Farini was no longer with a photography outfit and had a wooden leg; a log sliding down the mountain side had smashed into him. By early Spring, I was back in Ostende and commenced the finishing touches to my ship. A friend from the Société Littéraire lent me a French play to read called *L'Insoumise*.[4] There was my name for my ship! *L'Insoumise*, the unsubdued, the unruly. The sort of epithet a nursemaid might use about a naughty child. There was no ship of that name in Lloyd's,[5] so I got her registered in that name in Belgium.

My son, Michael,[6] joined me later. I did not think the arrangement would work, as he had practically never before been under my control. Also, I was rather under the impression that the admirable training and discipline of the Nautical College, Pangbourne, where he had passed three years, went for very little on board the merchant vessels the young fellows then found themselves in on going to sea. The life of an apprentice on board a large passenger and cargo-carrying steam ship is not too hard, but, according to Mike, it is not exactly what they had expected it to be; if they were provided with fairly roomy accommodation, separated from the crew and fed as well as the officers, the greater part of their work was similar to that of an ordinary seaman and consisted largely of scrubbing decks and cleaning paintwork or hogging out boats; no attempt was

4 In English '*insoumise*' is variously translated as 'rebellious', 'unsubjugated', 'insubordinate' and 'unbowed'.

5 Lloyd's Register Group is a maritime classification society. The organisation dates to 1760.

6 Michael Cumberlege (1905–45). After Pangbourne, he joined the Aberdeen Line in 1922. He remained with the line as an apprentice for three years. This short period in *L'Insoumise* in 1924 must have been during a leave period.

made to give them instruction in navigation. The young chaps – there were six in Mike's ship – came to regard themselves as belonging to the crew rather than as young officers. The average apprentice, therefore, did not have much affection for his superiors and developed a rather 'bolshie' outlook. It was all quite understandable and a great pity.

There were compensations, and the open-air life at least had a good effect on the average healthy boy. Michael arrived on my ship after several voyages to Australia and back – a perfect young Hercules at the age of about 19 with hands like hams, an inside knowledge of paintwork, a dislike for authority and a book on Impressionist art. At about the same time, the father of another young man, Raymond, approached me to ask if I would take his son, claiming that the fellow had a passion for the sea and spent most of his spare time in North Sea fishing craft. Apparently this lad had just left a Guards regiment because he wanted to 'see the world'. I said I would take him on trial. He came and stayed a fortnight or so. His father gave him pocket money and insisted on paying for his keep. I agreed to take a couple of pounds a week. He arrived with his gear – guns, rifles, harpoons (for whaling!), a high-speed car and a saxophone. I liked him awfully, and his love of salt water was absolutely genuine. I visualised getting hold of one or two others of similar ilk.

Alas, Raymond was no longer my guest but now my paying guest, quite another cup of tea. The saxophone droned on till 3:00 am in the jazz band of an Ostend *boîte*. The Salmson[7] car buzzed about the flat roads of Belgium. At 9:00 or 10:00 am he was often dead to the world in his bunk. His admirable social qualities made up a lot for his lack of interest in the work of an ordinary Able Seaman, and his company was the best. The ship was never dull. Michael and Raymond got on famously, both being thorough bolshies although, at bottom, loyal to the ship. Mike was a far more knowledgeable sailor than Raymond, and the work came naturally to him – and, of course, he thought he knew a great deal more about seafaring than I did. But both were damned young and I very soon determined that the general arrangements would not work. Had we been ready for sea, things might have been different.

Our fitting-out was completed eventually. We moored near the Royal Ostend Yacht Club. One afternoon, three American destroyers came into harbour, passing within 100 yards of us. I ordered Michael to dip our red ensign. No notice was taken of it by the men-of-war. We kept our flag at the dip for 20 minutes and I then re-hoisted it, the destroyers by then having secured alongside the wall close to us. That evening, I went to bed fairly early before the boys returned from the shore. In the middle of the night I woke, hearing the patter of bare feet on the deck above me. Wondering who this might be, I jumped out of bed and ran on deck. I found Michael dragging a huge wicker fish basket while Raymond waited for him in a dinghy over the stern. 'What's the game?' said I. 'Oh, nothing, Dad. Don't worry. We're just going for a row in the harbour. We shan't be long!' I ought to have ordered them to bed, but I had got so bored with their manners and customs that I made some remark about it being their own funeral, and retired.

Next morning, coming on deck at about 7:00 am and, glancing across at the destroyers, I saw most of the ship's company on the forecastle and bridge of the Commodore's ship, looking up at their topmast head. On it, securely lashed, was a dirty old fish basket! I held a dictator's court martial there and then. 'Well, Dad, either they hadn't the decency to answer our salute or they kept a really bad lookout. So we thought we'd make sure which it was,' Michael explained. 'But how did you get it (the basket) up there?' Mike had shinned up a boat hook hooked into a scuttle, while Raymond had remained in the dinghy to pick Mike up in case he had had to dive overboard. He had then hoisted the huge basket to the masthead by the signal halliards and,

7 The French company Salmson emerged as an automobile manufacturer in 1919–22. During the mid-1920s it specialised in small cars with advanced features such as a twin overhead camshaft and overhead valves.

not content with that, shinned up the rigging after it. Hauling up the bight of the signal halliards, he had lashed the basket so that it was impossible to lower it from the deck. Slipping down to the deck, he was over the side and gone; and nobody was the wiser until the morning. I made the pair remain on board during the next four days while the destroyers were in harbour, and made the boys keep night watches in case the Americans suspected us, but we saw no sign of them having done so.

We left Ostend on a lovely day in a light breeze, and ran the engine to help us get out on the flood tide. The engine conked out as we got between the pier heads but the breeze freshened and we headed off to Calais. As evening came, though, along with falling rain, I decided to spend the night in Dunkerque. Next day we sailed to Dieppe but had to anchor offshore for the night due to a contrary tide. It was at Dieppe that I learnt that Raymond had, unbeknown to me, left his car at Calais; he went there by train, picked up the car and drove it back to Ostend, then rejoined us. I realised I would not get far with this crew.

In Dieppe I was joined by Arthur Marsden,[8] now a retired Commander, who immediately saw the lie of the land as regards the crew. Soon after, Raymond quit at his own request; life at sea had not come up to his expectations. Michael also left with a view to passing his 2nd Mate's examinations. Shortly after, he went to sea as 5th Officer in a Clan Line ship.

I brought *L'Insoumise* over to England with Marsden and one of my Ostende workers. We sailed to Shoreham, or rather into the canal at Southwick – a good place to lie up, as there is little rise and fall from the tide and one can secure to the wall as in Mediterranean harbours. I lived there uneventfully that Winter.

CLC at the wheel of *L'Insoumise* (Family collection)

8 See Chapter 7.

CHAPTER 15

Enjoying Life

A pattern to Cumberlege's new life began to emerge. He sailed south in L'Insoumise *along the French and Spanish coasts with a variety of paying guests and crew. His son Michael and daughter Diana visited.*

In Southwick I found a most able man, Mr. Munn. In early Spring 1925 we set out on a trial run with Munn as Bosun, Commander Mellin as a paying passenger,[1] Diana, my daughter,[2] a young friend of hers, another young fellow, Olive, who did everything for us, and myself as skipper. We sailed to France and back, to the Isle of Wight, and westward to Plymouth and Falmouth.

2nd Baron Michelham (NPG)

Before this, we ventured across the Channel to Le Havre and Deauville at the start of Spring before the real season commenced. Getting to Deauville early, we had the pick of the berths and spent one of the jolliest couple of months I had in my life. Next to us was a 700-ton steamer chartered by Lord Michelham.[3] Mich showed me over his ship. One evening at about ten, Diana dressed up in plus fours as a Duke, with her friend in a frock as a Duchess, and we went over to Mich's *bateau*. I called the watchman at the gangway and asked him to tell My Lord that the Duque and Duquesa de Monte Blanca were calling. Mich sprang up from his chair, rang a bell and gave instructions to a steward, who immediately came out to receive his distinguished visitors. A couple of quarts of champagne appeared, before we all burst out laughing. Mich could not very well send the pop [alcohol] away! Later that same night the 'Duke and Duchess' volunteered to buy cigarettes for me in town. They were away a long time, eventually returning with that look of lovely innocence which usually conceals some dark deed. According to Di, they had hijacked an H6[4] (I did not own a car) which had then broken down at the casino, blocking the way for the Rolls Royces; it had taken intervention by the [French] army to get it [a heavy vehicle] going again, with a bang. I never knew who owned the car they had 'borrowed'.

These happy days came to an end. Olive had to go home, and one of my crew got homesick. I suddenly remembered meeting a very enthusiastic young Swiss

1 Arthur Mellin, DSO (1870–1948) commanded the special service vessel *Sabrina II*, later called *Q3*, on 21 March 1916. In October 1916 he was thanked by the Admiralty for his work in an engagement with an enemy submarine. His DSO was awarded on the same basis. He was promoted to commander on 12 November 1917 in recognition of his wartime service, and he retired from the RN after the war.

2 Diana was 15 or 16 at the time.

3 Herman Alfred Stern, 2nd Baron Michelham (1900–84).

4 A luxury car produced by Hispano-Suiza, mostly found in France. Introduced at the 1919 Paris Motor Show, the 6-litre H6 was made until 1933. Roughly 2,350 H6s were produced.

THE TWO GIRLS OF THE *INSOUMISE*

(L–R) Ella Maillart and Diana (PD)

Diana in the Maillart book (PD)

Arthur Marsden when an MP (NPG)

skier in the Alps called Ella Maillart[5] who told me, among other things, about a voyage she and three other girls had made from Marseilles to Athens. She also told me she was terribly keen on seafaring and would come to my ship in any capacity if I sent her a wire. She claimed that one of her strong points was cooking. I sent the wire. She was on board within 48 hours, and also produced a young man, Van den Berg, who said he wanted to go to sea and see things. Not to be unmatey, I took him too. I liked Van, but my paying passengers – Arthur Mellin and Fred Ashe (a retired banker, who had joined him) – could not stand him.

As we wafted across the Bay of Biscay,[6] imagine Ella shucking peas, Van den Berg helping Diana pulling in a few unartful mackerel, Mellin sitting on the wheel box twiddling the wheel as occasion required and Fred Ashe reading his 365th detective story. A lovely day at sea with another to follow, and then mountains. Biarritz, shimmering with [gin] palaces. St-Jean-de-Luz looking too good to miss. And so we came to the worst port in the world, which ought to be one of the best. This place suited my paying passengers, who were golfers. It also suited Diana; there was safety in numbers and a lot of Latin youths. It also suited me, because I could sit in the bars in the sunshine and regard the world. Everybody was rich, except me who must be rich because I lived on a yacht. I enjoyed meeting all sorts of people; there wasn't an Englishmen there under the age of 80, and they lived at the golf hotel. We were only a matter of 300 yards from the beach. What a collection of young people used to swim to us and come aboard! Every day the sun shone. Sometimes the Atlantic rolled, but no gale. All my parties were impromptu, and sometimes Mellin and Ashe would turn up for dinner after golf and have to make themselves pleasant to a bevy of lovelies.

5 Ella Maillart (1903–1997) was a Swiss adventurer, travel writer and photographer, as well as a sportswoman. At the age of 20 she and three girlfriends sailed from Cannes to Greece. She then competed in the 1924 Summer Olympics as a sailor. She was also the captain of the Swiss women's field hockey team. From the 1930s onwards she spent years exploring the Muslim republics of the USSR as well as other parts of Asia, and published a series of books which, like her photographs, are today considered valuable historical testimonies. In 1942 her book, *Gypsy Afloat*, with a couple of chapters on her *L'Insoumise* experiences included, was published – to the irritation of the admiral, who was keen at the time to get this memoir published. She had first met him in the French Alpine skiing resort of Megève. She wrote: 'I was talking to a man of striking looks who was sitting at the table next to ours; tall, grey-haired, with steel-blue eyes in the middle of a sun-burnt, deeply-lined face. I would have guessed he was a sailor even if he had not worn a high-necked, navy-blue jersey. Detached and aloof, he seemed to be a spectator of his own life and of the world in general. He was a retired admiral who had decided to live all the year round on board his yacht, the *Insoumise*.' After the book appeared, Nancy Cumberlege wrote in 1942 to Mike Cumberlege, saying that Maillart had 'got the Skipper right' in her description of the admiral.

6 Maillart, a notable sailor, describes a rough transit sailing head-on into a westerly gale: 'We all looked as if we needed a rest' by the time *L'Insoumise* reached St Jean de Luz.

Arthur Marsden came to stay again. One afternoon, while I was walking with him along the seaport, we saw a blonde and a brunette sitting on the wall. We nudged each other and went on. Next day I looked over the side and there was the blonde swimming. 'Won't you come on board and repose a moment, Madam?' I said in French. 'Thanks,' she replied in English. I gave her a hand up the ladder. The sea unshipped her starboard shoulder strap and she stepped aboard with one of the loveliest breasts pointing to the skies. Arthur, with unexpected propriety, rushed up with a towel. Refusing it, to my intense delight, she sat down on the quarterdeck utterly unconscious that she was a trifle *déshabillée*. Or was she? What fun we had! Every day she swam over from the yacht she was on; always that shoulder strap slipped. It completely bouleversed me [bowled me over]. God bless you, Mélanie, for giving me wonderful days and exquisite nights thanks to that slipped shoulder strap. She left me for a Dutchman later.

Ella proved to be the worst cook in the world, and took hours to do the marketing. She was a lovely girl physically and I didn't mind, but my older guests were a bit put out when Ella, in her bathing suit, slapped down cold ham and tongue every day of the week instead of doing her duty. One morning, we assembled for breakfast in the saloon. Mellin simply hated Ella, and I must admit that his plate was dirty. It was Ella's duty to cook and lay the table. Mellin said: 'Ella, this plate is dirty.' Ella leant over him with a platter of eggs and bacon. 'God, so it is,' she said, and whisked it away from under his nose, rubbed it on the seat of her lousy pyjamas and put it back.[7]

I never gambled, but I did go to the casino, a ramshackle place called the Pergola. One evening I was strolling towards the baccarat tables when I ran into a very old friend of my youth who I had not seen for 25 years – Charlie Larios. We flung our arms round each other. Immediately he said: 'Come with me. You must tell me who that exquisite girl is in a red taffeta dress.' I'd designed that dress myself. It was my Diana! Charlie was then registered as Uncle Charlie. On board, Ashe's and Mellin's faces grew longer and longer. I trusted Di, by then 17, to innumerable *señores* and their high-speed Bugattis. You can't drive a Bugatti at 60 mph and make love, I figured. An intelligent French boy fell in love with her; marriage was his idea. He was utterly spurned. I told one Bolivian boy I would knock his two eyes into one if I ever saw him talking to Di again.

On another occasion I was dining at a most exclusive restaurant with some American friends and spotted Diana with a Venezuelan and an Argentine. Shortly after, she was alone, but motioned to say 'Don't bother. I'm O.K.' Next time I looked over, the youths were back. One was mopping a bloody nose, the other nursing a black eye. She explained later that each had fondly thought they were caressing her hand under the table but in fact had got hold of each other – and then gone outside to fight it out. Not long after this, Di fell for the leader of an American college band which was playing its way around Europe. He said he was going back to America and if he felt the same way about her when he got home as he did then, he would ask her to marry him. He went. She never heard from him again. What a time I had with this lovely daughter! But I judged her well. Eventually, she really fell for a young Spaniard called José – nothing to look at, but sound as a bell.

---

7 Maillart more or less confirms this account in her book. She had boarded in Deauville with Van, her Dutch friend, on the basis that she could cook. She found Ashe 'quite charming but very deaf'. Mellin was 'rather fierce … a woman-hater'. She shared a cabin with Diana: 'I looked at her with pleasure. She was younger than myself, but I had always been impressed by the calm of her smooth forehead. She had a delicate chin, cheeks like peaches, and dark blue eyes under wide-set eyebrows. Her Eton crop and her small upturned nose were most attractive … I think Diana was pleased to see me. She said at once that the elderly gentlemen were a nuisance as they did nothing but complain. Diana is the most reserved person I have ever met.'

St-Jean-de-Luz in the mid-1920s (PD)

It was a fine life, that summer in St-Jean-de-Luz. Mellin and Ashe were consumed with golf. Diana was safe with a hoard of palpitating South Americans. Ella, neglecting the cooking, was God knew where.[8] Mélanie would swim over in the cool of the evening and I would give her a blazing vermilion pair of Chinese trousers to wear, and we would eat great slabs of fresh pâté de foie gras cooked in port wine. Sometimes we took to the deck under the pale moon and played Ravel's 'Bolero' on the gramophone. Mélanie would snap her fingers and do the steps. I'm sure she had creole blood for all her curly golden hair. And when nature could have no refusal, somehow we found ourselves in that big blue room decorated with the golden and red Spanish ships on the walls. I had never dreamt of such a lovely scene.

September came. My guests left me, promising to return. We sailed north for Bayonne and the Adour river.[9] We arrived too late to enter, and anchored outside, in the fiendish Bay of Biscay. Fortunately, we had a calm night. I arranged for a St-Jean-de-Luz steam tunny-man [tuna-fishing boat] to give me a tow next day as my engine had refused duty. All went well until we got into those three great rollers on the [sand] bar, where the tow rope parted. We got another tow, which luckily did not part. A cold fog rolled down the river just as we secured up to seven rows of elm trees. Bayonne proved to be a beautiful and friendly port; even the local brothel was housed in an 18th-century building on the ancient walls.

Mrs. Munn came out to relieve Ella Maillart as cook. I was sorry she had to go, because of her pretty figure. 'Farewell, Ella,' I said, as I put her on the train. 'I hope one of these days you will come back as my honoured guest, but never, never again as my cook.' Since those days, she has done some remarkable trips in the wildest parts of China and written books about them.[10] A damned fine girl.

Diana and I were now alone except for Mr. and Mrs. Munn. We lived well; Mrs. Munn fed us like fighting cocks. Once a week Di and I would go over to meretricious Biarritz and dine at the Café de Paris for a change. I took these opportunities to instruct Diana a little, after a couple of glasses of champagne. 'I shall do exactly as I please with my own body,' was her outlook. 'Of course, dear. But I only want to put you wise

---

8 She writes that she would often sleep only four or five hours, but got breakfast promptly at nine o'clock each morning. She would then spend an hour on the beach planning the day with Diana. In the afternoon she spent time at the building [like a squash court] where the Basques played pelota. In the evenings, having put food on the table, she and Di would head off to dance to La Réserve, a Spanish band. The Admiral tried to prevent them going ashore so often, but the pair resorted to swimming ashore carrying smuggled dresses!

9 The Adour is in south-western France. It is 192 miles long; it rises in High-Bigorre (Pyrenees) and flows into the Atlantic Ocean (Bay of Biscay) near Bayonne; on its final stretch it defines the border between the northern Basque country and the Landes region.

10 Maillart was getting tired of her cooking job – and anyway had been told that *L'Insoumise* was heading for Gibraltar. Once the paying guests left, she thought that the admiral could not face an autumn gale at sea and so had decided to anchor in Bayonne for the winter. 'A last chocolat,' she wrote, 'was drunk in the small confiserie darkened by the low arcades of the old houses. The Admiral said: "Maybe we shall meet on the snow once more. Anyhow, come back here when you want to, and sail with us next Spring." I left for Geneva ... Six years were to go by before I saw my friends again. [In about 1935] I was steering a racing yacht and managed one black night to get her inside Port Sóller on the north coast of Majorca. On a neighbouring yacht I saw a familiar silhouette disappear down the companion. I boarded her and found the Admiral warming a feeding-bottle. His baby son [Mistral] was toddling about stark naked. I remained speechless with astonishment. The *Insoumise* had been exchanged for a very handy Newfoundland schooner which a small crew could sail easily Presently, the Admiral's wife came back, a young and cheerful person. With her was Diana, looking as charming as when I had last seen her. José, her husband, was carrying their son in his arms. He looked tired and worried; there was trouble brewing in Spain ... I know nothing more about these friends who were my shipmates on the stout *L'Insoumise*.'

to the pitfalls that are in your way.' She answered: 'I didn't ask to be brought into this world, and I don't see that I have anything to thank you for in consequence.' I refilled her glass and mellowed her outlook. We got pretty close in the end.

In Bayonne that Winter I met and made friends with an honest old naval pensioner who was *capitaine* of the port. His pay amounted to 1,000 francs or about £8 a month. He had a wife and seven children. I left a couple of hundred francs in an envelope at his little office on the quayside at Christmas. Then disaster struck. Mrs. Munn was taken severely ill and had to go home with Mr. Munn in charge. Bang went our cooking. Soon after, Olive returned. Then, one day a slight, red-faced, blue-eyed man with a ferocious moustache turned up at the quayside. He enquired if there was a job going for a seaman. I liked the look of him. He was 40 and came from Guilvenic in north-west France. He was a Breton who had gone to sea when he was ten. He had been working on the tunny boats but violence had broken out between the Bretons and the Basques. His name was Louis Leroux,[11] and soon he was overhauling the rigging. 'Haven't you got a wife somewhere?' I asked one day. '*Mais oui, Monsieur.* My Marie is staying with her uncle.' Can she cook?' '*Merde alors*, she wouldn't be my wife if she couldn't,' exclaimed Louis. Marie arrived in 50 petticoats, a white lace coif and three front teeth missing. Did we eat! Olive was relieved to be able to pay more attention to our creature comforts. I soon found that the Lerouxs had a daughter. Regina arrived, and the family settled in the forecastle. They were simple days. We passed the Winter happily.

Thanks to the icy flood of the Adour river charged with snow water, our copper on the bottom of *L'Insoumise* was spotless next Spring, which spared me the necessity of docking. St-Jean-de-Luz was again our headquarters during a glorious summer. But there was a difference. We had become an institution and were expected. Meantime, new toilets were being put up on shore, new villas erected, roads surfaced, and water and light and post offices provided for the comfort of the wealthy. Only the honest tars seemed to be overlooked. I thought there was some short-sightedness in this. So I got all municipal-minded. It struck me that a few of the million francs being spent onshore could be diverted into forming a safe harbour, which would be a tremendous benefit to everybody in the town, including the seamen. I got hold of the mayor, Joseph Garat (who later did two years in gaol for complicity in the 1934 Stavisky financial scandal, when worthless bonds were sold in Bayonne) and adumbrated my scheme. Garat twigged that there ought to be a local Cowes somewhere in the region. St-Jean-de-Luz was all but ready-made. Being a most forceful character, he called a meeting with other local mayors and influential hoteliers and others; he told me that if he could get the mayors and others to see eye-to-eye with him, they could touch the government for 10–15 million francs in addition to anything the various towns could put up. It was unanimously agreed that St-Jean-de-Luz was the proper spot to attract the peerage of England and top dogs of America with their yachts, not to mention anybody else. Having outlined the idea, I faded away. How far it went, I do not know – and these sorts of things take time. Before long a deep slump arrived, which queered everything. I remained in these lovely waters long enough to become one of the many first honorary vice presidents of the first yacht club in St-

Joseph Garat, Mayor of Bayonne (PD)

11 Leroux sailed with the admiral off and on for about ten years. Then he joined the admiral's son, Mike, when he was skippering the glamorous American-owned yacht *Landfall* in the Mediterranean 1937–39. Leroux returned to Brittany in 1940 after the German–Italian invasion of France in 1940.

'Skipper' in Maillart's book (PD)

Diana with a young admirer, Jorge Dibos, on *L'Insoumise* (Family collection)

Jean-de-Luz.

September came again and the limitless Atlantic rolled in her waves, and back we fled to Bayonne. The ship passed the Winter (1928–29) there; we had a stretch in the Haute-Savoie at the Three Pigeons. Spring arrived, and we resumed our station in St-Jean-de-Luz harbour. Michael re-joined, a new man. A couple of years tramping right round the world had made him see things more in reason. He was charming, and such a seaman. Louis stuck to me, with Regina and Marie. One fine afternoon on a leading wind, we sailed away and never went back.

On board I had my regulars – Mélanie, Marsden and Ashe, and Diana and her sleek-haired admirers (Michael arranged things badly with two of the most permanently-waved ones). It was a lovely night, and we wafted along the Spanish coast under a gorgeous moon. I chose the middle watch. The saloon was full of young people, mattresses on the floor, all very proper and youthful and lively. The following afternoon we hove to, out of the way, while 6-metre yachts passed on a race, with the Spanish king in one of them and his queen in another. It was the last of all the royal parties. I met Miguel Primo de Riviera[12] on board HMS *Royal Oak*. I was walking round the ship with the Commander, with the King and the Captain in front of us. Primo spotted one of the burnished steel clips used to shut a water-tight door. He moved it up and down and, turning to the Commander, said in admiration: 'How beautiful ... works, too!'

And so westward to Cape Finisterre with an anxious evening offshore. Calm, and a heavy swell. Every time I took a squint at the lighthouse we were nearer. No possibility of anchoring owing to the great depth. Waiting, anxiously waiting, for a breath of wind off the land. 'Come on, Mike. Let's get the 60-footer up.' It was a vast sort of topmast staysail, a fly jib, 60 feet in the hoist. It filled. I went to bed. At dawn a violent thunderstorm blew up and the huge sail had to come down instantly. Not a bit of it. The halliards[13] had somehow jerked off the sheave [pulley wheel] in the topmast head and jammed. Mike, having been hoisted up to the topmast in a bosun's chair and, fighting like a tiger, was able to wrap the sail round and about. Then the wind came fair and gently took us around Finisterre. Shortly after, we were becalmed; the Portuguese trade [wind] had petered out. We ran into fog and were surrounded by traffic, all unseen. We were utterly out of control, enveloped in fog and just swinging around the compass. I had a magnificent German wartime trench siren acquired in Ostend and Louis operated it to sound the 'Not Under Control' signal [*daah dit dit*]. A large mail boat must have heard it, as she altered course away from

12 Miguel Primo de Rivera (1870–1930), was a dictator, aristocrat and military officer who from 1923 to 1930 served as Prime Minister of Spain. His slogan was 'Country, Religion, Monarchy'. Historians depict him as inept, and lacking ideas and political acumen. He ended up alienating the army and the monarchy, and was forced out of office by an economic crisis in 1930. He died in exile six weeks later in Paris.

13 A halliard is a line or rope used to hoist a ladder, sail, flag or yard. The term comes from the phrase 'haul yards'. Halliards, like most parts of the rigging, were usually made of natural fibre like manila or hemp.

Diana aboard *L'Insoumise*
(Family collection)

us. A great steamer drifted slowly past, no more than 100 yards away. Off the Burlings[14] we were becalmed in divine weather for 48 hours. Steamers would pass close, their passengers lining the side as Diana plunged overboard into the broad Atlantic. There was no hurry; we just drifted, or sailed if a breeze sprang up. We were well out of sight of the land so I decided to check our dead reckoning with a slow old French tramp steamer. Michael took her signals down under my eye. We were 60 miles out in our reckoning. Suddenly, we got the breeze. The Tagus River was under our lee. That night we anchored at Cascais.

Next day, we sailed up to Lisbon. We flew all possible sail and left a 6-metre yacht trailing. *L'Insoumise* was showing off. Somewhere off the square, we dropped the hook. Several motor boats came near offering their services. One gentleman handed me *The Times* and other papers. He was Mr. Elias, ship chandler of Lisbon – the only really honest ship chandler I ever met. For the fortnight we were there he did everything for us, topping it off with a charming dinner party at his country house downriver. Michael spent hours in Cintra [now Sintra], where Vasco de Gama and Prince Henry and Juana the Loca rest in peace. And we spent a week on the other side of the Tagus, where we cleaned our propeller when the tide went down.

One day we sailed away, passing Cape St Vincent and making for Trafalgar. Suddenly, trouble came in the shape of wind from the south-west. The 60-footer came down, some chains parted, then the huge bowsprit parted [broke] and we had to lower the jib as well. Luckily, Cadiz was just to leeward, so we bore into that port under mainsail, mizen and staysail. A pilot boarded us and asked me to tack with a view to entering the passage into the anchorage. This would have been a very chancy manoeuvre given the nasty sea and strong wind. We disagreed. The pilot said: 'Very well. Take my steamer as a tug.' He said it would cost nothing. We were towed comfortably into Cadiz. I found a beautiful pitch pine spar here, and within a week we had replaced the bowsprit and fitted a new black iron chain bobstay in place of the galvanised one that had parted.

We sailed on to Gibraltar. I didn't like the billet we received, alongside the gun wharf at the Ragged Staff; I knew of old that in a westerly gale the sea could be tricky in that corner. Without mentioning the matter to the dockyard, I laid out a stream anchor and chain on my port quarter. Soon after, as it started to blow from the south-west, I was very glad I had done so. What a night! The sea rolled in from the Straits, and by midnight several destroyers, having slipped their moorings, were lying inside the moles. One had

14 Now called the Berlengas: a Portuguese archipelago of small, uninhabited Atlantic islands 6–10 miles off the coast of Peniche, a promontory north of Lisbon.

lost a propeller, and a light cruiser alongside the oil wharf had done considerable damage to herself. We were fairly safe until the huge iron mooring ring, to which *L'Insoumise* was attached on her port bow, broke. Then we began pitching heavily, and at each pitch the bowsprit just missed the wall. My trusty anchor held. At 3:00 am I got the girls up in the deck house and, with Louis Leroux, set about arranging a derrick so that I could swing them ashore; if my stern anchor had parted, there would have been very little left of the ship in the morning. A policeman came by and I asked him to go round to the nearest ship and see if they would send some men to lend me a hand. The Captain turned out to be my old friend, Robin Dalgleish.[15] In a quarter of an hour, 20 men and a young officer arrived. We managed to shift the outside bow hawsers to another ring that was intact, and were in comparative safety. The girls got to work, and the sailors had cooked eggs and bacon at about daylight. We did £70[16] damage. Fortunately, I was insured.

Captain Robin Dalgleish (PD)

A few days later, after nearly three years and true to her first love, Diana married her Spaniard, Don José-Maria Avial, at the Roman Catholic cathedral in Gib.[17] We had a grand wedding. The RC Bishop had made a bit of a song-and-dance about a Catholic marrying a Protestant and said there would be no music or flowers. I had countered this by hiring the local piano organ, pulled by a donkey, to play outside. This altered his outlook. I had to pay off my donkey, but the church was a mass of flowers, and champagne flowed in traditional style at the reception on board *L'Insoumise*.

I spent the next Winter in Gib. doing endless work on the ship with Louis Leroux, including a refit – sail-making, and resetting the rigging. We were never idle. Mélanie and old Ashe and his daughter stayed for a time, and then Spring came and we took to sea again. My crew now consisted of myself; Louis the Breton; Marie Leroux, a very acute and enthusiastic young Gibraltarian of 14 years; Regina, now about 13; and a young gunner subaltern. This last was a great lad, but he was in a parlous state financially with three months' leave due, and knew that if he remained in Gib. an army of creditors would immediately descend on his doorstep, and that would mean the end of any leave. It seemed better if he took passage with us to France, and from there he could jump lorries to Boulogne and thence to his mother's home in England, where he would be able to repair his shattered fortunes. He stole aboard one May evening under the cover of darkness[18] and next morning we were beating out of Gibraltar dockyard with a south-west breeze. Then at Cape de Gat [Cabo de Gata, Almeria] we ran into a high swell and strong breeze from the north-east. This lasted for seven days; we ended up close to the African shore. Eventually we got north to the small Spanish port of Denia, edging into the little harbour after deliberately going into the mud, sliding out into deep water and rattling out the cable. Here we were lucky to find a sailmaker, Tio Pépé, who brought out his two pretty nieces. The three of them set about the extensive repairs necessary to the sails after the nine-day blow.

15 Rear Admiral Robin Dalglish (1880–1934) was appointed commander of the light cruiser *Centaur* in 1928.

16 About £4,800 today.

17 In later life Diana told the story that José had chased *L'Insoumise* along all the ports from Bayonne to the Mediterranean in his Bugatti. Finally catching up with her in St Tropez, he invited her to lunch. They drove off in the Bugatti. He started accelerating, going faster and faster. Diana pleaded with him to slow down as they came to a curve in the road. He replied that he would if she would marry him. She accepted.

18 This is the last reference to the subaltern.

The month was May, when we might have expected fairly settled weather, but it was not to be. We left Denia, and a day later we were hove to for seven days in as hard and continuous a blow as I have ever experienced. I found anchorage in Rosas Bay.[19] This second blow was too much for Marie Leroux, so I decided to send the Lerouxs home to Brittany overland. I also discovered that my big mizen mast was very badly cracked about 10 feet above the deck. Using some hardwood I found onshore and had cut into strips, I was able to bind round the mast with iron bands set up with nuts and bolts.

On shore, I found a tiny little pub frequented by fisherfolk. The proprietor's daughter, Rosita, an extremely pretty child of maybe 17 years, served me good Catalan wine. I explained that I needed a couple of her best boy friends to work for me as sailors; at 7:00 am next morning 40 splendid young fellows were assembled on my quarterdeck. I chose, at random, 'Pedro of Tarragona' and 'Ramon of Rosas'. These were the names registered later at the post office. Never have I sailed with more honest, pleasant-natured and more efficient seamen. They were not yachtsmen cleaning bright work for the sake of it, they never wanted to go ashore, and they spent most of their leisure washing themselves or their clothes. They found the handling of my huge gaff mainsail child's play after dealing with the archaic lateens[20] of their fishing boats. They stayed with me for the whole season and left in October only for an extraordinary reason; they had bound themselves to act as beaters annually in November to an old Spanish nobleman for his yearly wild boar hunting in the Catalan mountains.

We set off for Toulon, keeping well to windward in case the Mistral, or NW wind, got up in the Gulf of Lyons. It did, with a bang and a crash out of a sunny blue sky. We made a fair wind of it and romped along the French coast, turning up into Toulon Roads and getting inside the naval harbour, where the Mistral was blocked by high buildings and I could drop my hooks, swing to the wall and tie up in front of the excellent Café de la Rade. Toulon has an attractive space reserved for yachts, because no wheeled traffic may pass along the waterfront. It is no Cannes or Monte Carlo, and bars are closed by 10:00 pm, but we stayed here for some weeks. When a tramp steamer came into port, I took the opportunity to persuade her amiable skipper to hoist out my wounded mizzen mast for nothing. Despite my extensive knowledge of the Mediterranean, Toulon was actually the first port on the French Riviera that I had visited, except for Marseilles; if ever I had had a choice, I favoured less sophisticated and more remote parts. Now I found myself at the beginning of the Côte d'Azur. An American yacht came in. Her owner knew the coast and recommended the little port of St Tropez.

19 The Gulf of Roses, north of Barcelona, is the most northerly bay on the Catalan coast of Spain. It is 10 miles wide.

20 A triangular sail on a long yard at an angle of 45 degrees to the mast.

CHAPTER 16

L'Amiral de St Tropez

For the next three years the Admiral made St Tropez his headquarters. He was his own master. His estranged wife Laetitia died in 1930. In 1931 he swapped L'Insoumise *for a smaller boat.*

We sailed one summer's day along the Côte d'Azur, and on a soft afternoon cast our anchor in the tiny but fine harbour of St Tropez, spotting a place to moor ten paces from M. Aristide Madre's hospitable Café de Paris. I remained there not three days but three years. Gaunt 17th and 18th-century houses, attractive *tartarnes* [fishing boats] with their inimical crews who became good comrades, great tuns [barrels] of wine rolled on the quays, a policeman sporting the Distinguished Service ribbon of England on his chest, an old harbour pilot sporting the same ribbon for a devoted act at Gallipoli – they are all amongst the host of memories and friends I have. There were also the aliens – more or less permanent residents whose meagre means of livelihood ranged between poetry, painting and sculpture; half a dozen *artistes* were scattered round the port making pictures of the tartarnes. The legs of beauties rubbed hips with the barons of the press. Scions of royalty and *vedettes* [stars] of the screen hovered. Strange persons with lip-sticked lovers came – and went – leaving us to our drop of *pastis* and our game of *belote* and the blasts of the merciless Mistral.

St Tropez and the Café de Paris in the 1930s (Mary Evans)

CLC dressed for work (Family collection)

Here, at last, was peace. St Tropez pleased me. Was I 'on holiday'? Perhaps I was. I did not think so because my ship work was endless. But I enjoyed the work, and I could drop it at any moment. I was my own master. If at noon I tired of painting the ship's side, I could stroll across to M. Madre's café for a long, cold draught of beer or hail Manoel, his waiter, to bring a dozen cocktails on board for sudden arrivals. It was I who gave the orders to go to sea, and equally it was I who countermanded them. A man called Mullins looked after the cooking, and Ramon and Pcdro looked after the deck. The harbour was safe, clean and generally suitable for any craft not too big. There was never any swell, and

A George Barne still life painting (Charleston)

ships could lie with their heads NNW so that even in a stiff Mistral one could lie head-to-wind. The one thing to ensure was to lay out plenty of chain; there is at least 4 fathoms of water inside the harbour.

George Barne[1] became a great crony of mine. He lived in one room in a back street, or rather he slept the last few hours of darkness there. At 10:00 am he used to enter the hospitable portals of the Café de Paris. 'You see,' he explained once, 'my landlady is an old fool.' 'Does she drive you out of the house?' I inquired. 'What an idea! Certainly not, certainly not. But nothing I can say will make her replace the broken light bulb in the toilet!'

George's speciality with the brush was 'still life' – the mackerel of the pavement artist. One of his paintings, 'Red Mullet on a Plate', got as far as the cellars of the Tate Gallery. Once, Mullins received a slimy conger eel wrapped in a newspaper followed a few days later by an octopus; both were thrown over the side. In the evening I walked into the Café de Paris and took a seat at George's table. He was frigid, silent for minutes. At length, he broke the silence. 'It appears,' he said, 'that you do not appreciate Mediterranean fish.' 'Oh? What makes you think that?' 'Well, I've sent you fish and you cast them in the sea.' There was no answer to that. Silence reigned. Eventually, I rose to go. Suddenly, the frown left his forehead and was replaced by the gentlest of smiles on his lips. 'My father presented my brother Harry and myself with a Bible each. In mine he wrote: 'Let not the sun go down on your wrath.' Hailing Manoel, George said: 'I pray you, enquire of the Admiral what he would like to take!' In 1914 George had been studying in Paris, a gentle, delicate youth unsuited to war's alarms. He had to join up, he was gassed, he caught malaria and in fact was utterly ruined – more of a menace to his own side than to the enemy. 'I was a bombardier in the Royal Regiment of Artillery,' he told me. 'I was quite incapable of giving anybody an order.' His brother Harry was a judge in Alexandria. He turned up once on his way home from Egypt – a very respectable Mr. Pickwick to George's Mr. Micawber in his most disreputable form.

Not long after my arrival in St Tropez, a French submarine came into harbour. I got to know the genial Commander. A French lady I knew called Stella, who had a business running a motor speedboat for hire, asked me if I could arrange for her to look round the submarine. Commander Lancelot proved amenable, and I had cocktails on the deck with him while Stella made her visit. A few days later, she came into the Café de Paris in the evening and sat with me and George. She pointed to a man with a walrus moustache sitting in a corner – either a retired policeman or a *gendarme* – and told me that earlier that evening she had been dining in the café when the man approached and started asking her about an English Admiral in a yacht. Had he been on board the submarine? Spy fever was rampant, and Stella was frank with him. A little later, a young French couple I knew slightly arrived in town in a very smart car and brought a friend on *L'Insoumise* with them. He had a very expensive German camera and said he wanted to snap me on my ship. I was manoeuvred

1 George Hume Barne (1882–1935) was born in Bristol but in 1917 was living in Paris. His work was included in the London Artists' Association Exhibition in 1929. In a letter dated 26 August 1917 Roger Fry comments: 'Barne is very good. He lives in Paris and works with intense deliberation, taking about 3 months over a single still life.'

around. He said he would be back in a week or so and would bring the photos with him. In the meantime, I made discreet enquiries and discovered that the man was one of France's most important 'agents'. He arrived with his postcard-size photos. I laid them out in the saloon and said: 'Very good. What do they remind you of? They only need a fingerprint and a number, and they'd look fine in the Rogue's Gallery.' He laughed. After a pause, he said: 'Oh well, Admiral, take it from me that these photos have done you no harm.' 'Perfect,' I said.

St Tropez, then, was my headquarters with trips from end to end of the Riviera, Italy and Corsica. In Winter I would go to the Haute-Savoie for skiing. From time to time, I took a run home for a few days to visit my mother and to spend 48 hours in town. I would go to my club, the Senior,[2] early, and bathe in a great bath while a valet put out my clothes. In the W.C.s there was a selection of three sorts of toilet paper, but the club refused to open the bar until 12 noon.

All sorts of personages crossed my path in St Tropez. One day in the Autumn of 1930 *Peau Brune*, a big, heavy schooner with a black mainsail and a big red patch came in and secured near us. The owners were a couple of interesting middle-aged men in seamen's' jumpers. Mélanie and I were invited over. The older one told us that he was carrying out a lifelong desire to cruise in the South Pacific. After a diesel engine was installed, they hoped to set off early next year. Their business was producing luxury art books in Paris. One they showed me sold for a mere 150,000 francs.[3] The slump arrived; their business went to pot. The schooner was sold.

That Winter it snowed in St Tropez. We were bidden to dinner (and a fat goose) at friend Serries' place. He had flown in the French air force in the war. He talked German like a native. His particular role had been to get himself landed behind German lines by a colleague and gain information, being picked up by pre-arrangement. He carried out this amazing performance a dozen times. On November 10th 1918 he was caught and hurriedly sentenced to death as a spy – but as the Armistice arrived next day, his life was saved. Sometimes I went ashore to take a humble meal at Madam Jeanne le Duc's curious restaurant. I met all sorts there, from film stars to ministers of state, British seamen, lovelies out for the evening, writers and poets and painters. One night a magnificent Juno of a blonde plus gigolo was at the next table. She had a yacht. I invited her to take a look at mine. She was enchanted by the idea, came aboard and left after midnight. I warned her to be careful in her high heels going down the gangway. She plunged with her thousand-guinea furs into the cold embrace of the harbour. So did the gigolo. I hauled them both out. Next day I pulled the fur out of 20 feet of water with a fish hook.

Another lady, Sappho, became one of my best friends. She intimated that she thought she would marry me on return from a visit to Paris. The slump killed that idea too. She lost half her income and told me on her return that she could not possibly keep a husband now. Another time, a fine schooner came in; I knew the American owner. On board were 20 guests including a nice-looking young woman. She told me her grandfather was known as P.L. 'Prince Louis of Battenberg!' I exclaimed. 'To know him was to love him.' I took another look at the girl. 'The last time we met I bathed you.' 'Bathed me?!' 'Yes, it was 25 years ago, in HMS *Hussar*. Your mother and your sister and you came on board in Patras and we sailed to Malta in dreadful weather.' I took her to *L'Insoumise* and unhooked a water colour of *Hussar* and gave it to her to take home to her mother.

---

2 The United Service Club. founded in 1815 for the use of senior officers in the British Army and Royal Navy and accordingly known to members as 'The Senior'. Because of its emphasis on senior officers it was considered the most prestigious of London's military clubs. It closed in 1978, and the building at 116 Pall Mall was acquired by the Institute of Directors.

3 150,000 francs in 1930 is worth about £1,200 today.

Such was my life for about three years,[4] but the Man with the Scythe carved a gap in my existence in St Tropez early on. It was late Spring 1930. A telegram rushed me to Paris. My wife had had a sudden operation in the wonderful American hospital. How good they were! I was given a spare room. 'Perhaps we cut too deep. Anyhow, a germ has been released, I'm afraid …' said the senior surgeon. It was the old trouble come back,[5] poor dear. I kept her going for a whole month, but the fever would not be allayed. At the end of June, I kissed her goodnight and she fell asleep in my arms for ever. If 25 years previously we had loved with a love that was more than love, we parted the fastest of friends.[6]

Winter 1930–31 came. My two anchors were down to 70 fathoms on chain on each, and the stern of *L'Insoumise* was secured to the quay at St Tropez. I took stock. A new mainsail, hundreds of fathoms of best manilla rope and a hundred and one other things must be found and the crew paid. In the Spring I would need to pay for docking. Where was the money coming from?

One evening, in torrential rain, Peter Blos,[7] the artist, came aboard. 'Stay, Peter,' I said. 'You can't sleep under that fir tree of yours in this weather.' He accepted, and camped in the deckhouse, as I supposed, for the night. Next day I took myself off to the snows of Savoie to forget my [money] difficulties. Three months later Jean, my man, welcomed me back: 'Monsieur Peter left a couple of days ago,' he told me. 'Oh, I'm sorry,' I said, thinking that Jean meant that Peter had left the country. 'Yes,' said Jean. 'I think he was sorry to go. At any rate, he was very well satisfied. He only found fault with the wine so I got him another brand.'

L'Insoumise, though, was in apple-pie order. Spring arrived, and one day a nice American couple came aboard. They had a yacht lying at Bayonne which they had sailed across the Atlantic – a schooner of 60 or so tons. I must have told them that I was wondering if I could ever afford to fit out my ship again; she was really too big for me – or, rather, for my pocket. Suddenly, the young woman had a brainwave. 'How would you like to make a swap?' she said. I had never thought of getting rid of my old craft; something might turn up, and I could always live in her. I thought for a while, then replied: 'Look, the season is just commencing. You're fitted out already and have made your arrangements for a cruise round Spain and into the Mediterranean. Why spoil your cruise? Go back to your ship, have fun and in six months' time come back and ask me again.'

Six months later the schooner *Westward* was lying alongside my ship in St Tropez harbour. 'Come on, now,' the Americans said. 'What about it?' I replied, 'She's yours.' I walked into *Westward* and they walked in *L'Insoumise*. *Westward* was some 70 tons displacement, *L'Insoumise* was 170 tons. *Westward*'s age was 5 years, *L'Insoumise* about 30. *L'Insoumise* was built to last, bar accidents, for 100 years, *Westward* was yacht-built. They got what they wanted, I got what I could deal with. For nearly 10 years I had banged about in the magnificent old barkie [barque], but I knew I could not go on.

---

4 In his book *Jolly Brise* Robin Bryer writes that Admiral Cumberlege became 'a legendary character in the harbours of the South of France … he who had a quayside restaurant named after him in one of the ports which he frequented.' Claudine Cumberlege recalls that the first night club opened in St Tropez was called L'Amiral in honour of 'the beautiful admiral who lives on his yacht'!

5 Cancer of the stomach.

6 Daughter Diana Cumberlege, who had accompanied Laetitia to Sydney in 1919–20, referred in later life to Laetitia and Claude having divorced. According to Diana, Laetitia had met 'a military fellow' during Claude's long absence in the First World War. When Claude turned up at the American Hospital in Paris in 1930 he met Laetitia's new companion, and the two of them cried together and held hands at her bedside as she died. Claude later invited the man to 'to have a few drinks' with him to console each other and then invited the man to stay on *L'Insoumise*. History does not recount if this ever happened.

7 Peter Blos (1903–86) was born in Munich, Germany, the son of portraitist Carl Blos. He studied art in Munich and Paris. In 1931 he emigrated to California where he painted portraits. From 1932 he made more than 35 trips to the south-western United States to paint the Hopi and Navajo tribes and the landscapes of Utah and Colorado. His posters are collector items.

Fleur de Lys at anchor (Family collection)

The Americans took her away. After spending a lot of money on *L'Insoumise,* by one of those appalling strokes of bad luck, they got her on the rocks in Agay Roads, 30 miles from St Tropez, on pretty well her first trip. It cost the underwriters £4,000-odd[8] to get her off and repair damages. Danish salvagers nailed planks over the holes, caulked them up, pumped her dry and towed her away to Marseilles on a calm night where she was dry-docked and repaired. The work of the Danes was beyond praise. The owner put in twin diesel engines after that. Luckily, the ship was fully insured and is still (1937–38) going strong.

I took out a British registration for *Westward*, changing the name to *Fleur de Lys*, and moved in. She was much smaller than *L'Insoumise*, and more economical to run, but not lightly built or 'yachty'. Designed by a well-known American and built in Connecticut, she had lines based on the Gloucester fishing schooners – that is to say, built for fair, but not racing, speed. She was 62 feet in length, had a 15-foot beam and a draught of 8 feet 6 inches. The rig was the same as that of a traditional schooner – shortish bowsprit, fore staysail on a boom, foresail and mainsail, no topsails, comparatively high masts. In ordinary weather this rig worked very well.

Really bad weather at sea, however, finds most men and ships out. In a terrific gale in November 1932, in which several ships and steamers were lost, my son Michael was at sea, as a leading member of the crew of a yacht bound from St Malo to Lisbon. After 21 days she was reported overdue. 'Admiral's son feared lost,' ran a headline in an English newspaper. In fact, the little craft, only 50–60 tons, had been hove to for 17 or 18 days under close-reefed foresail and fore staysail. The chronometers were pitched out of their specially-arranged boxes, which did not help. Nineteen days out from St Malo, land was spotted – Biarritz, the owner thought – and decided to run up the coast for the Bayonne River and go below for a bit of sleep. Michael was not so sure, and checked on the chart. It was Santander, not Biarritz, a matter of 150 miles to the westward. Failing to wake the owner, he wisely took the law into his own hands and hauled his wind for Bilbao. Mike took some amazing photos from water level of terrific seas on this voyage – evidence of the power of nature, a good advertisement for the vessel and a witness to the *sang froid* and pluck of the young man who took them. It was in a similar gale that same Autumn that something like 300 Breton fishermen lost their lives when 30 tunny boats were lost. All these vessels were much larger and heavier, and carrying much bigger and more experienced crews than Mike's little sailing ship. But they could not have been 'well found' – unsuitable topmasts and bowsprits, and ballast carelessly stowed.

Fleur de Lys had a 6-cylinder high-speed American diesel engine of 60 hp. It could turn the propeller at 500 revolutions. It was complicated, and the previous owner had given it up as a bad job. I tried to repair it, but by the time I had finished, the front end of the engine was wrecked beyond repair. We committed the damned thing to the deep. It was replaced by a very efficient Parsons petrol paraffin engine which only gave me 3½ knots and was hideously uneconomical on fuel. In the end, I bought it for £10 and sold it for £20.

8 Worth about £240,000 today.

I made some fairly drastic alterations down below with a view to gaining more space; it was my only home. The saloon now had one large-sized bed at settee height on the starboard side. There was a comfortable toilet and wash place leading out of the saloon. A ladder led out of the saloon through a sliding hatch onto the deck. On the starboard side aft there was a roomy, wide-berthed single cabin, a very large after-cabin with its own lavatory and wash place, and a big outlet into the cockpit. The forecastle had two berths for crew and its own toilet. The large kitchen housed both the engine and all necessary appliances. In all, there were ten actual sleeping berths, so arranged that there were no compartments split into potty little cabins. Most of my old furniture had to go, but I retained my 200-year-old brass-bound Dutch coffer as a super wash-deck locked on the upper deck.

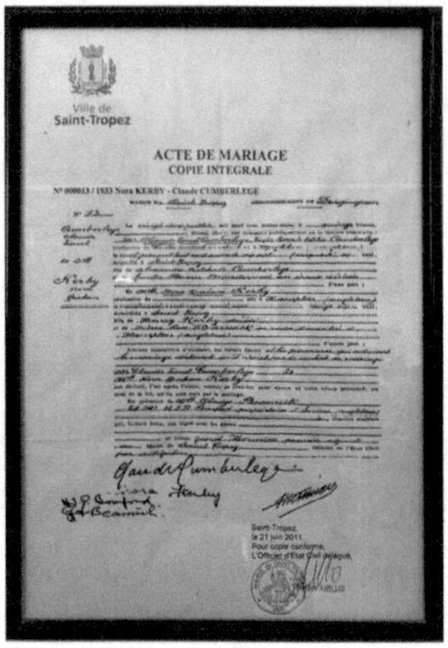
Ville de
Saint-Tropez

ACTE DE MARIAGE
COPIE INTEGRALE

N° 000013 / 1933 Nora KERBY - Claude CUMBERLEGE

Saint-Tropez,
le 21 juin 2011
Pour copie conforme,
L'Officier d'Etat Civil délégué,

Marriage of the Admiral to Nora Kirby, 27 July 1933 (Family collection)

I had an ideal ship for a long voyage, and *Fleur de Lys*, being only five years old, was well found. I could afford to keep two paid hands, and only needed one or two friends

Nora and Claude in 1935–36 (Family collection)

who were good amateur seamen to make up a crew for a voyage to the South Seas. But, as I discovered, it was not easy to find paid hands prepared to sign on for a three-year voyage. Nor could I find friends who were able to get away for so long. I looked vaguely for a partner prepared to take a share in the ship and contented myself with dreams.

These were suddenly interrupted by the arrival of a good-sized motor yacht in St Tropez rented by a friend of mine. He invited me over for a drink. Going on deck, I was presented to a young lady who did not seem to belong *'dans cette galère'* [in this group]. I said so. She responded that she had come aboard with a girlfriend for 'tea' with the idea of taking a short trip to sea and back. Now she was 50 or 60 miles from her point of embarkation and without hope of returning to base for days. Her name was Nora Kirby.[9] She took my advice, hopped ashore and boarded my ship, where I had several useful friends who might help. The result of this manoeuvre was that after a winter's trip to Austria with her own friends in 1932, and a visit to her mother in England, she returned to me and my ship. The Mayor of St Tropez spliced [married] us for a matter of 30 francs, and presented me with a *Livret de Famille*[10] gratis, and ever since I have done my best to abide by the instructions embodied in this tome but, to date [1938], have only managed to complete two of the vacant spaces marked 'Fils'.[11] We had a glorious honeymoon in a gem of a schooner called *Marie Lys* belonging to a French friend. But the Pacific Island trip had to be abandoned, although Nora had been all for it. Nature had stepped in.

That Spring and Summer (1933), we cruised the coast. Nora had done a good deal of small boat sailing and she took to *Fleur de Lys* in no time. Straight away I made her take the wheel on entering and leaving harbour; this gave her confidence and left me free to operate the sails. The summer drifted into autumn and it was time to lay up the ship; our baby's arrival was becoming imminent. We returned to St Tropez. I made a little hammock and bought a sack of bran. Mme. Normand, the policeman's wife, was warned to stand by. Doctor Damon (he had pulled Nora through a nasty go of paratyphoid) was bespoke.

On September 19th 1933, during the heaviest north-west gale of the year, a violent Mistral blew up out of a wonderful blue sky. Our anchor chains were as taut as bars. By midnight it was blowing a full gale. The harbour seas were breaking over the quay just astern of us and scattering spray on the doors of M. Madre's well-lit café. In the galley, Mme. Normand was quite unaffected, and was boiling odd bits of steel in enamelled pans. Nora, who was never seasick, lay on a mattress arranged on the saloon table and was as comfortable as she could be in the circumstances. Dr. Damon was the colour of a frog's armpit and rocking himself on the settee, his head in his hands. On deck, the Mistral thundered. Then, a little piping wail – the *vox humana*! I handed a tiny dark-haired boy to Mme. Normand, who promptly fetched him a smack across his little face. Did he yell! I carried Nora to her comfortable big bed as cheerful as a cricket, and now, beside her in his little hammock, lay the baby, covered with bran. The sea was steely calm, there was not a breath of wind. I walked across the gangway. There were dozens of people waiting. I spotted George Barne. 'George,' I said. 'A lovely boy.' George rose slowly on his poor old legs, put his long white hands on my shoulders and said, 'Then you will permit me, well, I mean to say …' and kissed me on both cheeks, dropped into his chair and burst into tears. I took a quart of beer in a jug on board for Mme. Normand.

9 Nora was 30 years younger than Claude.

10 A *Livret de famille* is an official document issued at the birth of the first child or at the time of marriage. It must be updated on the occasion of any event occurring after its issue (marriage of parents, birth, adoption, divorce, death etc.). It contains texts on French family law.

11 Mistral (born 1933); Tarik (born 1936).

A few days later I called in at the Mairie with my *Livret de famille* and registered the arrival of Mistral. In the fish market they thought the name of the boy *gentil* [pleasing]. The assistant chief of police said that it was 'a rascal of a name'. The tartaners said the name meant trouble later. A wonderful autumn followed, with Norah doing all the nursing and me in charge of the bran. The rain came down solidly in November followed by snow in December – very unusual in these latitudes. I made a snowman three feet high on my quarterdeck. At this point we bought tickets for the train which passes from France into Italy and thence to Kitzbühel in Austria. But … we had forgotten Nora's passport. However, she still had one in her maiden name. I took her photograph out of it and stuck it alongside mine in my passport, then cut up a blank cheque form with her new name printed on it and pasted it underneath. There was no deception intended; we had my *Livret de Famille*, which proved she was my wife. Off we went – Nora, Misty, myself and Dick. Dick was a most beautiful North African Sluky [saluki] dog, as big as a camel.

We rolled to Ventimiglia, the Italian frontier. Instructing Nora to follow me with Dick while I took charge of Master Mistral, we walked along from our second-class compartment as the train pulled up, then stepped out onto the platform from one marked first class. I gave the fascist salute and we were instantly surrounded by several fine-looking uniformed gentlemen. My baby was torn from my arms and the men all surrounded the infant. I cannot speak much Italian, but could easily understand most of the remarks that followed along the lines of 'What a baby! What a perfectly lovely child!' Diffidently, I produced the passport with a questioning air. '*Oh, che? Oh, passaporta,* no matter! *Che bambino, che bellissimo*! Pass by 'ere. Fineesh *passaporta*.' We were escorted across the platform to our next train. An officious-looking conductor arrived, saw the baby, halted, kissed his own fingers and joined the chorus. He threw open the train door, and we and our bags and dog were ushered into a compartment. We were comfortably in Austria next morning.

I had never been to Kitzbühel before – it was a lovely place. We found a tip-top pub, took a two-room suite, and for the next three months had a charming holiday. It was March [1934], and the roofs were dripping before we tore ourselves away from our sunbathed little chalet. We left Dick the Sluky behind with a pretty girl who had made friends with him; a yacht is no place for such a long-legged animal.

Back we went to *Fleur de Lys*. We fitted out for another season. Suddenly a currency crisis; the pound tumbled. We kept the home together with unaccustomed economy, and increasingly faded away in the café and left somebody else to pay for the drinks. France became exorbitantly expensive.[12] So we sailed away, wandering down the Spanish coast and at length made Barcelona – a fine town, but I always felt there was something wrong about its social system – and anchored off the yacht club. Daughter Diana and her little boy came to see us from Talavera.[13] There were rumours of revolution – but, we thought, that did not concern us.

12 The USA came off the gold standard in 1934 and the French franc rose in value. So did the British pound, but not by as much.

13 Diana's husband José owned a 10,000-acre cash-poor estate in Castile-La-Mancha, and was seemingly respected by his workforce. He studiously kept out of politics and thought that calm diplomacy would suffice to keep his workers content. It was not to be.

CHAPTER 17

A Spanish Interlude

For financial reasons Cumberlege kept Fleur de Lys *in the western Mediterranean. In 1935 he went ashore in Spain, and in July 1936 he witnessed the start of the Spanish Civil War. He left for Gibraltar.*

Sóller, Majorca (PD)

Southward we sailed on a calm, still evening. We found anchorage in Sóller, a village in north-west Majorca. We were happy in this tiny place, although Mistral at nine months was a menace, tottering naked into the warm sea. Now and again a dainty yacht would put into the exquisite, out-of-the-way harbour, but most of the time we had it to ourselves. Autumn came, and we sailed round to Palma with its good inside anchorage for yachts. Here we met *Jolie Brise*, which was undergoing a refit in the charge of Michael.[1] Then, leaving our own boat in the hands of a young Englishman, we took a steamer to England to show off Mistral to his grandparents. We took a flat in Surbiton to be near the family. I enjoyed my fire and, apart from visits to my mother, rarely went outside for the next five months. In the Spring [1935] we returned to *Fleur de Lys*, and sailed to Ibiza and then to the Spanish coast.

Our first port of call was Cartagena in Murcia; the atmosphere there was too rosy [red] for our liking. The local functionary had the manners of a pig. Here was none of the 'courtly Spanish grace' of a retired Naval Captain one usually found in these billets. He looked like a retired plumber pitchforked into the job because of his political leanings. In fluent Spanish, I ended up telling him exactly what I thought of him and threatening to report him to the British embassy in Madrid and to the Spanish admiral whose flag flew from a dirty-looking man-of-war. He was flabbergasted. The town was a fly-blown place and 'savages' stood in rows around us while we made simple purchases in the shops. We were glad to get back on board. For five days we sailed south in summer weather about 7 miles offshore. No

1 The Admiral was a friend of a wealthy American called Stanley Mortimer whose motor yacht exploded somewhere near St Tropez in 1933, and the Admiral suggested to Mortimer that his son Mike should go to England to find him a replacement sailing boat. Mortimer agreed, and Mike unearthed a 56-foot Le Havre pilot cutter in need of modernisation. Mortimer gave Mike the job of refitting *Jolly Brise*. In the summer of 1934 he sailed *Jolly Brise* south to Palma, Majorca, and the work was done there by the Ballester Yard in the winter of 1934–35.

wireless, no news, but very happy. Nan[2] thought of putting on the gramophone; she was one of those lovely girls who dressed by gramophone. One day Manoel was steering the ship when suddenly he asked me to kill him. He had a bad case of sunstroke. We got him to turn in to his bunk.

Next morning, Manoel was up; I took his temperature, found it slightly under normal and told him to sit quietly in the shade. The girls dived overboard and swam around until I spotted a huge basking shark idly cruising about 100 yards from the yacht. Not a breath of wind. For the next three days and nights we lay in about the same spot – ideal, had it not been for our patient. At last, a little breeze came up and I laid a course for Malaga before turning in. Nora and Nan stayed up, 'gramophoning' in the balmy night air. Manoel was safe in bed, and the second sailor simply had to follow the course. Suddenly, I woke up on the floor and guessed that the yacht had jibbed.[3] In the saloon I found the girls poring over a chart. 'What's the game?' I enquired. They didn't think we were heading for Malaga at all. I relieved the second sailor and at dawn we were off Malaga. On arrival I sent the two young men to a doctor, who diagnosed sunstroke. There was a steamer sailing for Barcelona the next day; both of them went home by it.

If Cartagena had been pink, Malaga was a more sinister shade: crimson. Boys amused themselves by heaving stones from the quayside into our cockpit; a policeman who remonstrated faintly with them at my request was treated with scorn and derision. When his back was turned I went ashore and knocked two of their heads together. After that, we were left alone. This was July, a year before the Civil War broke out. We left Malaga after recruiting a couple of locals who called themselves seamen – not bad lads, but not yacht hands. The 60 sea miles to Gibraltar – a three-hour trip 30 years before – took us five days and got our sails blown away. We tied up in the little camber where three decades earlier I had anchored my torpedo flotilla. Normally, a retired Rear Admiral might expect to have his call on the Governor returned by at least one of the man's under-strappers. Nothing of the sort was done by the bumptious fellow who was in office at the time.[4] The local Admiral, though, was an old friend.[5] We were in clover.

Nora now thought that she would like to live ashore for a change. I agreed, subject to suitable lodging. In a very dubious frame of mind, I was dragged off to a spot in the mountains some seven miles beyond Algeciras – a beautiful place. The house consisted of half a dozen old farm buildings banged into shape and joined up, the whole forming an irregular three-sided erection surrounding a patio, except to the south, where there was an uninterrupted view over forest falling gradually by 1,000 feet to the Straits of Gibraltar. A vast piscine, or bathing pool, filled the immediate foreground. I hesitated, wondering if, even at almost the eleventh hour, whether some Spanish man of good will would emerge for the Right. I thought of the Byron lines, 'Ah, sweeter than accents of lovers' farewell are the songs they sing and the tales that they tell.'[6] 'Take it, my dear,' I said. 'Let's get in tomorrow.'

Mistral lived night and day in his birthday suit, so I rigged a guesswarp[7] of two-inch rope around the pool. If he fell in, he could yell and hang onto the warp. Maria took on the role of cook. Juanillo became the

2 In 1936 Nancy Wooler (1915–1989), a Canadian, married Michael (1905–45), Cumberlege's older son by his first marriage. She loved sailing and got on well with the Admiral but less well with Nora. During the Second World War she shared a house in Sussex with the Admiral and his wife. After Mike was murdered in Sachsenhausen concentration camp in 1945, she married Lennox Livingstone-Learmonth in 1947 and lived for some years in southern Ireland.

3 Gybed; when sailing downwind, turned abruptly – and in this case probably inadvertently.

4 General Sir Charles Harington, GCB, GBE, DSO (1872–1940) was noted for his record during the First World War in a staff capacity, as Chief of Staff to General Herbert Plumer and the 2nd Army. He became Governor of Gibraltar in 1933 and retired in 1938.

5 Vice Admiral Sir James Murray Pipon, KBE, CB (1882–1971) was promoted to Rear Admiral in 1932 and Vice Admiral in December 1936, and retired from the RN soon after.

6 Lord Byron (1788–1824). *Bride of Abydos*, Canto i, Stanza 1.

7 A line that leads from a ship through a fairlead on a boat boom which is used for small boats to make fast.

gardener; his main duties came to be pulling Mistral out of soggy pools. Baltazar came with the house; he did anything I put to him, and nothing if I forgot to give instructions. Gorgeous summer ran into autumn. I knew there were snags but suppressed the knowledge. Strange signs in blood-red paint appeared on white cottage walls nearby – 'Death to landowners' 'Pay no taxes'. The sun shone and the eagles circled and the nightingales sang. Surely, here was peace? Autumn came, and Winter. The chestnut logs roared in the open chimney. One day, after early night had fallen, two dark men in black corduroy-coated suits called at Maria's bolted and barred kitchen entrance. She came in to our saloon with a brace of woodcock in her hand. Did we want them? Of course, we did. It was a hard and bitter Winter; the road was undermined in several places and a lorry went over the edge. But we were never without a brace of woodcock a week that Winter. Wild rabbits supplemented our diet boiled in red wine and shoved in strange fungus recommended by the poachers. How we fed!

The name of our pretty place was El Canuto, while the name for the whole valley was El Canuto de los Arcos, the Valley of Folds in the Hills of the Archways. By then, though, there were no archways – that is, the supports of Roman-era aqueducts carrying water from the hills to Algeciras and maybe as far as Carteia, the Roman city that used to stand near Gibraltar.

Spring 1936 arrived with all the flowers and birds known to man. Now and again, we went to Gibraltar by car to get money from the bank and do a little tobacco smuggling. It was only on those occasions that I noticed the signs, painted on the walls of houses, of the general discomfort and unrest brewing around us. I did not draw Nora's attention to them as she would be busy driving. The general view was that nothing was likely to happen until after the harvest in October. In the towns of Andalucía, though, the workers and seafarers were seething with discontent. Nora was going to have a baby in August; night after night, I wondered to myself if it would not be wiser to clear out. We had no stake in this country – but as soon as morning dawned, I forgot I had even thought of leaving such a lovely, peaceful spot. Time went on; one gets rather *mañana-ish* living in Spain.

Diana, my daughter, married to José, a landowner, wrote to say that they hoped to come down to see us soon, but at the moment the crops – their only source of livelihood – were not harvested. Things were difficult for them. The 10,000-acre estate – much of which was forest – had a certain amount of grazing and

Left: Diana with her daughter and José Avial at Malpartida 1935–36 (Family collection)
Right: Diana with her son José Maria (Joe) (Family collection)

arable land. José worked like a slave himself and was popular, but every penny he had went into the pockets of labour and none was left for improvements such as irrigation. The only cash resources of this young couple with two small children (a boy of five and a girl of three) were £1 a week plus any proceeds from the pawning of Diana's few pieces of jewellery. Their home consisted of a huge, old-fashioned farmhouse, a corner of which they had transformed into a small but comfortable home. The nearest town was Talavera – 10 miles away across a plateau. A small, poverty-stricken village of 250 souls was two or three miles away. A tributary of the Tagus River bounded one side of their domain. The nearest building was that in which the Iron Duke [Duke of Wellington] had had his headquarters during the battle of Talavera.[8] It was unoccupied except for caretakers. This sort of property might be found across Spain, but rarely with the owner living on it. More likely, he would be sitting in a Biarritz café, and his administrator would be paying out half the basic wage ordered by the Republican government of six pesetas a day – and his workers would sign for three rather than get the sack. Such owners got no more than they deserved if they lost their all.

To me, the Civil War was the result of lack of education, for which the Catholic church was mainly responsible, as well as foreign propaganda, absentee landlords and selfish politicians. In my peaceful, exquisite Canuto, all seemed well with the world – for the next three months anyhow. Nora was determined to give birth in this lovely spot, and we found various people to help as required. The Red rising was not due until October, I thought. I had taken some precautions, planning a getaway in two earmarked lorries. Then, one day, we ran into a sudden strike in Algeciras, and a most pathetic demonstration by the wives and families of fishermen, filing along dressed in any old rags or cast-offs. No noise, no excitement, just a drove of hopeless, miserable people and their wretched babies. May I never see anything like it again. Soon after, one calm and sunlit Sunday, we had been out to the ocean beach beyond Tarifa when we met a tribe of a dozen or so children seemingly returning home from Sunday school. They gave us the clenched fist of the communist salute. Oh well, I thought, we should be out of here in a couple of months.

One morning a cabalistic sign in red paint was painted on our white wall. I left it; I wasn't sure what it meant, but we were well considered in the neighbourhood. On another occasion, I went to Gibraltar by the steamer to get some cash. Nora was to meet me in Algeciras on my return by the 5:00 pm ship. She was stopped entering town. There were no taxis. The cafés were closed. Soldiers were everywhere, and machine guns pointed up each street. I had Juanillo with me. 'Come on Juanillo,' I said. 'This is where we foot it.' 'Nothing new to me, Señor Almirante,' he responded. Off we set. It was a long, long climb and it took us an hour and a half. Not a soul did we meet until the village of Pelayo, where we ran into some friendly *Carabineros* [policemen]. 'What is the news, Señor Almirante?' I could only tell them what I had seen.

Later I learnt that a Colonel commanding the troops in Algeciras had taken charge, anticipating trouble. Not a shot had been fired. 'I knew you would be all right and would get home somehow,' said Nora. 'I haven't worried. Mistral is in bed.'

That night, every man in the village, including Juanillo and Baltazar, fled into the cold Sierras 1,000 feet above us. They must have spent a most uncomfortable night. The women preferred to remain at home. Little Maria stuck to us. There was nothing to be done. The Moors[9] arrived; a posse was sent to Pelayo to

8 The Battle of Talavera (27–28 July 1809) was fought outside the town of Talavera de la Reina, Spain, 75 miles south-west of Madrid, during the Peninsular War. An Anglo-Spanish army under Sir Arthur Wellesley joined a Spanish army under General Cuesta in operations against French-occupied Madrid. The French army withdrew at night after its attacks were repulsed. At daylight next day the British and Spanish discovered that the French force had gone, leaving their wounded and two brigades of artillery in the field. Wellesley was ennobled as Viscount Wellington of Talavera and of Wellington for the action.

9 Soldiers from Franco's army based in Morocco.

reassure the inhabitants. There were rumours of bloodthirsty doings in San Roque and La Linea, towns we would have to pass through *en route* to Gibraltar. Algeciras was bombed again. I still felt the best thing to do was to remain quietly where we were. Three or four days later, at 5:00 in the evening, we heard a car on our private track. It was the British Consul from Algeciras, come to tell us that a dockyard tug had been sent over from Gibraltar to evacuate British folk in the area. We were not ordered to leave, but told this was the only opportunity available to do so. Nora was eight months pregnant by now. Not wishing to embarrass the authorities in Gibraltar, and realising the improbability of getting transport for the doctor to be with us, I decided to quit.

'How long have we got?' I asked the Consul. 'Well, my orders were not to keep the tug more than half an hour and it's taken that long to get here!' We piled into the old Austin Seven and hid our new second-hand Humber Snipe amongst the trees. We stowed all we could, wrapped up in sheets and blankets in the back of the car and said farewell to Canuto. It was very sad. The whole village came out to say goodbye. My friends the Carabineros gravely grasped my hand. 'Shove off, Nora. I can't stand this sort of thing.' Nora was all but in tears. The Carabineros slapped their shouldered rifles. Even the one-legged man and the spotted-faced barman rushed out from the Venta bar. We rolled down the hill. 'Adios,' said Misty, gravely. We boarded the tug, where there were already some 50 British subjects, with our gear, and the old car was taken away by a friend of the Consul and garaged in Algeciras.

We arrived at Gibraltar about 8:00 pm. Admiral Pipon's Flag Lieutenant met us with an ultimatum: Nora was to go to The Mount [the Admiral's house] with Mistral. The building was already full, but no refusal was entertained. I went to *Fleur de Lys*. My friends knew that Nora was due, almost overdue. So it came to pass that while I went back to England to make arrangements for Diana and her family, Tarik was born at The Mount and Nora stayed in the most perfect comfort. One does not forget that sort of hospitality.

James Pipon, Flag Admiral Gibraltar, when he was Captain of HMS *Delhi* (PD)

One morning, James Pipon came aboard himself and said, 'Look here, old chap. Diana's quite all right, but bad news about José.' He handed me a wireless message he had received from the *Devonshire* cruiser which had got it by some means from the embassy in Madrid. 'José-Maria killed yesterday. Diana proceeding home via Marseilles.'

From Diana, I heard what had happened in Talavera:

> We were at Malpatida [their home] when the troubles commenced. We remained there for several days and were threatened by the nearby villagers continually, but nothing happened except that the servants drifted away. José eventually took the car to Talavera and saw the captain of the Guardia Civil, who was a friend of ours. Talavera de la Reina had gone completely Red, but this captain had maintained order and urged José to come into Talavera where he could guarantee our safety, but said it was impossible to do so if we stayed at Malpatida. So we took a few things and went into Talavera and stayed quietly with a friend of ours, a wealthy man who for 25 years had made it his business to look after the poor of the city. All went well for a few days. Then one day the captain came to our house and told us that Franco's armies would be arriving in a few days, but meanwhile he and his men had secret orders to go to Toledo to help loyalists there. That night the captain and all his men left Talavera.

Diana's home at Malpartida, Talavera de la Reina, Toledo, Spain (Family collection)

A day or two passed and Franco's men did not arrive. The Reds got nasty. We, and all other well-to-do folk, were dragged before the Red tribunal and questioned, not once or twice a day but 20 times a day. Then we were sent home for an hour or two before being lugged back for further questioning. At night, every night, we heard executions, which took place in the Alameda not three minutes from the house. This went on for ten days until José was so utterly tired of it all that I believe he rather hoped the next time would be the last.

One night, it was. After midnight, a crowd came to the door and demanded admission. When they got in, they said that they wanted our host and his young son and José to go to the tribunal for more questioning. José got up and dressed and went downstairs. I followed, but was stopped on the stairs by a young man who was very agitated and forbade me to go any further, saying 'Whatever you do, don't show your face outside the house.' I asked what was going on, and the man said 'Nothing. Only taking them to the tribunal for more questioning.' I felt, I knew, this was the end. The daughter of the house and I sat together watching the clock. It was three o'clock. At five minutes past three we heard the shots.

The girl and I went out. It was just dawn. We searched the Alameda, the morgue, enquired at the hospital. Nobody knew anything, until I saw a Red I knew by sight. He told us we might as well go home as he had personally seen the bodies flung on a lorry which was driven off into the country. I went to the Red tribunal where they just laughed at me when I asked 'Why did you murder such men who have done nothing but good to their people and had carefully avoided all politics?' The only answer I got was 'That is the very reason we shot them.' I realised it was no good staying. Seeing a man in the office whom I knew slightly, I asked him to get me a permit to clear out of Talavera. There was no sort of law or order in the place; this man merely went to a drawer, pulled out the office stamp and stamped a permit and gave it to me. Armed with this I went out to Malpartida, which was untouched, and packed up some things and luckily found a few pesetas in an old box; otherwise, I hadn't a penny. Taking the baby and accompanied by a young fellow who had been a great friend of José's and for whom José had done a lot,[10] I got to the station at Talavera and had just enough money to buy tickets to Madrid.

10 Tomas Herrero, later manager of the Malpartida Estate.

> I told the boy to pretend he was English, although he couldn't talk a word of the language. I told him I would chat to him in English and he must answer me with the English titles of the gramophone records which he used to put on for us. The carriage was crowded. Sitting opposite us were some Red militia men with rifles. They actually mentioned José-Maria's name and agreed that a terrible mistake had been made by bumping off such a universally popular man!
>
> I arrived in Madrid with a Spanish penny and a halfpenny, and went to the British Embassy. Here they took charge of me and, eventually, I was sent by train to Valencia and put on board Devonshire.[11] But not before I had had to go and see poor Minuto's [José's] mother and break the news to her. Minuto was the old lady's favourite child. It all but broke her heart.

That is Diana's story. Pretty grim. Fortunately, she had sent her little boy, José Maria (Joe), aged five, to England a month before the troubles began. Shortly after, her poor mother-in-law, no longer young, a widow and almost an invalid, was imprisoned in Madrid. There she stayed for the best part of a year until her devoted Irish secretary – who had been governess to her three children and who had taken refuge in the embassy – managed to get her out. Just a quiet, very pious, even old-fashioned Spanish lady. So much for the Spain we are backing.[12]

Meantime, we refugees were perfectly comfortable once more under the Union Jack [moored in Gibraltar], even if I had to pay exorbitant charges for the use of moorings nobody else needed.

---

11 The *Daily Express* newspaper of 6 August 1936 carried a story about Diana's escape to England on page 9, claiming in the headline that she had reached the UK 'on forged papers'. She was remarkably calm in an interview with the reporter, expressed no bitterness towards those who had murdered her husband, and said that she hoped to return to Spain and the farm to pick up her life there.

12 This is a reference to UK policy during the Spanish Civil War; British leaders believed that the Spanish Republican government was the puppet of extreme-left socialists and communists. The UK government proclaimed neutrality; its objective was that in a future European war the UK would enjoy good relations with whichever side won in Spain. It was also concerned about the fascists, and concluded that in the Spain of 1936–38 no desirable basis of government was possible.

CHAPTER 18

Cap d'Antibes 1937–1938

The Cumberlege caravan in the Mediterranean rolled on. The Admiral gave up his life on board, settling onshore in Cap d'Antibes, France, in late 1937. He lived there until Italy invaded in 1940.

We set up home once more on board *Fleur de Lys,* and were very happy. The new baby was christened Tarik – the name of the first-known Moorish chieftain who had given his name to Gibraltar.[1] An interlude occurred when I went to Malta in the greatest comfort with a friend, Captain John Godfrey[2], the skipper of *Repulse*, with a view to seeing Mike and his wife, Nan, who were looking after an American gentleman's yacht called *Landfall* which was laid up there. A delightful trip. I had always loved Malta; it had not changed much, and it was a grand pleasure to meet my old friends after an interval of some 20 years. Then I went back to Gibraltar in the hospitable *Resource* and joined my family in *Fleur de Lys.* I set about finding a crew. Gibraltarians were useless; their sole desire was to get a job in the dockyards. I tried Spaniards without success. For the time being I gave up the unequal contest – with Spain unsafe and Italy behaving like a spoilt child, there was not much point in leaving Gibraltar.

John Godfrey, Captain of HMS *Repulse* and later Director of Naval Intelligence 1938–42 (IWM)

Then Mistral fell overboard and all but drowned. He was three years old. He was not allowed on deck without his lifebelt on, but one early morning he tried to climb the ladder on to the upper deck in his pyjamas. We got him down. He must have gone into the forecastle. Suddenly, I heard a splash. It was not Misty but Manoel. A young Spaniard 30 yards away, engaged in cleaning, had looked across and seen something floating face downward in the sea. Realising it was a boy, he had yelled out to Manoel. who instantly jumped overboard and got Misty on deck. His great blue eyes were wide open, his head lolled. He seemed as dead as mutton. Nora rushed up in her nightshirt and dashed ashore to the nearby doctor's door opposite. Meanwhile, I turned

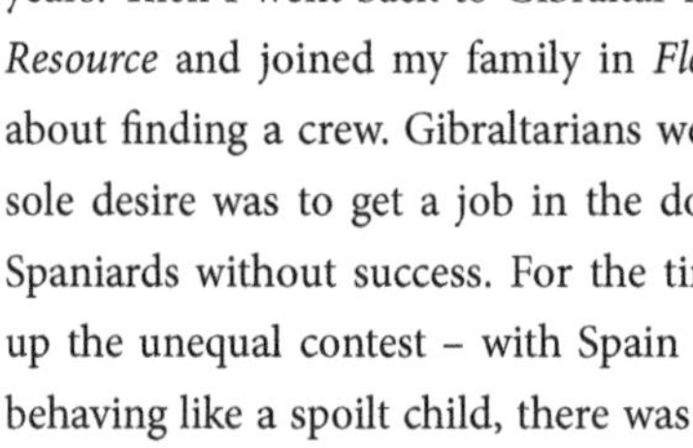

Mike at the helm of *Landfall* (Paine Family)

1 Gibraltar comes from the Moorish name 'Gabel Tarik – the hill of Tarik'.

2 Vice Admiral John Godfrey (1888–1970) commanded the battle-cruiser *Repulse* from 1936 to 1939, then served as Director of Naval Intelligence 1939–42. From 1943 to 1946 he was Flag Officer Commanding the Royal Indian Navy.

Misty upside down and water ran out of his stomach. I squeezed his tiny ribs and lungs again and again and again. Eventually a great spurt of white foam gushed out of his lungs through his mouth, and he caught a breath and let off a yell. I rushed him below, wrapped him in a blanket and added a hot water bottle. Nora returned with Dr. Gill. He was very grave. We waited. Misty was just about able to breathe. The doctor advised against hospital and felt the best thing to do was to leave him lying quietly. His lungs were virtually full of water. In the evening, his temperature had climbed to 104 degrees. He began to labour and was in a bad way. I took matters into my own hands and rubbed him all over with a bottle of Sloan's liniment.[3] Within a quarter of an hour, believe it or not, his temperature was normal. He still had a lot of water in his lungs, but in a day or so he was swimming around the ship in his belt. An inquest ensued. We concluded that his thick camel-haired dressing-gown had helped him by acting as a sort of life buoy. But it was only the alertness of that man in the next ship that had saved him.

We decided to take no more chances; until a certain age, children simply do not realise any sort of danger. It was the Summer of 1937. We decided to go ashore for a bit. The south coast of Portugal, by road through Andalucía, appealed to us. I called on the Algeciras command and asked it if they had any objections to my projected passage through Nationalist territory. They had none, and said they would be glad to give every assistance. I was told to call in at the Algeciras office on the day before we planned to start the journey, and I would be given a safe conduct passage as far as Seville. There, I would need a new pass to the Portuguese frontier.

We set off. I had fashioned a railing on the car within which we stowed half a dozen suitcases. Nora was the chauffeur, Nurse and two children sat behind her with Sheba, the dog. In Algeciras our safe conduct pass was delivered by the Duque de Seville in five minutes. From there to the 'very royal and very loyal city of Tarifa', as a sign proclaimed. Near Vejer we topped up with petrol and lunched in a cool spot on cold chicken, an icy melon and a flagon of wine. At the Seville–Cadiz–Algeciras crossroads we were held up by a large guard of soldiers; Tarik, a platinum-blond baby, charmed the ragged troops and officials. Next, Jerez de la Frontera. In Seville we rolled slowly through the lovely gardens, thronged on this Sunday evening hour with countless folk, pulled up at a hotel I knew and dined very well that night.

Next morning, I visited the British Consulate, where I was informed that I would certainly get permission to proceed to Portugal but might well have to wait for it for some time. The Vice Consul came with me to the Commandancia office. Here we were informed that now, since the previous day, all applications to leave the country had to be made to the central government in Salamanca. This did not disturb me. The official said he would telegraph my request and ring me at the hotel as soon as permission was received. We made the best of things, enjoying the magnificence of the cathedral. It now occurred to me, however, that in view of this new order it might be even more difficult to get back from Portugal into Spain when we wished to return to Gibraltar and the yacht. So I began the process of getting a safe conduct pass to proceed from Seville back to Algeciras. Eventually it appeared. Our return journey was as pleasant as our outward. Once more we found ourselves in the silence and comfort of our floating home.

By that time, one year after the outbreak of the Civil War, order and peace reigned in Andalucía. But the trip in Spain gave us time to think. Perhaps, after all, a longer tour in inimical Italy might lead to a humorous adventure? I had never regarded the country as a whole as unfriendly, and saw Mussolini as the biggest bluffer in the world. We [the British] simply did nothing but talk as the gangster's stupidities

3 Sloan's Liniment is used for the relief of muscle or joint pain caused by strains, sprains, arthritis, bruising or backaches. Capsaicin, from chili peppers, is the active ingredient; it causes a sensation of heat that activates nerve cells, providing the relief.

grew. 'Let's go to Italy,' I thought. A friend had just motored from Naples through Italy to England and reported nothing but kindness and courtesy. So we shipped on board a Japanese steamer, complete with dog and Humber Snipe car – an enjoyable passage. We were on the ship for about four days, and arrived at Naples early one morning. An Automobile Association representative helped me land the car and go through customs. I bought tourist *lire*, hotel coupons and enough petrol coupons to cover about six weeks' touring. Throughout our time in Italy, we rarely saw another British car or person or ship flying the British ensign; a friend of mine had actually had a guard put on board his yacht in port, such was the suspicion. But everywhere we went on land we had a delightful time. In Rome, soldiers were everywhere. But we had the luck to see Gangster Ben [Benito Mussolini] and hear him screaming from his balcony until a passing brass band utterly ruined the effect. He seemed to be amused.

After eight weeks we left Italy with broad smiles and crossed the French frontier. Nice housed us for a week until we found a small place to rent on Cap d'Antibes, and here we are today. The house has central heating, is under fir trees and in sight and sound of the sea. The half-acre garden has half a dozen golden genistas,[4] some peach trees and a couple of oleanders growing in its red soil. There are a lot of birds, partly due to a magnificent lighthouse above us. Mistral scatters bread everywhere. We have a Swiss mademoiselle who rules the children with a rod of iron. I find the locals grasping and jealous. There is no village, and the post office is never open. Two shops supply our needs and hate each other. I have borrowed a bicycle so that I may pedal down to Juan-les-Pins, two miles away, to fetch a doctor when needed. Nora is expecting again; she never ceases buying cradles and baby carriages and knitting things. We hope it will be a girl.[5] Mistral is now nearly five years old; Tarik is 18 months; they both give me a great kick. Once Claudine is off the stocks, I am going to take a round turn and two half hitches in myself,[6] and that's it.

Cap d'Antibes, 1938

At Cap d'Antibes 1939 (L to R) Mike Cumberlege, Nora, unknown, CLC (Family collection)

4 Also known as the Mount Etna broom – a large flowering shrub or small tree associated in the Mediterranean with sunny open landscapes and poor stony soil.

5 It was. Claudine Cumberlege was born in 1939 and, like her brother Tarik, was christened in HMS *Repulse*. The rented villa was replaced by one that Claude and Nora built in 1939–40.

6 A vasectomy. Luis, the admiral's fourth child by his second marriage, was nevertheless born in England in 1941.

Afterword

From 1939 to his death in 1963 Claude Cumberlege continued his nomadic existence, spending the 1940–45 war in England, the 1945–59 period in France, and the last four years of his life in Majorca.

Sometime in 1939, following the birth of Claudine, the Admiral decided to build his own house in Cap d'Antibes. No attention was paid to the external circumstances as tensions rose across Europe in the wake of Hitler's dismemberment of Czechoslovakia and Mussolini's invasion of Albania. The French army numbered nearly one million men, and the supposedly impregnable Maginot Line had apparently been completed. Cap d'Antibes seemed far from any conceivable danger. Michael, his wife Nancy and their young son Marcus lived nearby when Mike was not away in the Mediterranean skippering a yacht for well-to-do American patrons; and the French Riviera had an abundance of rich and famous visitors each summer to amuse the endlessly sociable Claude and Nora.

Both were witty, irreverent storytellers. The Admiral, however, did tend to embellish his stories. A good example concerns Jack Kennedy, the future American President. In July/August 1939 the entire Kennedy clan, headed by father Joe Kennedy, then US Ambassador to the United Kingdom, descended on Antibes and the luxurious Hotel du Cap-Eden-Roc for a holiday. Jack Kennedy, aged 22 and at Harvard, was among them. According to Cumberlege, he was having a drink and holding court at his favourite café in Cap d'Antibes when the proprietor came up to him and said in French: 'There are a couple of drunk American sailors [*sic*] who insist I serve them more drinks. Can you explain to them that I cannot do this because they can't have any more? I don't speak English.' The Admiral obliged and, making use of his considerable presence, politely asked the two not to insist on asking for more booze. They, equally politely, insisted on having more. So the Admiral suggested the following: 'We shall let you have more to drink if you pass a test.' They agreed. This test consisted of standing on one leg, drawing the other leg upwards, bending down and with one hand touching the nose with one hand and the uplifted leg with the other. If they did this without stumbling or falling, they would get more drink. The first American tried and failed. The second tried and succeeded. Shortly after, Cumberlege chatted with the winner and told him that he was a retired admiral. To which the young man replied,

The Kennedy family at the Hotel du Cap Eden Roc, July–August 1939. John F. Kennedy is in the front row, extreme left.
[Notes: Blemishes and spotting are original to the negative.]
(John F. Kennedy Library)

'U.S. Navy Ensign, John Fitzgerald Kennedy.' The only problem with this tale is that Jack Kennedy did not enlist in the US Navy until October 1941. But he *had* been in Cap d'Antibes in 1939.

France and the UK went to war with Germany in September 1939, but the next six months lulled the Cumberleges into another false sense of security. Son Michael was called up at the start of 1940 and, thanks to John Godfrey, the Admiral's friend who by then Director of Naval Intelligence, was posted to Marseille on Contraband Control Duties – in reality, checking on the activities of the French Fleet based there. By early May, the fighting in northern France had begun to intrude into life on the Riviera. The Admiral remained blithely unconcerned.

On 10 June 1940 Italy declared war on France and Britain. A couple of weeks later Mike and Nancy were bombed by the Italian air force while staying in Mike's apartment in Marseille, but survived. Back in Antibes that afternoon, 120 miles away, the Admiral was busying himself in his new garden wearing only the bottom half of his pyjamas when, as Mike recounted in a letter,

> a taxi rolled up, and two very definitive personages, including the local mayor dressed in funereal black with his badge of office, top hat and white-gloved hands, bore down on the Skipper [as the Admiral's children called him]. The Admiral was not at all put out by his scanty costume. The mayor delivered a magnificent speech, the gist of which was 'Courage ... I am the harbinger of bad tidings. Your son is dead.' 'Dead? Well, I don't believe it,' Father replied. 'You couldn't kill him with a poleaxe.' The mayor then showed him the telegram he had received from Marseilles. The Admiral read it and realised it referred to his cook's son. It had been ambiguously worded. So they all went into the house together and had a cognac, and everything was okay.

Next day, the Admiral's stubbornness in the face of negative war news reached new heights. Nancy had returned to Cap d'Antibes. That afternoon Mike received orders to leave France. He hurried back to Cap d'Antibes, woke Nancy and told her that she had to pack up their home and return to Marseilles with him, ready to board a vessel to take them to Gibraltar. Meantime, he went to see his father, informed him that the news was rather bad – he was not permitted to be more specific – and that he should prepare for worse news. The Admiral responded by pulling a blanket over his head and saying, 'You're a damn fool. How could *you* know, anyway?' He said he would make his own arrangements and 'to hell with everybody'. Mike replied that he might not see him again, and left.

Later that evening, the Admiral turned up at Mike's home. He still refused to believe the news of the rapid German advance through France. Early next morning, as Mike and Nancy were pulling out, the Admiral and Nora came to say goodbye; Mike offered them use of his flat in Marseille, but they refused it. The Admiral and his family then hung on until July, when the Vichy government gave all British citizens a week to leave. Then the Italians gave all British subjects in southern France 48 hours to leave, and a difficult trek through southern France towards Biarritz ensued.

Here Cumberlege's path again crossed that of his elder daughter, Diana. After the murder of her husband José-Maria Avial in the summer of 1936, and her escape via the UK embassy in Madrid and HMS *Devonshire*, she had reached London penniless and homeless with her daughter, Paloma, in early August, along with 60 other refugees. Next day, the *Daily Express* ran a feature about the first British casualties of the Spanish Civil War reaching England. A wealthy Peruvian, Jorge Dibos Valdeavellano, one of her admirers when *L'Insoumise* had been anchored in St-Jean-de-Luz in the summer of 1927, was living

MOTHER, WIDOWED BY REDS—COMES HOME ON FORGED PAPERS

MRS. DIANA AVIAL, British-born widow of a Spanish landowner, arrived in London yesterday with sixty other refugees from the Spanish Terror.

She brought with her her daughter, aged three and a half, and a wooden suitcase tied with orange rope. She declared to the Customs an empty jewel case, a few clothes, one toy.

It was all she had in the world.

She is the daughter of Rear-Admiral C. L. Cumberlege. She married Don José Avial. They lived on a farm near Talavera de la Reina, a hundred miles west of Madrid.

She said: "We had been expecting it for months. A fortnight before it began we hid with friends until July 18. Then the rebel guard marched away.

"They said reinforcements were coming—but they never arrived. The town was taken by the mob—young boys so hysterical they did not know which was friend or foe.

"For them, my husband was a capitalist, they were Communists. They forgot his friendship for them, his work for them. Two poachers betrayed him. They took him away. We heard the shot.... That's all.

"I hid with a servant. She stamped my papers with the town hall stamp when no one was looking.

"I have come through fire, death, destruction. You cannot tell which side is which. Brother fights brother. Whichever party emerges, the destruction of all Spain is there.

"I am not bitter. The boys did not know what they were doing. They shoot any one.

"I shall go back, look for the farm, pick up the ruins—and start again."

Daily Express exclusive pictures show Mrs. Avial and Paloma, her daughter, at Victoria.

Millionaire's Wife, Fined For Theft, Flies To Liner

Mrs. Mildred Wilson O'Neill, forty-two-year-old wife of an American millionaire, who had spent several weeks in London, passed part of her last night in England in a small, white-tiled room with a wooden bench and two rough blankets—a prison cell.

Yesterday Mrs. O'Neill dashed from Marylebone Police Court to Croydon, chartered a special air-plane to Cherbourg and boarded the Queen Mary. It was a race against time because her mother-in-law is

The *Daily Express* story about Diana's escape from Spain (*Daily Express*)

in London at the time. He saw the article and sought out Diana. Within a year, she had remarried.

Although in 1938 she purchased a house on the outskirts of Ifield, West Sussex, she moved with Jorge Dibos to his large residence, with 75 acres, near Biarritz. In July 1940 he arranged for the Cumberlege family to be guided from his house over the Pyrenees to Spain. They journeyed to Algeciras and thence across the bay to Gibraltar. Here they boarded a MacAndrews Line[1] ship to Liverpool before finally reaching The Hyde, Diana's house in Ifield, where they remained until 1945.

A few hours after the family had said goodbye to Diana and Jorge, German troops arrived at Biarritz. Diana, now with a Peruvian passport, avoided internment. But Wehrmacht officers lived in their house, festooned Nazi flags from the windows, held parades outside the front door and hung washing over the rose bushes and terraces – and, in Diana's words, 'made themselves loathsomely objectionable in every way'. In mid-October the couple left, making their way to Lima via Portugal and New York.

In Sussex, after the Cumberleges had moved into Diana's spacious house, Nancy Cumberlege, who had left London during the Blitz, went to live there too with her young son, Marcus. The house was adjacent to a golf course and an RAF airfield, and almost next door was the Officers' Mess of 239 Squadron, commanded at the time by Wing Commander Peter Donkin. Nancy worked in the canteen once or twice a week to keep boredom in check and her spirits up, and to earn some money. Nora was

The Hyde, Ifield, Sussex (Family collection)

Diana in 1968. She lived in Peru for the rest of her life (Family collection)

1 The MacAndrews Line was founded in 1857. In 1927 it became part of the Royal Mail group. In 1938 it began a passenger/cargo service between the UK and Gibraltar/Spain. In 1939 nine of the company's twenty ships were requisitioned by the Admiralty as anti-aircraft and convoy rescue ships, and in 1939–45 ten ships were lost to enemy action. After the war the line survived to 1979.

Left: CLC in his Home Guard uniform (Family collection).
Right: CLC in the Home Guard (seated, second left) in 1943 (Family collection)

always partying, sometimes away for days at a time in London, to the discomfort of her husband. In 1941 she unexpectedly gave birth to her fourth child, Luis, and was very ill for a time afterwards. That year, too, Nora's niece, Betty Cox, married Donkin.

In 1939 the Admiral offered his services to the Royal Navy, only to be informed that there were no appointments for him. So he joined a local Home Guard unit. Detail about his life in Sussex, however, is sparse. Just about the only source is the letters that Nancy Cumberlege wrote regularly to her husband, Mike, abroad on active service until he was captured in April 1943. On 24 February 1941 she wrote that Claude had not said a word about his new son with his jet-black eyes. but 'did remark to me this morning that it was very odd how none of his children bore the slightest resemblance to each other, and none except Claudine to himself![2] Poor old Skipper; he is just the same, pretty miserable, but busy on [building] rabbit hutches. He has turned his room into a workshop.'

The grass of the lawn at The Hyde was allowed to grow long to provide hay for the rabbits in winter. The Admiral then decided to decorate the lounge of Diana's house, and painted the walls yellow and orange and adorned them with a willow tree, a pagoda and a junk with flags flying. After this, in black ink, he decorated a lampshade with the outline of ships – *Fleur de Lys* and *Landfall* and a dirty British coaster. Around this time, too, he invested £1,000 in war bonds[3] despite the family's increasing need for income from capital to cover everyday expenses.

In late April or early May 1941 the Admiral was operated on, probably for cancer. Nancy wrote, after visiting him in hospital in Brighton some days after the operation: 'Skipper is very well and looks better than he's looked since France … I am so relieved. I really did think there might be difficulties, and he was drinking a lot just before the operation … He told us that none of us would ever know what he had been through in these last three months – which is a very great deal for him to say.' Nancy reckoned he looked younger by 20 years when he got back to Ifield in mid-May. Yet by the start of 1942 he was unwell again. 'He's the most awful colour, a yellowy grey, and has to stay in bed for two days every ten days or so, and otherwise just sleeps all day and feels miserable.' Nora's erratic behaviour, usually caused by alcohol, passed the Admiral by except for an occasion when he caught her alone in a car with a 'mad Irishman'.

2 The question of Luis' paternity upset Nancy Cumberlege, who was convinced that the Admiral was not the father. In one letter to her husband, she wrote: 'It's all I can do to keep quiet about it … I feel Nora deserves a lot of punishment.'

3 Equivalent to £53,000 today.

A wartime Christmas card from the Admiral in 1943 (Family collection)

Mike in a cafe in Croatia in 1939 (Family collection)

With Nora and Claudine in *Tatler* in the early 1950s (*Tatler*)

From May 1943 Cumberlege worried about the fate of his eldest son. Michael, a Lieutenant Commander RNR, had been captured by the Germans at the end of April during an undercover mission by the SOE[4] in the Aegean to blow up the Corinth Canal. The family knew he was alive, captured, but no more. The war in Europe ended without further word of Mike.

A desperate search began, led by Nancy. The Admiral pulled all the strings he could, contacting the admiral commanding the RNR, the UK Naval Commander-in-Chief Germany and an old friend, General Lewis Lynne, the commandant of the British sector in Berlin. It turned out that Michael, tortured in Mauthausen concentration camp, had spent 15 months in harsh conditions and solitary confinement in Sachsenhausen concentration camp near Berlin. Lynne in turn approached his Russian opposite number, as Sachsenhausen by then was in the Soviet section of the divided city. To no avail. Not until November 1946 was Mike, having been murdered by the SS in February–March 1945, declared dead by the Admiralty. An authentic war hero, he was awarded the DSO & Bar, and the Greek Medal of Honour.

By 1945, somewhat against the odds, the Admiral and his wife remained together. Nora returned to Cap d'Antibes soon after the end of fighting in Europe to see how the house she and Claude had built had fared. The garden was so overgrown that she had trouble finding the place. But once she did get her bearings and settled in, she rapidly struck up friendships with new acquaintances, including a Dominican diplomat called Porfirio Rubirosa,[5] known as one of the great lotharios of the 20th century. A short while later, the Admiral returned with three of the children; he was not impressed with Rubirosa.

Needing income to recreate their pre-war lifestyle, Claude and Nora invested in various businesses such as bars, discos and property on the French Riviera and in the ski resorts of the Haute-Savoie. They also became leading lights in the post-war social life of Antibes, meeting and mixing with many of its most prominent visitors, including the Duke and Duchess of Windsor, Noel Coward, Rita Hayworth and Prince Aly Khan. Tarik, Claudine and Luis went to the village school in Cap d'Antibes and soon became fluent in French. Later, Claudine attended the local College

4 Special Operations Executive formed in mid-1940 to conduct espionage and sabotage in Europe against the Axis powers, and to aid local resistance movements.

5 Porfirio Rubirosa Ariza (1909–1965) was a Dominican diplomat, racing car driver, soldier and polo player. He was a supporter of dictator Rafael Trujillo, and was also rumoured to be a political assassin under his regime. Rubirosa made his mark as an international playboy for his jetsetting lifestyle and his legendary sexual prowess with women. His five wives included two of the richest women in the world at the time, among them Barbara Hutton.

Left: Claudine aged 19 with Sean Connery (Family collection)
Right: At the Sea Club with Nora and Louis (Family collection)

des Filles while the boys went to a school for boys. Mistral remained in England at a boarding school for a few years before completing his education in Antibes. Claudine recalls how indulgent the Admiral was with her, in contrast to the strict way he had tried to bring up Diana.

A drastic French currency reform in 1958 brought an end to this existence. The house in Cap d'Antibes was rented out, and the family moved, initially to the cheaper Costa Brava. In 1960 Nora and Claude upsticked again and arrived in Majorca with their four children.[6] Here they fell in love with a colonial-style property with whitewashed walls in Cala Ratjada on the north-east coast, overlooking the Admiral's beloved Mediterranean. The building was purchased in 1962. The following year Claude died, aged 86.[7] Nora added a swimming pool and other facilities, and opened the 17-room establishment to visitors in 1964. She died in 1992, but the Sea Club flourished through word-of-mouth recommendation and remains in business to this day, still in the ownership and management of the Cumberlege family.

Robin Knight, London 2023

A bust of Claude Lionel Cumberlege (Family collection)

6 Mistral Cumberlege (1933–2019) lived all over the world before settling in California. His death notice states: 'Everywhere he went, he made many lasting friends. He loved sailing and skiing … He touched many hearts with his good humour and kind ways.' Tarik Cumberlege (1936–2011) lived much of his life in Stockton, California, where he was a businessman. Claudine Cumberlege (born 1939) lives in the Palma neighbourhood of Genova, Majorca. At age 21, she became Sean Connery's girlfriend for a year, having met the actor at a party in London. They reconnected once in the mid-1960s at the Sea Club, when Connery was filming in Majorca. Luis Cumberlege (1941–2020) ran the Sea Club once Nora died, and made many renovations. Today the club is run by his sons.

7 The Admiral's oldest son by his first marriage, Michael (born 1905), was executed in Sachsenhausen concentration camp by the German SS in early 1945. He had one son, Marcus, who died in 2019. Diana Dibos Valdeavellano (born 1910), his daughter by his first marriage, died in Lima, Peru, on 15 August 1989; she had cancer of the stomach and passed away just five weeks after the diagnosis. Her mother, Laetitia, had also died of cancer of the stomach. Diana had five children, two by her first marriage and three by her second, including Juan Dibos.

BIBLIOGRAPHY

Primary Sources

The National Archive
ADM 116/1686
ADM 1/8430/235
ADM 1/8548/8
ADM 137/5
ADM 137/7/1
ADM 137/7/6
ADM 137/7/7
ADM 137/11/1
ADM 196/44
ADM 196/90
ADM 196/125
ADM 196/141
ADM 196/44/332
OEL/1
HD/1915/277

Others
http://dreadnoughtproject.org/tfs/index.php/Claude_Lionel_Cumberlege
https://www.awm.gov.au/collection/E84727
https://www.navy.gov.au/biography/rear-admiral-john-saumarez-dumaresq
https://en-wikipedia.org/wiki/John_Saumarez_Dumaresq
https://www.navyhistory.org.au/admiral-dumaresq-a-son-of-australia/
Papers and letters of the Cumberlege family
T.J. Rodoni Archive, University of Newcastle (Australia) Library

Books & Articles

Bryer, Robin, *Jolie Brise* (London: Martin, Secker & Warburg, 1982)
Burnell, F.S., *How Australia Took German New Guinea* (Sydney: 1915)
Craig, B. & Winter, C., *Richard Thurnwald and Thomas James Rodoni in the Upper Sepik Region of New Guinea 1914* (South Australia Museum & Flinders University, 65pp paper, 2016)
Cumberbatch Family History (Robert Cumberbatch, USA, 2010)
Cumberlege, C.L., 'Report of *Warrego* Sepik River Expedition December 1914' (*AWM* 33, Item 64/3)
Cumberlege, Claude Lionel, *Master Mariner* (London: Paul Davies, 1936)
Hadler, Robert, *Mutineers* (Melbourne: Wilkinson Publishing, 2021)
José, Arthur W., *The Royal Australian Navy 1914–1918* (Sydney: Angus & Robertson, 1928)

Knight, Robin, *The Extraordinary Life of Mike Cumberlege SOE* (London: Fonthill Media, 2018)
Mackenzie, S.S., The Australians at Rabaul. Vol X. The Official History of Australia in the War of 1914–1918 (Sydney: Angus & Robertson, 1938)
Maillart, Ella, *Gypsy Afloat* (London: W. Heinemann, 1942)
Muhlhauser, George, *The Cruise of the Amaryllis* (London: John Lane, 1924)
Osborne, P.J.B., *Some Family History* (Canberra and District Historical Society 1958)
Pixley, Norman S., *The Bells and 'Coochin Coochin'* (Historical Society of Queensland, 1968)
Raffin, Greg, *Australia's Real Baptism of Fire* (Seven Hills, NSW, Australia, 2013)
Reeves, L.C., *Australians in Action* (Sydney: Australasian News, 1915)
Smith, John, *Archives* (Naval Historical Society of Australia, 2017)
Wilson, Graham, 'A Soldier's Perspective: the HMAS Australia Mutiny' (*Journal of the Australian Naval Institute*, May/July 1996)

INDEX